Words Well Spoken

Studies in Rhetoric and Religion 8

EDITORIAL BOARD

MARTIN J. MEDHURST
Editorial Board Chair
Baylor University

VANESSA B. BEASLEY
Vanderbilt University

RANDALL L. BYTWERK
Calvin College

JAMES M. FARRELL
University of New Hampshire

JAMES A. HERRICK
Hope College

MICHAEL J. HYDE
Wake Forest University

THOMAS M. LESSL
University of Georgia

Words Well Spoken

GEORGE KENNEDY'S RHETORIC OF THE NEW TESTAMENT

C. CLIFTON BLACK & DUANE F. WATSON
editors

BAYLOR UNIVERSITY PRESS

© 2008 by Baylor University Press
Waco, Texas 76798

All Rights Reserved. No part of this publication may be reproduced, stored in a retrieval system, or transmitted, in any form or by any means, electronic, mechanical, photocopying, recording or otherwise, without the prior permission in writing of Baylor University Press.

Cover design: Joan Osth
Cover image: Italian School, *Roman Orator*, from L'Antica Roma, 1825. Used by permission of the Bridgeman Art Library.

The Library of Congress has catalogued the hardcover edition as follows:

Library of Congress Cataloging-in-Publication Data

Words well spoken : George Kennedy's rhetoric of the New Testament / C. Clifton Black and Duane F. Watson, editors.
   p. cm. -- (Studies in rhetoric and religion ; 8)
Includes bibliographical references and indexes.
ISBN 978-1-60258-064-0 (hardback : alk. paper)
 1. Bible. N.T.--Criticism, interpretation, etc. 2. Kennedy, George Alexander, 1928- 3. Bible. N.T.--Language, style. I. Black, C. Clifton (Carl Clifton), 1955- II. Watson, Duane Frederick.

BS2361.3.W67 2008
225.6'6092--dc22
                                2008010609

The ISBN for the 2017 paperback edition is 978-1-4813-0821-2.

Printed in the United States of America on acid-free paper.

To Vernon K. Robbins
*Whose friendship and scholarly collaboration
have greatly enriched my life*
D. F. W.

and

To Fred L. Horton Jr. and Charles H. Talbert
*Exacting, encouraging teachers who
introduced me to the art of biblical interpretation*
C. C. B.

CONTENTS

Abbreviations		ix
Acknowledgments		xiii
1	Introduction *C. Clifton Black and Duane F. Watson*	1
2	The Recollection of Rhetoric: A Brief History *Margaret D. Zulick*	7
3	George Kennedy's Scholarship in the Context of North American Rhetorical Studies *Thomas H. Olbricht*	21
4	The Influence of George Kennedy on Rhetorical Criticism of the New Testament *Duane F. Watson*	41
5	Kennedy and the Gospels: An Ambiguous Legacy, a Promising Bequest *C. Clifton Black*	63
6	Rhetography: A New Way of Seeing the Familiar Text *Vernon K. Robbins*	81
7	George Kennedy's Influence on Rhetorical Interpretation of the Acts of the Apostles *Blake Shipp*	107
8	George Kennedy's Contribution to Rhetorical Criticism of the Pauline Letters *Frank W. Hughes*	125

9	Kennedy and the Reading of Paul: The Energy of Communication *James D. Hester*	139
10	Moving an Audience: One Aspect of Pathos in the Book of Revelation *Greg Carey*	163
11	Afterword *George A. Kennedy*	179
Curriculum Vitae: George Alexander Kennedy		193
Bibliography		205
List of Contributors		235
Index of Primary Sources		237
Subject Index		243

ABBREVIATIONS

AI	Arbeiten zur Interkulturalität
AJT	*American Journal of Theology*
Ars Rhet.	Aristotle, *Ars Rhetorica*
BETL	Bibliotheca ephemeridum theologicarum lovaniensium
Bib	*Biblica*
BibInt	*Biblical Interpretation*
BIS	Biblical Interpretation Series
BTB	*Biblical Theology Bulletin*
BZNW	Beihefte zur Zeitschrift für die neutestamentliche Wissenschaft
CBET	Contributions to Biblical Exegesis and Theology
CBQ	*Catholic Biblical Quarterly*
CM	*Communication Monographs*
ConBNT	Coniectanea biblica: New Testament Series
CSSJ	*Central States Speech Journal*
CV	*Communio viatorum*
CW	*Classical World*
De or.	Cicero, *De oratore*
DJG	*Dictionary of Jesus and the Gospels*
ESEC	Emory Studies in Early Christianity
FFNT	Foundations and Facets, New Testament
GBSNTS	Guides to Biblical Scholarship New Testament Series
GBSOTS	Guides to Biblical Scholarship Old Testament Series
GTA	Göttinger theologische Arbeiten
HUT	Hermeneutische Untersuchungen zur Theologie
HTR	*Harvard Theological Review*

ICC	International Critical Commentary
IDB	*The Interpreter's Dictionary of the Bible*
Inst.	Quintilian, *Institutio oratoria*
Inv.	Cicero, *De inventione*
IOS	*Israel Oriental Studies*
ISBE	*International Standard Bible Encyclopedia*
JBL	*Journal of Biblical Literature*
JSNT	*Journal for the Study of the New Testament*
JSNTSup	Journal for the Study of the New Testament: Supplement Series
JSOTSup	Journal for the Study of the Old Testament: Supplement Series
JTS	*Journal of Theological Studies*
LA	Library of America
LCL	Loeb Classical Library
LEC	Library of Early Christianity
LJ	*Modern Language Journal*
MTSR	*Method and Theory in the Study of Religion*
Neot	*Neotestamentica*
NHMS	Nag Hammadi and Manichean Studies
NIGTC	New International Greek Testament Commentary
NRSV	New Revised Standard Version
NTL	New Testament Library
NTS	*New Testament Studies*
PR	*Philosophy and Rhetoric*
PRS	*Perspectives in Religious Studies*
QJS	*Quarterly Journal of Speech*
RC	*The Review of Communication*
Rhet	*Rhetorica*
Rhet. Her.	*Rhetorica ad Herennium*
RRA	Rhetoric of Religious Antiquity
RSV	Revised Standard Version
SBLDS	Society of Biblical Literature Dissertation Series
SBLMS	Society of Biblical Literature Monograph Series
SBLSBS	Society of Biblical Literature Sources for Biblical Study
SBLSP	*Society of Biblical Literature Seminar Papers*
SBLSymS	Society of Biblical Literature Symposium Series
SNTSMS	Society for New Testament Studies Monograph Series

SP	Sacra Pagina
SpT	*The Speech Teacher*
StABH	Studies in American Biblical Hermeneutics
ThH	Théologie historique
ThQ	*Theologische Quartalschrift*
TZ	*Theologische Zeitung*
WBC	Word Biblical Commentary
WGRW	Writings from the Greco-Roman World
WUNT	Wissenschaftliche Untersuchungen zum Neuen Testament
ZNW	*Zeitschrift für die neutestamentliche Wissenschaft und die Kunde der älteren Kirche*

ACKNOWLEDGMENTS

The editors sincerely thank this volume's contributors, without whose distinctive, valuable offerings the book could not have achieved the breadth and richness for which we aspired.

Deeper than the capacity of speech to capture is our gratitude to all of the following:

- George A. Kennedy—erstwhile instructor, now senior collaborator—whose creative scholarship has inspired this account, whose unwavering support has bolstered its completion, and whose afterword crowns the entire enterprise.

- L. Gregory Bloomquist, Saint Paul University of Ottawa, Ontario, who in 2005 was instrumental in organizing a session at the Annual Meeting of the Society of Biblical Literature, in which a Rhetoric and the New Testament Section began to take serious measure of Kennedy's work for biblical interpretation.

- Carey C. Newman, director of Baylor University Press, who immediately recognized this volume's potential to enrich conversations among a range of scholars in the humanities.

- Martin J. Medhurst, general editor of BUP's Studies in Rhetoric and Religion, who generously accepted the present volume as a member of that distinguished series and whose acute editorial board summoned all the book's contributors to greater clarity and coherence.

- Laura C. Sweat, candidate for the Ph.D. in New Testament at Princeton Theological Seminary, who expedited this volume's completion in ways beyond reckoning, with timely attention to detail and unflagging good cheer.

- Harriet and Caroline Black, who graciously acquiesced to yet another book's distractions of their husband and father; and Dr. JoAnn Ford Watson and Christina Watson, who did the same for theirs.

C. C. B.
D. F. W.
4 December 2007

CHAPTER 1

INTRODUCTION

C. Clifton Black and Duane F. Watson

Of interdisciplinary studies one is tempted to grouse as did Mark Twain on a different subject: "Everybody talks about the weather, but nobody does anything about it."[1] If that estimate seems hyperbolic, perhaps Hamlet's rueful comment (I. IV.) was more apt in speaking of

> ... a custom
> More honoured in the breach than the observance.

For our intellectual failings the reasons are more transparent than immediately remedied. In every area of human inquiry, whether in the sciences or the humanities, knowledge multiplies rapidly and exponentially. Unless the furrow one tends is either very short or very shallow, or both, it is no longer possible for even acknowledged experts to stay abreast of all developments. To ask them to maintain credibility in their native fields, while crossing boundaries into foreign terrain, seems at best supererogatory and at worst naive. More is the pity, for most of us would concede that some of the most innovative and productive scholarship happens when investigators venture beyond the zones of their academic comfort, learning from others who examine intersecting phenomena from different angles of inquiry.

The work of George A. Kennedy, Paddison Professor of Classics Emeritus at the University of North Carolina at Chapel Hill, exemplifies such teaching and research. Firmly rooted in the teeming literature of western antiquity, Kennedy early on concentrated his prodigious intellect and industry on ancient rhetoric at a time when that subject was a neglected stepchild among his peers in the guild.

After mastering the history of rhetoric,[2] compressing that history into manageable size for interested nonspecialists,[3] and translating many of its primary sources, both famous and little known,[4] Kennedy could easily have spent his remaining years puttering in the garden and polishing his accolades. This he has resolutely refused to do, for reasons that say something about the nature of his discipline and much about the gentleman's own character. Rhetoric's earliest theorists claimed that it was dealing with a subject of universal, transcultural human significance—a thesis that one of Kennedy's most recent monographs has put to the test.[5] Kennedy himself, however, is as generous a listener and amiable a collaborator as any scholar could ever hope to meet. His academic passport is covered with the smudged stamps of custodians in a broad array of expertise: specialists in speech communication, homileticians, biblical exegetes, anthropologists, philosophers, and theologians. For colleagues in these disciplines and others, Kennedy's work has the extraordinary capacity to open up frontiers instead of shutting conversations down.

Some of that intellectual stimulation, we hope, crackles in this volume's chapters. The book as a whole cannot take full measure of Kennedy's influence in all disciplines cognate with classics, nor does it try. Its distinctive coloration bespeaks its origins in a symposium sponsored by the Rhetoric and the New Testament Section of the Society of Biblical Literature in Philadelphia, November 2005. At that time early versions of four of this book's chapters addressed "The Impact of George Kennedy's Work for the Rhetorical Analysis of the New Testament." Quickly it became evident that those essays alone were inadequate to the task, for large chunks of Christian Scripture went uninvestigated, more recent excursions beyond Kennedy's enterprise needed engagement, and the larger intellectual currents buoying his own research had receded from view. To these ends, new chapters were commissioned for the present book. The editors stand indebted to all contributors who carved time from their already overburdened schedules to support our aspiration for a full-orbed volume. Though it remains incomplete in some important respects—we think especially of rhetoric's philosophical underpinnings and political implications—one book cannot do everything, save perhaps to serve as impetus for continued study. As it stands, the present work offers some early-twenty-first-century snapshots of rhetorical analysis of New Testament texts, with considered reflections on how its practitioners have, for now, arrived where they have. These distinctly Christian documents are more than historical artifacts, but stand prominently among the charter documents that still inform a goodly number of the world's religious adherents. So it is for the editors a source of high gratification that this book has found inclusion in a distinguished series devoted to rhetoric and religion. That topical marriage makes sense: as a missionary enterprise Christianity has always been in the business of persuasive discourse (see Matt 28:18-20; John 20:30-31; Rom 10:14-17) even as rhetoric, both practiced and theorized, has often been driven by religious impulses (e.g., "Longinus," *On the Sublime* [first c. C.E.]; John Chrysostom [347–407]; Augustine [354–430]; Hugh Blair [1718–1800]).

The reader may benefit from some general guidance on what he may and may not encounter in the pages that follow. First, while many of its contributors duly express appreciation for Kennedy's inspiration and encouragement of their own work, the present volume does not intend to be a *Festschrift*. Kennedy has already been twice honored with such volumes.[6] Here, sheer celebration of a senior scholar's mentorship is not the order of the day. Rather, our aim is to take his contributions seriously, to note different and provocative phases in his own work's development, and to observe how other scholars are responding to its challenges in the field of biblical exegesis. Not every author represented here is of the same mind in assessing Kennedy's impact; that, arguably, is a stimulating and beneficial outcome. For all its consistency across the years, Kennedy's own mind has been changed, following new thoughts down fresh paths. Taken collectively, the contributors to this volume are evincing much the same, notwithstanding all points on which they might agree with Kennedy and with one another.

Another collective is potentially misleading and invites clarification: The New Testament is itself not a unitary work but a significant corpus of first- and early-second-century literature of various genres, themselves consisting of manifold literary forms. While one can speak meaningfully of "early Christian rhetoric,"[7] that coinage probably obscures as much as it reveals. Thus, to thumb this book's pages—from James Hester's deft handling of Paul's volatile letter to the Galatians, to Blake Shipp's thoughtful consideration of the rhetorically punctuated romance of the Acts of the Apostles, and from there to Greg Carey's luminous estimate of pathos in the Revelation to John—requires no small mental agility. The same intellectual suppleness will well serve one beginning rhetorical study when Vernon Robbins invites such a novice to stretch her mind into "rhetography," a cognitive picturing of context. Every chapter in this book takes Kennedy's approach to rhetoric as a touchstone; many nudge rhetorical study in new directions, as Kennedy himself is doing.

Several of these contributions trace ample swaths of the history of rhetorical interpretation, whether of the New Testament generally (Duane Watson) or rhetorical instruction in the early American republic, based on classical antecedents (Margaret Zulick). For readers eager to get down to specific texts—Luke's infancy narrative, for instance—such chapters may at first seem distracting, overwrought window-dressing. Think again: without a tradition of practical discourse, mediated across the centuries, none of us would know how to pluck well-seasoned rhetorical fruits as well as those bursting afresh. Kennedy no more sprang fully armed from Aristotle's brow than did Athena from Zeus. Rather than begrudge particular authors their interests, the specialist in speech communication has much to learn from Frank Witt Hughes's assessment of Pauline rhetorical criticism, even as the biblical critic will never enjoy a better fireside chat than Thomas Olbricht's richly detailed, curlicued tale of speech, composition, and classics in North American pedagogy. The study of rhetoric is a broad board to which the teacher of English, the poet, the preacher, the historian, and the biblical scholar can happily draw up a chair. Your editors are at best servants at table. As much as anyone, George Kennedy is its host.

Enjoy the feast!

Notes

[1] Quoted by Robert Underwood Johnson in *Remembered Yesterdays* (1923; repr., Whitefish, Mont.: Kessinger Publishing, 2004), 322.

[2] George A. Kennedy, *A History of Rhetoric* (Princeton: Princeton University Press): vol. 1: *The Art of Persuasion in Greece* (1963); vol. 2: *The Art of Rhetoric in the Roman World* (1972); vol. 3: *Greek Rhetoric under Christian Emperors* (1983).

[3] George A. Kennedy, *Classical Rhetoric and Its Christian and Secular Tradition from Ancient to Modern Times* (Chapel Hill: University of North Carolina Press, 1980); *A New History of Classical Rhetoric* (Princeton: Princeton University Press, 1994).

[4] Aristotle, *On Rhetoric: A Theory of Civic Discourse* (trans. with intro., notes, and appendices by George A. Kennedy; Oxford: Oxford University Press, 1991; 2nd rev. ed., 2006); George A. Kennedy, *Two Greek Rhetorical Treatises from the Roman Empire:*

Introduction, Text, and Translation of the "Arts of Rhetoric" Attributed to Anonymous Seuerianus and Apsines of Gadara (in collaboration with Melvin Dilts; Leiden: Brill, 1997); *Progymnasmata: Greek Textbooks of Prose Composition, Translated in English, with Introductions and Notes* (Atlanta and Leiden: Society of Biblical Literature/Brill, 2003); *Invention and Method: Two Rhetorical Treatises from the Hermogenic Corpus* (Atlanta and Leiden: Society of Biblical Literature/Brill, 2006).

[5] George A. Kennedy, *Comparative Rhetoric: An Historical and Cross-Cultural Introduction* (New York: Oxford University Press, 1998).

[6] Duane F. Watson, ed., *Persuasive Artistry: Studies in New Testament Rhetoric in Honor of George A. Kennedy* (Sheffield: JSOT Press, 1991); Cecil W. Wooten, ed., *The Orator in Action and Theory in Greece and Rome: Essays in Honor of George A. Kennedy* (Leiden: Brill, 2001).

[7] Amos N. Wilder, *Early Christian Rhetoric: The Language of the Gospel* (Cambridge: Harvard University Press, 1964).

Chapter 2

THE RECOLLECTION OF RHETORIC
A Brief History

Margaret D. Zulick

> *Even when narrowed to the field of religion and concentrated in New Testament studies, the study of rhetoric remains staggeringly vast. To get our bearings we begin with a contribution from expert cartographer Margaret Zulick, whose concise orientation compresses twenty-four centuries of rhetorical investigation into about as many paragraphs. En route Zulick directs our attention to many of the key thinkers in our aggregate intellectual heritage, not merely in Kennedy's alone: from Aristotle to* The Columbian Orator; *from Augustine to Kenneth Burke; from Judah Messer Leon to Karlyn Kohrs Campbell.*

Any essay assessing the work of George Kennedy and its bearing on religious rhetoric does well to emulate his ability to traverse disciplines in search of comparable ideas. My own career across disciplines could not have been done successfully, if at all, were it not for his trailblazing. In contemplating Kennedy's "post-biblical" influence, we turn immediately to the many disciplines in which rhetoric is now influential, having been given an identity and a body of work of its own. I therefore verge on autobiography in order to do justice to the bridges Kennedy's work has helped to build between rhetorical interests in biblical studies, communication, languages, and classics.

When James Muilenburg wrote "Form Criticism and Beyond," suggesting rhetorical criticism as a remedy for the purely historical approach to the study of Old Testament literary forms, he was working from a European-centered understanding of rhetoric as the study of prose style.[1] This conception of rhetoric, elaborated in the works of Muilenburg's noted student Phyllis Trible,[2] was what I knew of rhetoric when I started Ph.D. coursework at the then-interdisciplinary program in Religious Studies at Garrett-Northwestern. While looking for a field cognate to Hebrew Bible at Northwestern, I encountered some

New Testament students in the Garrett cafeteria and discovered that they were taking courses in a subject called rhetorical criticism. In this way I blundered into what was then the best rhetoric program in the country. For two full semesters I was unaware that I was in a communication department, not a rhetoric department, and I struggled to make sense of their approach to the classic rhetorical texts. Accustomed to close reading of fixed literary tradition as an end in itself, I encountered a group of people who, with less Greek than my own four semesters' worth, were mining Aristotle's rhetoric as a how-to manual for contemporary speech and disputation. At their elbows were Kennedy's volumes on classical rhetoric.[3] The idea was energizing—and this *energeia* induced me to make rhetoric my academic home.

Two qualities of Kennedy's thought have made it possible for rhetoricians trained in modern communication departments, without much background in classical languages, nevertheless to come to grips with the Greco-Roman rhetorical tradition: his copiousness and his sense of adventure in following the art of rhetoric wherever it leads, especially across long-standing disciplinary boundaries. Early reviews of *The Art of Persuasion in Greece* in communication journals testify to the sheer volume of information; in fact, they were agreed that the book had too much information for the nonspecialist.[4] In *New Testament Interpretation through Rhetorical Criticism*, Kennedy crossed not one but two disciplinary lines, for in outlining a rhetorical reading of the New Testament, he cited both Lloyd Bitzer and Kenneth Burke: Bitzer, a communication scholar; Burke, a critic without portfolio.[5]

What was the rhetoric I encountered in this foray toward the field of communication? For American communication scholars, rhetoric is a very different animal than it was for Muilenburg. For them, logical invention of arguments, not stylistic elegance, is the heart and soul of persuasion. In fact the two traditions of rhetoric—call them European and American—seemed largely unaware of each other. So I was set on the path to assist in bringing them back together, in recollecting the complete tradition. There was a pragmatic imperative to this goal as well. New Testament scholars enjoy a strong genetic liaison between the language of the New Testament and the rhetorical tradition. I needed to justify a rhetoric of the Old Testament, supposedly pre-Hellenic and Hebrew rather than Greek. The idea of rhetoric as a transhistorical theory of persuasion, an aspect of language as such in its function to persuade, was therefore essential to a rhetorical treatment of these texts.[6]

In the rest of this chapter I wish to rehearse briefly the historic process by which we came to these divergent views of rhetoric, its contents, and its purpose, and to assess Kennedy's role in helping us all to recollect the full tradition of rhetoric for biblical studies and communication, religious and otherwise.

CLASSICAL ORIGINS

In his attempt to rehabilitate rhetoric, Aristotle paradoxically laid the groundwork for rhetoric's dismemberment, by which I principally mean the bifurcation of invention and style. Plato's opposition of "rhetoric" and "sophistry" to "philosophy" and its method, "dialectic," had positioned rhetoric as the false art and dialectic as the true art of definition and division of arguments (*Phaedrus* 259e–264e). Therefore, the opening lines of Aristotle's *Rhetoric*, ἡ ῥητορική ἐστιν ἀντίστροφος τῇ διαλεκτικῇ ("Rhetoric is a counterpart to dialectic" [my translation]), are pointed directly at reassociating rhetoric with the invention of valid arguments in dialectic. Aristotle relegates style as an afterthought to the depths of book 3, while in book 1 he rules out of the province of art all save proofs: αἱ γὰρ πίστεις ἔντεχνόν ἐστι μόνον (*Rhetoric* 1354a) ("For only [logical] proofs are artistic" [my translation]). In order to further support this attachment of rhetoric to dialectic, Aristotle borrows the device of the enthymeme and redefines it as a truncated syllogism. Then he rules out of play direct appeals to emotion, even parts of speech outside the rules of art, concerned only with proofs (1354b–1355a). Despite this, Aristotle's *Rhetoric* does contain remarks on style and arrangement in book 3, which is surely evidence of the composite nature of this text. *Rhetoric* in fact appears to evince internal warfare between the book's two competing principles of organization: the Aristotelian division into the canons of invention, arrangement, and style; and the old handbook tradition of using the theory of arrangement to organize the presentation, treating both invention and style under their appropriate parts of speech.

Few Romans appear to have paid much attention to Aristotle: the Roman period yields copious treatments of invention and style, following the handbook tradition. Yet Aristotle's characteristic organization persists in two near-contemporaneous Hellenistic rhetorical studies, *Rhetorica ad Alexandrum* (fourth c. B.C.E.) and *Rhetorica ad Herennium* (first c. B.C.E.). And the young Cicero produced an entire treatise on rhetorical invention (*De inventione rhetorica*; early first c. B.C.E.).

PATRISTIC, MEDIEVAL, AND RENAISSANCE DEVELOPMENTS

After the end of the classical age and near the beginning of the Christian era, Augustine (354–430) faced an entirely different problem. In the face of attacks on rhetoric as exemplary of corrupt pagan culture in its entirety, he once again had to rehabilitate it for a Christian audience. He makes a strong case in book 4 of *De doctrina christiana* (begun 397; concluded 427) for continuing to study rhetoric despite its notorious ethical neutrality:

> For since by means of the art of rhetoric both truth and falsehood are urged, who would dare to say that truth should stand in the person of its defenders unarmed against lying, so that they who wish to urge falsehoods may know how to make their listeners benevolent, or attentive, or docile in their presentation, while the defenders of truth are ignorant of that art? (4.3; 118)[7]

Yet Augustine refuses to produce a full rhetoric, and the rest of book 4 consists mainly of examples of style: eloquence drawn from the letters of Paul and the Psalms. The still-rising centrality of style, and the altered situation of rhetoric, is further demonstrated by his lament for the situation of audience that had no mandate as an Athenian dicast to judge one way or another: "How do these help a man who both confesses the truth and praises the eloquence but still does not give his assent?" (4.29; 138).

Yet there is no invention of arguments for Augustine. On his own premises there cannot be, because Christian rhetoric relies on divine revelation instead of invention for the discovery of arguments. In place of invention is the treatise on signs, a complete ontology and epistemology with the paramount purpose of creating a set of safety rules for the interpretation of authoritative texts. Invention has been replaced by hermeneutics, for in a world in which God has already spoken, the only job for a Christian orator must be to translate and to contemplate the word already uttered.

The trajectory from Boethius (480–524) to Peter Ramus (1515–1572) has been clearly laid out by Kennedy. He notes that Boethius "subordinates the whole study of rhetoric to dialectic."[8] For Rudolph Agricola (1444–1485), probable argument is the matter of dialectic, while rhetoric is consigned to practice. Ramus follows suit, including a treatise on rhetoric after his work on dialectic; the rhetoric is devoted solely to style and delivery.[9] Kennedy also points out that rhetoric was traditionally taught after grammar and prior to dialectic, although it might be more logical to do the reverse.[10] This appears to explain why, as late as the nineteenth century in Germany, rhetoric was taught as a study of prose style, preparatory to philosophy. It is instructive, for instance, that by the twentieth century at least three semioticians—Barthes, Ricoeur, and Tudorov—thought it necessary to contribute rhetoric primers as *aides-mémoire* to an audience that no longer perfectly recalled its terminology.[11] Thus by the sixteenth century, the dismemberment of invention from style in rhetoric seems complete. The question remains: How do we come to have an American tradition that does retain the focus on invention?

The Italian humanists continued a more holistic approach to rhetoric as "a synthesis of wisdom and eloquence."[12] An example of this tradition in the annals of biblical criticism is the fifteenth-century Jewish treatise of Judah Messer Leon, *The Book of the Honeycomb's Flow*.[13] This fascinating volume draws up a complete art of rhetoric using examples of eloquence from the Hebrew Bible. It relies heavily on Cicero and Quintilian, even using a tissue of quotations to put the words of Scripture in their mouths.[14] The effect is to assert the power of biblical persuasion while at the same time defending the art of rhetoric. It is this humanist tradition that seems more properly to have been the precursor of the revival of rhetoric in revolutionary France, Britain, and America.

NEOCLASSICAL RHETORIC IN THE EARLY AMERICAN REPUBLIC

The humanist tradition of rhetoric flourished through the eighteenth century in England, which gave us, among other several rhetorical treatises, the work of Robert Lowth on Hebrew poetics.[15] The founders of the American republic would have known this tradition. While considering the classics of Greece and Rome for a model of democratic polity during the Federalist period, the founders also turned to the classics in forging a distinctively American public voice.[16] John Quincy Adams' treatise on rhetoric, written when he was the first holder of Harvard's Boylston chair in rhetoric and oratory in 1806, was a complete treatment after Cicero, Quintilian, and Aristotle. In going back to these classics, Adams bypassed more recent rhetorical treatments and texts on elocution from Britain.[17] He also situated his theory in a history of eloquence in his inaugural address. After flagging under the weight of centuries of corruption, rhetoric was revivified and given new purpose in the American experiment:

> Under governments purely republican, where every citizen has a deep interest in the affairs of the nation, and, in some form of public assembly or other, has the means and opportunity of delivering his opinions, and of communicating his sentiments by speech; where government itself has no arms but those of persuasion; where prejudice has not acquired an uncontrolled ascendency, and faction is yet confined within the barriers of peace; the voice of eloquence will not be heard in vain.[18]

More influential than Adams' lectures, however, was the schoolbook *The Columbian Orator*, published in many successive editions between 1797 and 1850.[19] This is the text from which Frederick Douglass learned to read, as he recounts in his autobiography.[20] Clearly, *The Columbian Orator* is already in the elocutionary tradition represented in eighteenth-century Britain by Thomas Sheridan.[21] This tradition was aimed entirely at teaching delivery. It was intensely pragmatic, developing elaborate notations for inflection, tone, and gesture to accompany specific emotions.[22] It lasted throughout the nineteenth century. Yet while some see the elocutionary movement as preempting the study of rhetorical theory, it does carry two important pieces of the complete tradition. First, American elocution specifically ties rhetorical practice—the act of speech—to the exercise of democracy. To perceive this, one must look beyond the technical introduction to the selection of texts for memory and performance. For instance, *The Columbian Orator* presents Whig speeches from the British House of Parliament rubbing shoulders with Cicero, Cato, Seneca, and George Washington, as well as orations on eloquence. Taken together, the extracts build up a vocabulary for American democracy. Almost a century later (1872), J. A. Lyons' selections produce a similar mosaic. The selections mix topics on eloquence, liberty and democracy, and classical learning in general. Clearly, the classical tradition has not been abandoned, but it is assumed that the matters of invention, arrangement, and style will be taken up elsewhere.

The second piece preserved in the American elocutionary movement is performance itself. Delivery is one of the five classical canons, yet neither the American nor the European school today builds it into theory. For Caleb Bingham, however, the act of speech was of the first importance:

> When Cicero, in the person of Crassus, has largely and elegantly discoursed upon all other parts of oratory, coming at last to speak of this, he says, "All the former have their effect as they are pronounced. It is the action alone which governs in speaking; without which the best orator is of no value; and is often defeated by one, in other respects, much his inferior." And he lets us know, that Demosthenes was of the same opinion; who, when he was asked what was the principal thing in oratory, replied, "Action"; and being asked again a second and a third time, what was next considerable, he still made the same answer.[23]

Yet despite this continuation of the tradition in secondary schools and private education, by the turn of the nineteenth century, rhetoric was dying out as a course of study in colleges and universities in America as well as in Europe. It was the nineteenth century, not the sixteenth, that threatened to put a final end to the rhetorical tradition with the rise of what Burke calls "The Adepts of Pure Literature" on the one hand and scientism on the other.[24]

RHETORIC IN MODERN AMERICA

Rhetoric fell out of favor as American universities expanded and created separate departments based on theoretically defined categories of knowledge.[25] Departments of English literature as well as departments of classics sought to build a literary canon in which rhetoric enjoyed at best second-class citizenship. The new social sciences developed more scientific ways of accounting for the effects of persuasion on audiences. By 1913 it was necessary for teachers of public speaking to declare independence from English.[26] The newly formed departments of speech aimed to bring to bear all the arts and social sciences available to examine the phenomenon of human communication. These departments needed a theoretical rationale for speech as a separate category of knowledge. Some faculty, notably the "Cornell school," turned to Aristotle, while others appealed to psychology and even physiology.[27]

The consequent "rediscovery" of classical rhetoric for modern speech tended to eschew the pragmatic focus on performance as rhetoricians distanced themselves from the old elocutionists. The "neo-Aristotelian" model was strongly audience-centered. For the first fifty years of the century, it was engaged in laying down standards of value, studying the speeches of great political orators, and developing a "canon" of public address, distinguished from that of belles lettres. All these purposes are evident in Herbert A. Wicheln's essay from 1925, "The Literary Criticism of Oratory."[28]

Bitzer's essay on "The Rhetorical Situation," published in 1968 as the inaugural essay in the journal *Philosophy and Rhetoric*, began a sea change in rhetorical criticism as practiced in communication departments. Not only is Bitzer's focus on audience-centered criticism; he also moves the unit of study itself from the speech to the social situation. The continuing influence of Aristotle and the absence of concern with eloquence are also palpable. Bitzer's three components of the "rhetorical situation"—exigence, audience, and constraints—neatly correspond to Aristotle's three forms of proof—ethos, pathos, and logos—themselves based on the parts of the speech-situation: speaker, audience, and speech.[29] But the new focus on audience and situation freed the field from its dependence on a canon of oratory and from a unit defined as either a single speech or speaker to encompass the controversies and nontraditional forms of communication that made 1968 a banner year in American political history. It is safe to say that this one essay has had more influence outside the field of communication than any other.

Bitzer's essay, nevertheless, was preceded and perhaps made possible by the introduction into communication of the writings of Burke. Burke has had perhaps more influence on the contemporary understanding of rhetoric than any thinker since Aristotle. After a spate of review essays in communication journals, his four-part essay "A Dramatistic View of the Origins of Language," published in successive issues of the *Quarterly Journal of Speech* during 1952–1953, ushered in an era in which the subject of rhetoric shifted away from the study of great orators to the study of human symbol-making.[30] As Burke himself announces in his essay "The Range of Rhetoric":

> Rhetoric as such is not rooted in any past condition of human society. It is rooted in an essential function of language itself, a function that

is wholly realistic, and is continually born anew; the use of language as a symbolic means of inducing cooperation in beings that by nature respond to symbols.[31]

While early appropriations of Burke's thought were reductive and derivative, his work fundamentally transformed the nature and function of rhetoric for the discipline of speech.

Beyond the academy's various departments of study, American political discourse has been heavily influenced by the too often overlooked tradition of Protestant preaching. Having considered this phenomenon elsewhere,[32] I shall not repeat all the particulars here. In general, however, American public discourse frequently draws from the Bible's prophetic and apocalyptic modes of speech, mediated by such traditions as those of the Puritans and the Quakers, which when adopted by the country's various cultural ideologies has lent religious authority to movements as diverse as nationalist "Manifest Destiny" and abolition of slavery in the nineteenth century, and McCarthyism and Vietnam protests in the twentieth.

AT PRESENT (AS OF 2007)

So where do we stand today? It seems to me that trends in biblical rhetoric to some extent parallel trends in rhetorical theory at large. For instance, in an exchange with Vernon Robbins, Elisabeth Schüssler Fiorenza distinguishes between, in her terms, "antiquarian" research and a fully ideological rhetoric of inquiry,[33] while Robbins argues for an intermediary, "interactionist" position.[34] Accepting three dimensions of rhetorical inquiry, we antiquarians wear that label, I hope, as a badge of honor and continue along the lines Kennedy outlined: investigating the rhetoric of eloquence, the organic relationship between the *technē* of Greco-Roman rhetoric, and the text of the New Testament. The socio-rhetorical school expands the critical interaction between text and audience to understand the New Testament's persuasive context in the spirit of Bitzer and Burke. The "full turn" toward a rhetoric of inquiry effectively enjoins the process of criticism itself to account for its political motives before a contemporary audience with emancipatory concerns.

This train of thought in New Testament rhetoric has been reflected in rhetorical theory as well. As outlined above, the discipline developed from a rediscovery of the rhetorical tradition, toward a more situated, audience-centered yet essentially neo-Aristotelian approach. But the political credentials of this approach were then challenged by a new wave of scholarship influenced by Burke and also by the ideological commitments of the New Left and the second wave of feminism. This occurred as early as 1972 in a landmark exchange between the liberal neo-Aristotelian Forbes Hill and the feminist Karlyn Kohrs Campbell.[35] This shot across the bow began an "ideological turn" toward critical rhetoric that persists.[36]

Perhaps this conflict is both healthy and inevitable. It is noticeable that no transition in the field to date has meant the death of a viable scholarly enterprise. Instead, different philosophies, projects, and purposes tend to continue side by side. Perhaps it is time, however, especially in view of the occasion for this essay, for yet another defense of rhetoric. Despite its undoubtedly masculinist and hegemonic antecedents, rhetoric carries with it the sophistic attitude toward knowledge with which it began. It knows itself as the art of invention. As an art, it assumes that those who study at the feet of *Peitho* will put her wisdom to uses that are both aesthetic and ethical.[37] Among many other things, this means that the critic must also be a practitioner and, therefore, cannot sustain critical distance from the object of study. As invention, rhetoric offers always the expectation that something new can and will be said.

I cannot presume to suggest a program for New Testament study based on foregrounding rhetoric as the art of invention. I do think that, in the spirit of Kennedy's work, more cross-disciplinary collaboration is called for. In traversing the three areas of inquiry I outlined at the start of this chapter—rhetorical theory, biblical rhetoric, and American public discourse—I have encountered insights and lacunae stemming directly from the scholarly firewalls that exist across the academy. Yet we are fast approaching a day when the rhetoric of eloquence, the rhetoric of audience, and the rhetoric of inquiry will no longer be read in isolation. The full arsenal of *Peitho* is once again available to us, in large part because for the last forty years Kennedy has been breaking all the rules. He chose a subject that was considered unworthy of significant attention, perhaps even a bit embarrassing, by many classicists and literary experts. He was chastised for putting too much information in his books on the subject—too many notes, as the Emperor said to Mozart. Kennedy bridged the divide between classics and biblical studies by writing a seminal book on rhetorical criticism of the New Testament. In that same book he crossed a chasm by engaging the literature of communication theory. And finally, when most people would have rested on their laurels after a dozen books, including a major new translation of Aristotle's *Rhetoric*,[38] he issued a new global theory of comparative rhetoric.[39]

It is with the concept of *energeia* from that book that I close. Kennedy defines rhetorical *energeia* as beginning with "a form of energy," a "natural phenomenon" in which a perceived crisis leads to utterance "aimed at affecting the situation."[40] I would like to conceive rhetorical *energeia* at the end of the process rather than at its beginning, as a restoration of the full critical capacity of rhetoric, in which style, argument, audience, and performance together produce the full music of eloquence.

Notes

[1] James Muilenburg, "Form Criticism and Beyond," *JBL* 88 (1969): 1–18, esp. 30–31.

[2] Phyllis Trible, *God and the Rhetoric of Sexuality* (Philadelphia: Fortress, 1978); idem, *Texts of Terror: Literary-Feminist Readings of Biblical Narratives* (Philadelphia: Fortress, 1984); *Rhetorical Criticism: Context, Method, and the Book of Jonah* (GBSOTS; Minneapolis: Fortress, 1994).

[3] George A. Kennedy, *The Art of Persuasion in Greece* (Princeton: Princeton University Press, 1963); idem, *The Art of Rhetoric in the Roman World: 300 B.C.–A.D. 300* (Princeton: Princeton University Press, 1972); idem, *Classical Rhetoric and Its Christian and Secular Tradition from Ancient to Modern Times* (Chapel Hill: University of North Carolina Press, 1980).

[4] William R. Carmack, "Studies in Classical Rhetoric," *QJS* 49 (1963): 325–28; Melvin Miller, review of George A. Kennedy, *The Art of Persuasion in Greece*, in *LJ* 48 (1964): 57–58.

[5] George A. Kennedy, *New Testament Interpretation through Rhetorical Criticism* (Chapel Hill: University of North Carolina Press, 1984), 34, 158; Lloyd Bitzer, "The Rhetorical Situation," *PR* 1 (1968): 1–14; Kenneth Burke, *The Rhetoric of Religion: Studies in Logography* (Berkeley and Los Angeles: University of California Press, 1970).

[6] I deal at greater length with the rhetoric of the Hebrew Bible in "The Active Force of Hearing: The Ancient Hebrew Language of Persuasion," *Rhet* 10 (1992): 367–80; and in "Rhetoric of Religion: A Map of the Territory" (forthcoming). Here let it suffice to say that the primary form of direct address recorded in the Hebrew Bible is prophecy; see Margaret D. Zulick, "The Agon of Jeremiah: On the Dialogic Invention of Prophetic Ethos," *QJS* 78 (1992): 125–48.

[7] All translations of *De doctrina christiana* come from *Augustine, On Christian Doctrine* (trans. D. W. Robertson Jr.; Library of the Liberal Arts; Indianapolis: Bobbs-Merrill, 1958). The page number follows the book and line numbers.

[8] Kennedy, *Classical Rhetoric and Its Christian and Secular Tradition*, 179.

[9] Cf. Conley's assessment ten years later: in synthesizing Aristotle and Cicero, "Boethius . . . makes rhetoric an appendage of dialectic," while Agricola and Ramus consign invention wholesale to dialectic, "assigning to rhetoric the task of teaching only the embellishments of speech." Ramus assigns to dialectic the task of "discovering truth," leaving rhetoric as only the "vehicle [of] transmission." See Thomas Conley, *Rhetoric in the European Tradition* (New York: Longman, 1990), 80, 127, 130.

[10] Kennedy, *Classical Rhetoric and Its Christian and Secular Tradition*, 209–11.

[11] Thus Paul Ricoeur: "[D]oes not the return of contemporary thinkers to the problem of metaphor commit them to the hopeless project of raising rhetoric from its ashes?" (*The Rule of Metaphor: Multidisciplinary Studies of the Creation of Meaning in Language* [trans. Robert Czerny, Kathleen McLaughlin, and John Costello; Toronto: University of Toronto Press, 1977], 9). Cf. Roland Barthes, "The Old Rhetoric: An Aide-Memoire," in *The Semiotic Challenge* (trans. Richard Howard; New York: Hill and Wang, 1988), 11–94.

[12] Kennedy, *Classical Rhetoric and Its Christian and Secular Tradition*, 197.

[13] Judah Messer Leon, *The Book of the Honeycomb's Flow (Sepher Nopheth Suphim)* (trans. Isaac Rabinowitz; Ithaca: Cornell University Press, 1982).

[14] Leon, *The Book of the Honeycomb's Flow*, 29.

[15] Robert Lowth, *De Sacra Poesi Hebraeorum. Praelectiones Academicae Oxonii Habitae a Roberto Lowth* (Oxford: Clarendon, 1753), 293–95. See also Roland Meynet, "Histoire de 'l'analyse rhétorique' en exégèse biblique," *Rhet* 8 (1990): 291–320.

[16] Carl J. Richard, *The Founders and the Classics: Greece, Rome, and the American Enlightenment* (Cambridge: Harvard University Press, 1994); Kenneth Cmiel, *Democratic Eloquence: The Fight over Popular Speech in Nineteenth-Century America* (New York: William Morrow, 1990), esp. 46.

[17] John P. Hoshor, "American Contributions to Rhetorical Theory and Homiletics," in *History of Speech Education in America: Background Studies* (ed. Karl R. Wallace; New York: Appleton–Century–Crofts, 1954), 129–52, esp. 130.

[18] John Quincy Adams, *Lectures on Rhetoric and Oratory* (2 vols.; Cambridge: Hilliard and Metcalf, 1810; repr., New York: Russell & Russell, 1962), 1.30–31.

[19] Caleb Bingham, *The Columbian Orator: Containing a Variety of Original and Selected Pieces; Together with Rules, Calculated to Improve Youth and Others in the Ornamental and Useful Art of Eloquence* (Boston: Caleb Bingham, 1797, 1815).

[20] Chapter 7 of *Narrative of the Life of Frederick Douglass, An American Slave*, in *Frederick Douglass: Autobiographies* (ed. Henry Louis Gates Jr.; LA; New York: Literary Classics of the United States, 1994), 41–42.

[21] Frederick W. Haberman, "English Sources of American Elocution," in *History of Speech Education in America: Background Studies* (ed. Karl R. Wallace; New York: Appleton–Century–Crofts, 1954), 105–26, esp. 115.

[22] Joseph A. Lyons, *The American Elocutionist and Dramatic Reader for the Use of Colleges, Academies, and Schools* (2nd rev. ed.; Philadelphia: Butler, 1872).

[23] Bingham, *The Columbian Orator*, 7.

[24] Kenneth Burke, "The Adepts of Pure Literature" in idem, *Counter-Statement* (3rd rev. ed.; Berkeley: University of California Press, 1968), 1–28.

[25] Thomas Olbricht traces this development in chapter 3 of the present volume.

[26] Donald K. Smith, "Origin and Development of Departments of Speech," in *History of Speech Education in America: Background Studies* (ed. Karl R. Wallace; New York: Appleton–Century–Crofts, 1954), 447–70, n.b. 455.

[27] Smith, "Origin and Development of Departments of Speech," 456–57.

[28] Herbert A. Wichelns, "The Literary Criticism of Oratory," in *Readings in Rhetorical Criticism* (3rd ed.; ed. Carl R. Burgchardt; State College, Pa.: Strata, 2005), 3–27.

[29] Bitzer, "The Rhetorical Situation," 6.

[30] Kenneth Burke, "A Dramatistic View of the Origins of Language," *QJS* 38.3 (1952): 251–64; 38.4 (1952): 446–60; 39.1 (1953): 79–91.

[31] Kenneth Burke, *A Rhetoric of Motives* (Englewood Cliffs, N.J.: Prentice-Hall, 1950; repr., Berkeley: University of California Press, 1969), 3–48, n.b. 43.

[32] See "Rhetoric of Religion" (above, n. 6).

[33] Elisabeth Schüssler Fiorenza, "Challenging the Rhetorical Half-Turn: Feminist and Rhetorical Biblical Criticism," in idem, *Rhetoric and Ethic: The Politics of Biblical Studies* (Minneapolis: Fortress, 1999), 83–104.

[34] Vernon K. Robbins, "The Rhetorical Full-Turn in Biblical Interpretation: Reconfiguring Rhetorical-Political Analysis," in *Rhetorical Criticism and the Bible* (ed. Stanley E. Porter, Dennis L. Stamps, and Thomas H. Olbricht; JSNTSup 195; Sheffield: Sheffield Academic, 2002), 48–60.

[35] Forbes Hill, "Conventional Wisdom—Traditional Form: The President's Message of November 3, 1969," *QJS* 58 (1972): 373–86; Karlyn Kohrs Campbell, "Conventional Wisdom—Traditional Form: A Rejoinder," *QJS* 58 (1972): 451–53; Hill, "Reply to Professor Campbell," *QJS* 58 (1972): 454–60.

[36] Raymie McKerrow, "Critical Rhetoric: Theory and Praxis," *CM* 56 (1989): 91–111; Philip Wander, "An Ideological Turn in Modern Criticism," *CSSJ* 34 (1983): 1–18.

[37] Margaret D. Zulick, "The Ethos of Invention: The Dialogue of Ethics and Aesthetics in Kenneth Burke and Mikhail Bakhtin," in *The Ethos of Rhetoric* (ed. Michael J. Hyde; Columbia: University of South Carolina Press, 2004), 34–55.

[38] Aristotle, *On Rhetoric: A Theory of Civic Discourse* (trans. with intro., notes, and appendices by George A. Kennedy; Oxford: Oxford University Press, 1991).

[39] George A. Kennedy, *Comparative Rhetoric: An Historical and Cross-Cultural Introduction* (New York: Oxford University Press, 1998).

[40] Kennedy, *Comparative Rhetoric*, 3–4.

CHAPTER 3

GEORGE KENNEDY'S SCHOLARSHIP IN THE CONTEXT OF NORTH AMERICAN RHETORICAL STUDIES

Thomas H. Olbricht

Scholarship remains aloft on two wings: exploration of the novel and remembrance of the past. Among this generation of rhetorical analysts, Tom Olbricht possesses a memory of elephantine proportions. Not only does he have at his fingertips the names and places and dates; better than most he understands how the study of rhetoric has flourished among, while cross-pollinating, multiple disciplines in the humanities: classics, English, speech communication, and religion. At the point where these luxuriant vines of inquiry entwine, Olbricht identifies one figure that, at least since the mid-twentieth century, has tilled the soil and cultivated the fruit: George Kennedy. Seat yourself on the bench beside Olbricht, and listen while he tells you the tale.

In the last two decades, studies in rhetoric broadly defined have come to the forefront worldwide in numerous academic disciplines. George Alexander Kennedy, Paddison Professor of Classics Emeritus at the University of North Carolina at Chapel Hill, has played a crucial role in offering classical and other insights into rhetoric. The key scholars in most efforts to undertake rhetorical assessments have engaged his works. In this chapter I shall set forth Kennedy's broad contribution to classics, speech communication, and English composition in North America within the context of those fields' respective developments. I shall also introduce his contributions to biblical studies, though other contributors to this volume will develop that aspect. In terms of honors bestowed, those in speech communication have likely heralded Kennedy to a degree greater than in other disciplines, though his work is highly regarded by biblical critics and has received wide recognition among classicists.

CLASSICAL STUDIES

Soon after their arrival in Boston Bay during the "great migration" of the 1630s, the Puritans set out to replicate the type of education with which they were familiar at Cambridge and Oxford. They did so first at Harvard, later at Yale and Princeton. Central to these studies was knowledge of Latin, Greek, and Hebrew, and the reading and translation of classical texts. Meyer Reinhold has described in detail the early history of these studies.[1] Some of the standard works that were mastered and translated were by Virgil, Cicero, Horace, Justinian, Tacitus, Herodotus, Plutarch, Lucretius, and Thucydides. By the first half of the nineteenth century, however, required immersion in the classics began to be challenged. Kennedy sets out the acceleration of these changes in an afterword to Reinhold's volume.[2]

Kennedy designates the period in which classical scholarship flowered in America as the last half of the nineteenth century: "The Age of Heroes." Within this era the American Philological Association was founded (1869), as well as the American School of Classical Studies in Athens (1881) and the American Academy in Rome (1894). Classics departments characterized by rigorous graduate study were created at Cornell, Johns Hopkins, Stanford, and Chicago all before the close of the nineteenth century.[3] Most of these programs' notable professors worked in both Latin and Greek and published classical texts and grammars: Basil L. Gildersleeve (Johns Hopkins), William Watson Goodwin (Harvard), Thomas Day Seymour (Yale), William Hale (Cornell and Chicago), Paul Shorey (Chicago), and Herbert Smyth (Harvard).[4] Many of these professors studied classics in Germany for a year or more and obtained a doctorate there.

Throughout the early half of the twentieth century, requirements in Latin steadily declined in North American high schools, while Latin and Greek as college and university requirements were also lifted. Nevertheless, departments of classics in major universities built on the solid foundations established by those professors during the "Age of Heroes." Several centers encouraging classical studies were established, which, according to Kennedy, helped to elevate American classical studies as equal to "that of the Old World."[5] One of the first was the Institute for Advanced Study at Princeton, followed by the Center for Byzantine Studies at Dumbarton Oaks, the Center for Hellenic

Studies in Washington, and the National Humanities Center in North Carolina. More recently, according to Kennedy,

> A very important influence on American understanding of the classics throughout the [first] two-thirds of the twentieth century has been the arrival here of scholars and teachers seeking freedom of thought and escape from persecution in Europe, especially Russia, Germany, and Austria. The great names are those of Michael Rostovzeff (1870–1952) and Werner Jaeger (1888–1961), but there have been many others with European training who have diversified and deepened American scholarship. There has also been an exodus from Britain as opportunities there decreased following the Second World War.[6]

It was during this postwar era that Kennedy's own higher education commenced:

> As an undergraduate at Princeton . . . I learned to read Plato and Demosthenes in Greek with the encouragement of A. E. Raubitschek. As a graduate student at Harvard I studied with Werner Jaeger, taking courses in Aristotle and Hellenistic Literature and a seminar on "Longinus." Jaeger did not share the general prejudice against rhetoric, encouraged my interest in it, and on the last occasion on which I saw him, laid his hand apostolically upon my shoulder and said, "I have written *Paideia*, you must write *Peitho*." As my interests in rhetoric became better known, encouragement came from others, including Harry Caplan, Friedrich Solmsen, and G. M. A. Grube. I also discovered that west of the Appalachians universities included whole departments of speech which took rhetoric seriously and were interested in what I was trying to do. Fred Haberman at Wisconsin was the first to seek me out, followed by Jack Matthews of Pittsburgh and Donald Bryant at Iowa. As the latter's guest in Iowa City, I found, to my astonishment, I could engage in a serious discussion of stasis theory which might well have taken place in the second century before Christ.[7]

Studying at Harvard with Jaeger, Sterling Dow, J. Peterson Elder, and others, Kennedy soon made his mark in classics with his work on ancient rhetoric. He obtained his Ph.D. from Harvard in 1954, writing on Quintilian's *Institutio oratoria*.[8] Before publishing his first book, Kennedy had seen into press essays and reviews on classical rhetoric in such journals as *Harvard Studies in Classical Philology, American Journal of Phi-*

lology, *Transactions of the American Philological Association*, *Classical Journal*, *Classical Weekly*, and *Classical World*.⁹ While drawing upon the works of Richard C. Jebb, Friedrich Solmsen, Leonhard von Spengel, and Christianus Walz,¹⁰ with *The Art of Persuasion in Greece* (Princeton, 1963) Kennedy claimed to have written the first detailed study of the history of Greek rhetoric. In 1972 Kennedy published a companion volume on the history of Roman rhetoric,¹¹ which at that time had even fewer predecessors to draw upon, though one may mention the works of Richard Volkmann, Eduard Norden, and G. M. A. Grube.¹²

Most of the major Greek and Latin rhetorical texts and translations in the Loeb Classical Library had been published before the appearance of Kennedy's major books on Greek and Roman rhetoric. Reprinted after the publication of Kennedy's volumes, those Loeb volumes recognized his first two major studies in their bibliographies.¹³ Also cited in later Loeb volumes is the volume Kennedy edited in *The Cambridge History of Literary Criticism*.¹⁴ More recently Kennedy has also published texts and translations: his commentary on Aristotle's rhetoric, *Two Greek Rhetorical Treatises from the Roman Empire*, *The Latin Iliad*, *Progymnasmata*, and *Invention and Method: Two Rhetorical Treatises from the Hermogenic Corpus*.¹⁵

Kennedy's work on classical rhetoric has received widespread recognition among classicists. For it he has received various awards and been elected to some of the highest professional offices, only some of which may be mentioned here. From the American Philological Association he received the Charles J. Goodwin Award of Merit (1975). His colleagues in classics honored him with a *Festschrift*, *The Orator in Action & Theory in Greece & Rome*.¹⁶ Editor (1989–1994) and honorary editor (1994–present) of the *American Journal of Philology*, he has also served the American Philological Association in practically every capacity, among others as its president (1978–1979) and as its delegate to the American Council of Learned Societies (1980–1983). Among the other learned organizations he has served are the American School of Classical Studies at Athens, the Center for Hellenic Studies (senior fellow, 1990–1995), and the Fédération Internationale des Associations des Études Classiques (vice-president, 1989–1994). Yet, as we now shall see, Kennedy's influence on the study of rhetoric transcends the bounds of the classicists' guild. To appreciate his particular contribution, however, a sense of the development of rhetoric within other academic disciplines is in order.

SPEECH COMMUNICATION

As we have seen, the hegemony of classical education waned after the American Civil War.[17] In the antebellum era very little curricular effort was exerted in English history, oratory, or literature either in England or the United States. After 1810 biblical studies began to draw on the new energies expended in Germany but focused on philological and grammatical concerns while manifesting little interest in rhetoric. Francis James Child, Boylston Professor of Rhetoric and Oratory since 1851, was appointed the first professor of English Literature at Harvard in 1876.[18] The Modern Language Association was established in 1883, three years after the founding of the Society of Biblical Literature.[19] Thomas E. Coulton identified seven departments of English in American colleges in 1870, and forty-five by 1900.[20] According to Harold M. Jordan,

> It was common practice to combine all rhetorical training under a single Department of English after 1890. Many colleges and universities divided the subject-matter of Rhetoric into two departments designated as Departments of English Language and Literature and Departments of Rhetoric and Oratory, during much of the latter half of the nineteenth century.[21]

By the early twentieth century, instruction in speech had often degenerated into elocution, emphasizing a dramatistic and often stilted delivery.[22] Within the organization of the National Council of the Teachers of English were certain professors who taught public speaking but opposed those elocutionary methods. Some of these professors also belonged to the National Association of Elocutionists. Because of their common interest in oratory and rhetoric, they believed they were entitled to sectional meetings at the conferences of the National Council of the Teachers of English, but they were denied such permission. As a result, teachers of public speaking voted in 1915 to found a new society, the National Association of Academic Teachers of Public Speaking, whose name was changed in 1945 to the Speech Association of America, later to the Speech Communication Association (1970), and ultimately (1998–present) the National Communication Association. That society's founding fathers, seventeen in number, taught at Carleton, Miami (Ohio), Winona State, Minnesota,

DePauw, Lombard, Northwestern, Wisconsin, Iowa, Illinois, Cincinnati, Cornell, and Harvard. Its three crucial leaders were James M. O'Neill (Wisconsin), Charles H. Woolbert (Illinois; later, Iowa), and James A. Winans (Cornell).[23] Glenn N. Merry of Iowa functioned as business manager, a critical position at that juncture.[24] In 1915 speech as a separate discipline took a giant step forward.

The outcome was that the teaching of rhetoric departed from English departments and fell into the hands of speech teachers. Writing in 1984, Robert Connors, Lisa Ede, and Andrea Lunsford observed:

> One of the primary elements in this rebirth [in Speech Communication] is the rediscovery by composition scholars of the tradition of classical rhetoric. This classical tradition, over twenty-five hundred years old and composed of theorists as divergent as Plato and Quintilian, had been nurtured in departments of speech after English departments rejected rhetoric in the early part of this century and only relatively recently has classical rhetoric come again to be an informing principle for the study of written—as opposed to oral—discourse. It was English departments' misfortune that classical doctrines were lost to them for so long, as we are learning now.[25]

Graduate work in speech began in America in the early part of the twentieth century. The Master of Arts in Public Speaking was conferred at the University of Iowa in 1902, 1903, and 1904, but most graduate degrees in the field were granted after 1920.[26] The University of Wisconsin's Speech Department conferred its first M.A. in 1920 and the first Ph.D. to be granted in speech in 1922. The first Ph.D. in speech at Cornell was conferred in 1926. Iowa's earliest Ph.D.s were granted in 1930. By 1936 90 percent of the graduate degrees in speech were completed at Michigan, Iowa, Wisconsin, Northwestern, Teachers College of Columbia, Cornell, and Southern California.[27]

Edward P. J. Corbett attributes the emphasis on classical rhetoric in speech departments generally to that at Cornell: "It was the Speech Department at Cornell University that fostered the resuscitation of classical rhetoric in our time. In the fall semester of 1920–21, Alexander Drummond and Everett Hunt established a seminar at Cornell in which the students read and discussed Aristotle's *Rhetoric*, Cicero's *De oratore*, and Quintilian's *Institutio oratoria*."[28] The faculty members of Cornell's Speech Department in 1920 were James A. Winans, the department's chairman; Lane Cooper, who translated Aristotle's *Rhetoric*; Alexander M. Drummond; Harry Caplan; and Herbert A. Wicheln. Instructors Caplan and Wicheln had been doctoral students of Cooper, who was a one-man department of comparative literature and classics. Caplan later became Goldwin Smith Professor of the Classical Languages and Literature at Cornell. Regarding the inception of one seminar there, Hoyt Hudson later wrote:

> Drummond took over the [department's] chairmanship that fall, and among other things, he wanted to build up the graduate work in rhetoric and public speaking. So he and Everett Hunt founded a seminar. They took a few of us through Aristotle's *Rhetoric* (it is quite possible that we were the only group in any American university then giving attention to what is now a perennial best-seller), Cicero's *De oratore*, and Quintilian's *Institutions*. The three works occupied most of the academic year, though somewhere early in it we also polished off Plato's *Phaedrus* and picked up something about Isocrates and the Sophists.[29]

It is clear that those who advanced rhetoric at Cornell were well grounded in the classics. Two key figures, Hunt and Hudson, were graduates of South Dakota's Huron College, both having majored in Greek and Latin.[30] Another Huron graduate, Lester Thonssen, later became interested in classical rhetoric, received his Ph.D. at Iowa in 1931, and published a rhetorical reader in 1942 and a book on speech criticism with Iowa's A. Craig Baird.[31]

The Cornell School centered on a rhetoric that drew strongly from classical roots. In his essay, "The Literary Criticism of Oratory" (1925), Wicheln cogently argues that rhetorical criticism is analytical. Wicheln focuses on the speaker's personality, public character, leading ideas, topics, his choice of the motives to which he appeals, the nature of his proofs, and his audience. Additionally, the critic must discuss the speech's arrangement and mode of expression, habits of preparation and delivery, style, and effects on the immediate hearers. The rhetoric of the Cornell School cared little for tropes and figures.[32]

Cornell's influence on rhetorically tinctured speech communication became increasingly pronounced in the American Midwest. H. Clay Harshbarger (Ph.D., Cornell, 1929) was in the same year appointed a professor at the University of Iowa. There he taught classical rhetoric during the 1930s but soon became interested in radio. Baird then took up the teaching of rhetoric at Iowa.[33] Baird, a graduate of Wabash College (1907), Union Theological Seminary (B.D., 1910), and Columbia (M.A., 1912), had come to Iowa in 1925 after teaching at Bates College. He was not specifically trained in rhetoric, but he read Greek and Latin. (Both Harshbarger and Baird were my own teachers at Iowa.) By 1951—a year in which the membership of the Speech Association of America numbered almost six thousand[34]—the University of Iowa offered one of the country's premier speech departments. Iowa, Cornell, Wisconsin, Illinois, Northwestern, and Minnesota hosted the flagship programs advancing the study of rhetoric.[35]

In 1951 the speech departments at Cornell and Iowa were the two chief centers at which classical studies in rhetoric were being pursued. Such classicists as Iowa's Gerald F. Else translated and analyzed ancient rhetorical documents but at that time tended not to offer courses in the field.[36] Donald C. Bryant (A.B., M.A., and Ph.D., Cornell, 1937), who came to Iowa as professor of speech in 1958, provided an additional link in the Cornell-Iowa connection. Working on their doctorates at Iowa in the 1950s were Lloyd Bitzer, now of the University of Wisconsin, and Walter Fisher, now an emeritus professor at the University of Southern California.[37] As early as 1944 Iowa and Michigan State offered courses in speech communication, which blended English composition and speech.[38]

Sensitive to its classical origins, scholars in speech communication soon recognized the work of Kennedy. As early as 1967 he published essays and reviews, especially on the history of Greek and Roman rhetoric, in various speech journals, including studies in *Philosophy and Rhetoric*, a journal founded jointly by scholars in philosophy and speech communication. His first two books on Greek and Roman rhetoric were included as required readings in graduate courses on rhetoric as soon as they were published. The Speech Communication Association awarded Kennedy the James A. Winans Award in 1973 and 1981. He also received the Distinguished Scholar Award from the Speech Communication Association in 1992. After his retirement from UNC-Chapel Hill, Kennedy was named a faculty affiliate in speech communication at Colorado State University in Fort Collins (1994–present).

ENGLISH COMPOSITION

By the early 1960s interest in rhetoric was ignited among teachers of English composition. Corbett, who is in some measure responsible for the recent flowering of rhetoric in English departments, pinpoints a critical year:

> The most significant development in rhetorical studies in recent years is the growth in the number of graduate programs in rhetoric in English departments. I have always designated 1963 as the year when English teachers manifested a sudden upsurge of interest in rhetoric, especially as it related to the teaching of composition.[39]

This date roughly coincides with the publication of Wayne Booth's *The Rhetoric of Fiction* (1961) and P. Albert Duhamel and Richard E. Hughes' *Rhetoric: Principles and Usage* (1962).[40] Corbett identified 1963 as foundational, because it was at that year's meeting of the Conference on College Composition and Communication (founded in 1949) that rhetoric became the hot topic. As Connors, Ede, and Lunsford observe:

> The impact of this rhetorical revival on composition studies was confirmed by the 1963 CCCC, the conference that most historians of rhetoric point to as the first gathering of the "modern" profession of composition studies. During that year's meeting, Wayne Booth gave his paper on "The Rhetorical Stance," Francis Christensen delivered his "Generative Rhetoric of the Sentence," and, most important for classical studies, Edward P. J. Corbett spoke on "The Usefulness of Classical Rhetoric."[41]

Considerable impulse for these new developments came from the so-called Chicago Formalists or Neo-Aristotelians, under the leadership of Richard McKeon and Ronald S. Crane, and later Richard Weaver, Duhamel, Corbett, and Booth.[42] In 1968 many scholars with these new rhetorical interests founded the Rhetorical Society of America. Its founding board of directors included Corbett, Booth, Henry W. Johnstone Jr. (about whom I shall say more presently), Bryant, and Harry Crosby, who earlier had been a supervisor of the communication skills program at Iowa.

At about the same time, Kennedy was active in the Society for the History of Rhetoric, serving as its vice-president (1979–1983) and president (1983–1985). The membership of this organization consisted principally of professors of English literature and composition. Especially after the appearance of his translation and commentary on Aristotle's *Rhetoric*, Kennedy was invited to participate in several of this society's panels.[43] In similar circles he also presented lectures that were subsequently published.[44]

During the 1960s interest in classical rhetoric had shifted among university departments of speech and English composition. Cornell, the premier school in the first half of the twentieth century, closed down its speech communication program in 1963. Pennsylvania State University emerged at the forefront, especially with regard to philosophy and rhetoric. In 1963 Carroll Arnold (Ph.D., Speech Communication, Iowa, 1943) moved from Cornell to Penn State.[45] There, from 1963 until 1977, Arnold taught rhetorical theory and criticism, beginning with classical rhetoricians. After retiring from Penn State in 1977, he also taught classical rhetoric for short periods elsewhere until 1982.

By the fall of 1962, Pennsylvania State University was one of the few places in the country where an attempt was made to bring together persons interested in philosophy and rhetoric. This was due mostly to Robert T. Oliver, then chairman of the school's Department of Speech. Oliver was perennially fascinated by the manner in which rhetoric had been influenced by other disciplines throughout history, and what such disciplines could learn from one another.[46] Beyond speech, he had conducted research in psychology and international studies. Oliver was an inveterate promoter—not only of speech, but also of collegiality. He approached Johnstone, serving in 1961 as acting chairman of Penn State's Philosophy Department, about appointing visiting professors in philosophy and rhetoric.[47] Johnstone had engaged in exchanges with Yale philosopher Maurice Natanson (1924–1996) on phenomenological matters and with Chaim Perelman regarding argumentation. Arrangements were made for Perelman, author of the landmark volume *The New Rhetoric*,[48] to offer a graduate course at Penn State as a visiting professor in the fall of 1962. In his volume's introduction, Perelman expressed appreciation to McKeon (Chicago) and to Oliver, Johnstone, and Olbricht (Penn State). Perelman had become interested in rhetoric as the result of his training in international law. The more he studied argumentation, the greater the help he found in classical rhetoric rather than in post-Cartesian developments in logic.[49] Though aware (as was Aristotle) of the emotional and personal dimensions of persuasion, Perelman devoted much of his attention to the logical aspects of argumentation. His lectures were the beginnings of a series of cross-disciplinary exchanges that contributed to the founding of *Philosophy and Rhetoric* (1968).

After a Penn State conference on philosophy and rhetoric in 1964 at which Kennedy was one of the presenters, I started a newsletter "Antistrophos" (after the Greek word translated "counterpart" in Aristotle's *Rhetoric* [1.1.1354a]: "Rhetoric is the counterpart of dialectic"). I anticipated that after a few years the newsletter would evolve into a journal.[50] With the coming of Stanley Paulson to Penn State in 1965 from the presidency of San Francisco State University, the wheels were set in motion to found a journal. We commonly agreed that it might be jointly edited by a philosopher and a rhetorician, both to be Penn State professors. Eventually, Johnstone was named editor of the journal, *Philosophy and Rhetoric*, with Arnold and me as associate editors.[51] Kennedy was appointed to the editorial board from the first issue in 1968 and continued to serve in that post for twenty years. *Philosophy and Rhetoric* has not offered concrete proposals for rhetorical methodology, but it has encouraged the philosophical guild to reflect on the foundations of rhetoric and rhetoricians to consider more seriously their presuppositions, exploring the various new rhetorics in the light of classical and modern rhetoric. The journal can take some credit for the growing interest in the nature and function of rhetoric in sociology, psychology, anthropology, and linguistics, as documented in a recent book edited by R. H. Roberts and J. M. M. Good, *The Recovery of Rhetoric: Persuasive Discourse and Disciplinarity in the Human Sciences*.[52]

RHETORICAL ANALYSIS OF SCRIPTURE

We turn, finally, to the beginnings of rhetorical analysis of Scripture. Though neglected in the English-speaking world until about four decades ago, scholars have been engaged in rhetorical criticism of Scripture since the beginning of modern biblical criticism. Among earlier investigations, one may mention Philip Melanchthon (1497–1560), who published *De rhetorical libri tres* (1519), *Institutiones rhetoricae* (1521), and *Elementa rhetorices* (1531); and J. C. G. Ernesti, especially his *Initia rhetorica* and his lexica of technical rhetorical terms in both Greek and Latin.[53] Perhaps some of the most creative work in the early part of the nineteenth century was that of Christian Gottlob Wilke (1786–1854) in *Die neutestamentliche Rhetorik: Ein Seitenstück zur Grammatik des neutestamentlichen Sprachidioms*.[54] Some of the rhetorical studies contributed at the turn of the twentieth century were produced by such leading figures as Johannes Weiss, E. W. Bullinger, Eduard König, Rudolf Bultmann, and Norden.[55]

In more recent years James D. Hester cites the challenge of the Society of Biblical Literature presidential address (December 1968) by Union Theological Seminary's Muilenburg as the start of his interest in rhetorical criticism.[56] Muilenburg was aware of classical rhetoric but was more interested in what he perceived to be the distinctive rhetoric of the Hebrew Scriptures. His address, "Form Criticism and Beyond,"[57] challenged the biblical guild to move beyond form criticism in order to assess larger literary features of the texts:

> What I am interested in, above all, is in understanding the nature of Hebrew literary composition, in exhibiting the structural patterns that are employed for the fashioning of a literary unit, whether in poetry or in prose, and in discerning the many and various devices by which the predications are formulated and ordered into a unified whole. Such an enterprise I should describe as rhetoric and the methodology as rhetorical criticism.[58]

A second major influence on rhetorical analysis in biblical studies was, of course, the work of Kennedy. In private correspondence to me some years ago, he describes the manner in which he entered a rapprochement with biblical critics:

> You asked about the inception of my book on the rhetorical criticism of the New Testament.[59] In the 1970s a series of students in the Graduate Program in Religion at Duke began to come to Chapel Hill to study with me, encouraged by Professor Moody Smith at Duke. Their program required an "outside minor" for the Ph.D. in Religion, and "rhetoric" was accepted as an option. The students usually took one or two courses with me and then I served on their doctoral oral exam and often also on their dissertation committees. Of these students, the one who took up my approaches most extensively has been Duane Watson. All of my students from Duke contributed papers to the *Festschrift* in my honor that Duane organized, published by Sheffield Academic Press in 1991 as *Persuasive Artistry*. As a result of the needs of these students, I had in the late 1970s decided to write an introduction to rhetorical interpretation of the NT,

which was published in 1984 by the University of North Carolina Press. It has continued to sell very well and seems to be used as a text in university and seminar courses. It in turn led to invitations to lecture on the subject and to contribute to collections of essays.[60]

Kennedy's publications have had a continuing influence on the rhetorical interpretation of the Scriptures, as the essays in this volume substantiate.

For many, a third impulse for rhetorical study of Scripture was the publication of Wilhelm Wuellner's "Paul's Rhetoric of Argumentation in Romans," which appeared in 1976.[61] When asked what whetted his appetite for Pauline rhetoric, Robert Jewett replied, "Without a doubt, it was the publication of Wilhelm Wuellner's article on Romans."[62] Wuellner's article evinced familiarity with classical rhetoric through such German philologists as Heinrich Lausberg,[63] the classically based "rhetorics of persons" of such scholars in English composition such as Corbett and W. J. Brandt,[64] and especially the new rhetoric of Perelman and Lucie Olbrechts-Tyteca. I myself was attracted to this article by Wuellner, because it seemed to me that he was one of the first in this country to employ both ancient and modern rhetoric creatively in assessing biblical documents, while at the same time retaining the insights of traditional, grammatically, and literarily oriented historical criticism. Wuellner was aware of the new interest of rhetoric in English departments but was apparently less well informed that American speech departments had borne the heat of the noonday sun in the fifty years between 1913 and 1963. In November 1993 a *Festschrift* in Wuellner's honor was presented to him in Berkeley, California. In its dedication I wrote:

> Professor Wuellner has been more active in the international promotion of rhetorical analysis of Scripture than any other person. While it cannot be said that he has created a school of rhetorical analysis, inasmuch as that implies a specific methodology and agenda, yet in the encouragement and, in certain cases, training of younger scholars, no one has expended more time and energy than Wilhelm. . . . More than anyone else, Professor Wuellner has been in contact with scholars in the United States, Canada, Europe, South Africa, Australia, Japan and elsewhere.[65]

By the time Hans Dieter Betz had published his landmark commentary on Galatians in 1979,[66] biblical critics were predisposed to treat Betz's comments on rhetoric with respect and even excitement. Betz drew mostly upon German studies in rhetoric. In his footnotes at least, he was oblivious to American rhetorical studies. His rhetorical focus was on arrangement, and he drew more on the Roman rhetorical tradition than on the Greek. In the 1980s a number of biblical scholars interested in rhetoric were partially trained by speech communication and English rhetoricians along with a few classicists, principally Kennedy. Here I may mention Frank W. Hughes, who studied with Michael C. Leff and Thomas B. Farrell at Northwestern, and Kennedy's protégé, Watson.[67]

Rhetorical criticism of the Bible has flowered in all sorts of directions these days, and new books with "rhetoric" in their titles are being announced monthly. Watson and Alan Hauser have compiled a two-hundred-page catalogue of *Rhetorical Criticism of the Bible*,[68] whose New Testament component Watson has lately updated and surveyed.[69] Pepperdine University has assumed leadership in sponsoring a series of international conferences on rhetorical analysis of the Scriptures, recently chronicled by Vernon Robbins.[70]

CONCLUSION

Who can say whether Kennedy exceeded Jaeger's expectations of him as a scholar? Beyond a doubt, however, Kennedy has far surpassed his mentor's vision by serving as a chief spokesperson for classical rhetoric in the multifaceted world of scholarship. Exercising leadership in most of the organizations and journals that seek to disseminate insight into classical rhetoric well into the third millennium, Kennedy has laid a solid foundation for scholarship on classical rhetoric in the twenty-first century.

Notes

[1] Meyer Reinhold, *Classica Americana: The Greek and Roman Heritage in the United States* (Detroit: Wayne State University Press, 1984).

[2] George A. Kennedy, "Afterword: An Essay on Classics in America since the Yale Report," in Reinhold, *Classica Americana*, 325–51.

[3] Kennedy, "Afterword," 325.

[4] Kennedy, "Afterword," 325–26, 336–37.

[5] Kennedy, "Afterword," 345.

[6] Kennedy, "Afterword," 348.

[7] George A. Kennedy, *Greek Rhetoric under Christian Emperors* (Princeton: Princeton University Press, 1983), xvi–xvii.

[8] George Alexander Kennedy, "Prolegomena and Commentary to Quintilian VIII (Pr. & 1–3)" (Ph.D. diss., Harvard University, 1954).

[9] For details, see Kennedy's bibliography in this volume.

[10] Richard Claverhouse Jebb, *The Attic Orators from Antiphon to Isaeos* (2 vols.; New York: Russell & Russell, 1962); Friedrich Solmsen, *Die Entwicklung der aristotelischen Logik und Rhetorik* (Berlin: Weidmann, 1929); Leonhard von Spengel, *Rhetores Graeci* (3 vols.; Leipzig: Teubner, 1854–1885); Christianus Walz, *Rhetores Graeci* (Stuttgart: J. G. Cottae, 1832–1836).

[11] *The Art of Rhetoric in the Roman World: 300 B.C.–A.D. 300* (Princeton: Princeton University Press, 1972).

[12] Richard Volkmann, *Die Rhetorik der Griechen und Römer* (Leipzig: Teubner, 1885); Eduard Norden, *Die antike Kunstprosa vom VI. Jahrhundert vor Christus in die Zeit der Renaissance* (2 vols.; Leipzig: Teubner, 1898); G. M. A. Grube, *The Greek and Roman Critics* (Toronto: University of Toronto Press, 1965).

[13] *Rhetorica ad Herennium* (trans. Harry Caplan; LCL; Cambridge and London: Harvard University Press/Heinemann, 1954), addendum (1981), xliv; *The Institutio Oratoria of Quintilian* (trans. H. E. Butler; LCL; Cambridge and London: Harvard University Press/Heinemann, 1920–1922), addendum (1980), xiii; Cicero, *De oratore* (trans. E. W. Sutton and H. Rackham; 2 vols.; LCL; Cambridge and London: Harvard University Press/Heinemann, 1942), addendum (1988), xxiv.

[14] George A. Kennedy, ed., *The Cambridge History of Literary Criticism*, Vol. 1: *Classical Criticism* (Cambridge: Cambridge University Press, 1989). To this volume Kennedy contributed an introduction and four chapters. This volume is cited in the following Loebs: Aristotle, *Poetics* (ed. and trans. Stephen Halliwell; Cambridge: Harvard University Press, 1995), 25; Longinus, *On the Sublime* (trans. W. H. Fyfe, rev. Donald Russell; Cambridge and London: Harvard University Press, 1995), 158; Demetrius, *On Style* (ed. and trans. Doreen C. Innes, based on W. Rhys Roberts; Cambridge and London: Harvard University Press, 1995), 339.

[15] Aristotle, *On Rhetoric: A Theory of Civic Discourse* (trans. with intro., notes, and appendices by George A. Kennedy; Oxford: Oxford University Press, 1991; 2nd rev. ed., 2006); George A. Kennedy, *Two Greek Rhetorical Treatises from the Roman Empire: Introduction, Text, and Translation of the Arts of Rhetoric Attributed to Anonymous Seguerianus and to Apsines of Gadara* (in collaboration with Mervin R. Dilts; Leiden: Brill, 1997); idem, *The Latin Iliad: Introduction, Text, Translation, and Notes* (privately printed; Fort Collins, Colo., 1998); idem, *Progymnasmata: Greek Textbooks of Prose Composition, Translated into English, with Introductions and Notes* (Atlanta and Leiden: Society of Biblical Literature/ Brill, 2003); idem, *Invention and Method: Two Rhetorical Treatises from the Hermogenic Corpus* (Atlanta and Leiden: Society of Biblical Literature, 2005/Brill, 2006).

[16] Cecil W. Wooten, ed., *The Orator in Action and Theory in Greece and Rome: Essays in Honor of George A. Kennedy* (Leiden: Brill, 2001).

[17] Some of the discussion that follows draws on Thomas H. Olbricht, "The Flowering of Rhetorical Criticism in America," in *The Rhetorical Analysis of Scripture:*

Essays from the 1995 London Conference (ed. Stanley E. Porter and Thomas H. Olbricht; JSNTSup 146; Sheffield: Sheffield Academic, 1997), 79–102.

[18] Warren Guthrie, "Rhetorical Theory in Colonial America," in *History of Speech Education in America: Background Studies* (ed. Karl R. Wallace; New York: Appleton–Century–Crofts, 1954), 48–59.

[19] William Riley Parker, "Where Do English Departments Come From?" *College English* 28 (1967): 339–51; repr. in *Essays on the Rhetoric of the Western World* (ed. Edward P. J. Corbett, James L. Golden, and Goodwin F. Berquist; Dubuque: Kendall/Hunt, 1990), 1–15.

[20] Thomas E. Coulton, "Trends in Speech Education in American Colleges" (Ph.D. diss., New York University, 1935), cited in Donald K. Smith, "Origin and Development of Departments of Speech," in Wallace, *History of Speech Education in America*, 462.

[21] Harold M. Jordan, "Rhetorical Education in American Colleges and University, 1850–1915" (Ph.D. diss., Northwestern University, 1952), 104, quoted in Smith, "Origin and Development," 468.

[22] On the beginning of the elocution movement in Great Britain and the United States, see Frederick W. Haberman, "The Elocution Movement in England, 1750–1785" (Ph.D. diss., Cornell University, 1947), quoted in Guthrie, "Rhetorical Theory in Colonial America," 55–58. See also Wayland M. Parrish, "Elocution—A Definition and a Challenge," *QJS* 43 (1957): 1–11.

[23] According to Carroll Arnold, Winans was not at the first meeting but soon became a member. In most accounts he is included among the seventeen founders (private correspondence with Arnold, 14 January 1994).

[24] Andrew Thomas Weaver, "Seventeen Who Made History—The Founders of the Association," *QJS* 45 (1959): 195–99.

[25] *Essays on Classical Rhetoric and Modern Discourse* (ed. Robert J. Conners, Lisa Ede, and Andrea Lunsford; Carbondale: Southern Illinois University Press, 1984), vii.

[26] H. Clay Harshbarger, *Some Highlights of the Department of Speech and Dramatic Art* (Iowa City: University of Iowa, 1976), 17–18.

[27] Smith, "Origin and Development," 466–67.

[28] Edward P. J. Corbett, *Classical Rhetoric for the Modern Student* (New York: Oxford University Press, 1965), 566–67.

[29] Hoyt H. Hudson, "Alexander M. Drummond," in *Studies in Speech and Drama in Honor of A. M. Drummond* (Ithaca: Cornell University Press, 1944), 4.

[30] Theodore Otto Windt Jr., "Everett Lee Hunt on Rhetoric," *SpT* 21 (1972): 177–92; idem, "Hoyt H. Hudson: Spokesman for the Cornell School of Rhetoric," *QJS* 68 (1982): 186–200.

[31] Lester Thonssen, *Selected Readings in Rhetoric and Public Speaking* (New York: H. W. Wilson, 1942); Lester Thonssen and A. Craig Baird, *Speech Criticism: The Development of Standards for Rhetorical Appraisal* (New York: The Ronald Press Company, 1948).

[32] Herbert A. Wicheln, "The Literary Criticism of Oratory," in *Studies in Rhetoric and Public Speaking in Honor of James Albert Winans* (New York: The Century Company, 1925), 212–13.

[33] This information was supplied to me by Carroll C. Arnold (Ph.D., Iowa, 1942) in a telephone conversation, 4 November 1993.

³⁴ William Work and Robert C. Jeffrey, eds., *The Past is Prologue: A 75th Anniversary Publication of the Speech Communication Association* (Annandale, Va.: The Speech Communication Association, 1989), 31.

³⁵ Herman Cohen, *The History of Speech Communication: The Emergence of a Discipline, 1914–1945* (Annandale, Va.: The Speech Communication Association, 1994), 109–18, 183–86, 235.

³⁶ Gerald F. Else, *Aristotle's Poetics: The Argument* (Cambridge: Harvard University Press, 1957). Though not particularly interested in either rhetoric or patristics, Else, my most demanding teacher at Iowa, was kind enough to read with me several writings of Basil the Great, which supported my dissertation "A Rhetorical Analysis of Representative Homilies of Basil the Great" (1959). Else later chaired the Classics Department at Michigan. During his retirement in Chapel Hill, North Carolina, he became a good friend of George Kennedy (from a telephone conversation with Kennedy, 4 November 1993).

³⁷ Bitzer is probably best known for his article, "The Rhetorical Situation," *PR* 1 (1968): 1–14, and for his edition of the classic work by George Campbell (1719–1796), *The Philosophy of Rhetoric* (Carbondale: Southern Illinois University Press, 1963). Those interested in narrative are familiar with Walter R. Fisher's *Human Communication as Narration: Toward a Philosophy of Reason, Value, and Action* (Columbia: University of South Carolina Press, 1987).

³⁸ See also Conners, Ede, and Lunsford, eds., *Essays on Classical Rhetoric*, 8.

³⁹ Edward P. J. Corbett, "The Cornell School of Rhetoric," in *Essays on the Rhetoric of the Western World* (ed. Corbett, Goodwin, and Berquist), 302.

⁴⁰ Wayne Booth, *The Rhetoric of Fiction* (Chicago: The University of Chicago Press, 1961); P. Albert Duhamel and Richard E. Hughes, *Rhetoric: Principles and Usage* (Englewood Cliffs, N.J.: Prentice-Hall, 1962).

⁴¹ Conners, Ede, and Lunsford, eds., *Essays on Classical Rhetoric*, 10. In "Some Issues in Dating the Birth of the New Rhetoric in Departments of English: A Contribution to a Developing Historiography," in *Defining the New Rhetorics* (ed. Theresa Enos and Stuart C. Brown; Newbury Park: Sage Publications, 1993), 22–43, Richard Young and Maureen Daly Goggin consider many other contributory factors, both before and after 1963.

⁴² Conners, Ede, and Lunsford, eds., *Essays on Classical Rhetoric*, 10.

⁴³ One such contribution was published as a "Response by George A. Kennedy at the Rhetoric Society of America's Meeting on His Translation of Aristotle's *Rhetoric*," in *Rhetoric in the Vortex of Cultural Studies: Proceedings of the Fifth Biennial Conference* (ed. Arthur Walzer; Minneapolis: Rhetoric Society of America, 1993), 244–46.

⁴⁴ George A. Kennedy, "Rhetoric and Culture/Rhetoric and Technology," Selections from the Charles Kneupper Memorial Lecture for the Rhetorical Society of America, 1998, in *Rhetoric, the Polis, and the Global Village* (ed. C. Jan Swearingen; Mahwah, N.J.: Lawrence Erlbaum Associates, 1999), 55–61.

⁴⁵ Arnold edited (1966–1968) the journal *Speech Monographs* (later, *CM*) and with John F. Wilson coauthored *Public Speaking as a Liberal Art* (Boston: Allyn & Bacon, 1964).

⁴⁶ President of the Speech Communication Association in 1964, Oliver was the author of numerous books, including *Culture and Communication: The Problem of Penetrating*

National and Cultural Boundaries (Springfield, Ill.: Thomas, 1962), and *Communication and Culture in Ancient India and China* (Syracuse, N.Y.: Syracuse University Press, 1971).

[47] Johnstone (1920–2000), an editor of *Philosophy and Rhetoric* (1967–1997), taught at Penn State from 1952 until 1984. For a more detailed account and bibliography, see Gerard A. Hauser, "Henry W. Johnstone, Jr.: Reviving the Dialogue of Philosophy and Rhetoric," *RC* 1 (2000): 1–25.

[48] Chaim Perelman and (his colleague) Lucie Olbrechts-Tyteca, *La Nouvelle Rhétorique: Traité de l'Argumentation* (Paris: Presses Universitaires de France, 1958), published in English as *The New Rhetoric: A Treatise on Argumentation* (trans. John Wilkinson and Purcell Weaver; Notre Dame: University of Notre Dame Press, 1969).

[49] Perelman and Olbrechts-Tyteca, *The New Rhetoric*, 1.

[50] In a letter (4 January 1994), James J. Murphy reminded me that the prospects for new activities in rhetoric were being discussed elsewhere. Murphy assembled a group of about ten rhetoricians, including Carroll Arnold and me, at a national meeting of Speech Communications in New York around 1965. According to Murphy we discussed a new rhetorical society and a new journal. The society was not launched at that time, but some encouragement was bolstered for the founding of *Philosophy and Rhetoric*.

[51] I have prepared a more detailed account of these beginnings, which are preserved in the archives of *Philosophy and Rhetoric* at Pennsylvania State University.

[52] R. H. Roberts and J. M. M. Good, eds. *The Recovery of Rhetoric: Persuasive Discourse and Disciplinarity in the Human Sciences* (Charlottesville: University of Virginia Press, 1993).

[53] See Carl Joachim Classen, "Paulus und die Antike Rhetorik," *ZNW* 82 (1991): 1–32; J. C. G. Ernesti, *Initia rhetorica* (Leipzig: Fritsch, 1784); idem, *Lexicon technologiae Graecorum rhetoricae* (Leipzig: Fritsch, 1795); and idem, *Lexicon technologiae Latinorum rhetoricae* (Leipzig: Fritsch, 1797).

[54] Christian Gottlob Wilke, *Die neutestamentliche Rhetorik: Ein Seitenstück zur Grammatik des neutestamentlichen Sprachidioms* (Dresden and Leipzig: Arnold, 1843).

[55] Johannes Weiss, "Beiträge zur Paulinischen Rhetorik," in *Theologische Studien: Herrn Wirkl. Oberkonsistorialrath Professor D. Bernhard Weiss zu seinem 70. Geburtstag* (ed. C. R. Gregory; Göttingen: Vandenhoeck and Ruprecht, 1897), 165–247; E. W. Bullinger, *Figures of Speech Used in the Bible* (London: Eyre and Spottiswoode, 1898); Eduard König, *Stilistik, Rhetorik, und Poetik in Bezug auf die biblische Literatur* (Leipzig: Weicher, 1900); Rudolf Bultmann, *Der Stil der paulinischen Predigt und die kynisch-stoische Diatribe* (Göttingen: Vandenhoeck and Ruprecht, 1910); Eduard Norden, *Agnostos Theos: Untersuchungen zur Formengeschichte religiöser Rede* (Leipzig and Berlin: Teubner, 1913). For further discussion, see Duane F. Watson, "Rhetorical Criticism," in *ISBE* (ed. Geoffrey W. Bromiley; Grand Rapids, Mich.: Eerdmans, 1988), 4:181–82; also idem, *Invention, Arrangement and Style: Rhetorical Criticism of Jude and 2 Peter* (SBLDS 104; Atlanta: Scholars Press, 1988), 1–8.

[56] Hester's works include "Placing the Blame: The Presence of Epideictic in Galatians 1 and 2," in *Persuasive Artistry: Studies in New Testament Rhetoric in Honor of George A. Kennedy* (ed. Duane F. Watson; JSNTSup 50; Sheffield: Sheffield Academic, 1991), 281–307; "The Rhetorical Structure of Galatians 1:11-2:14," *JBL* 103 (1984): 223–33; "The Use and Influence of Rhetoric in Galatians 2:1-14," *TZ* 42 (1986):

386–408, and, in the present volume, "Kennedy and the Reading of Paul: The Energy of Communication."

⁵⁷ Published in *JBL* 88 (1969): 1–18. Muilenburg began his academic career as an instructor of English at the University of Nebraska, where he received his M.A. in English history. Four years later he took his Ph.D. from Yale in the history and literature of early Christianity. See Phyllis Trible, "Muilenburg, James (1896–1974)," in *Dictionary of Biblical Interpretation* (ed. John H. Hayes; Nashville: Abingdon, 1999), 2.168–69.

⁵⁸ Muilenburg, "Form Criticism and Beyond," 8.

⁵⁹ George A. Kennedy, *New Testament Interpretation through Rhetorical Criticism* (Chapel Hill: University of North Carolina Press, 1984).

⁶⁰ Letter from George Kennedy to the author, 11 January 1994. Regarding *Persuasive Artistry*, see above, n. 56.

⁶¹ Wilhelm Wuellner, "Paul's Rhetoric of Argumentation in Romans: An Alternative to the Donfried-Karris Debate Over Romans," *CBQ* 38 (1976): 330–51; repr., *The Romans Debate* (ed. Karl P. Donfried; Philadelphia: Fortress, 1977). See also *Rhetorics and Hermeneutics: Wilhelm Wuellner and His Influence* (ed. James D. Hester and J. David Hester; New York: T&T Clark International, 2004).

⁶² In a telephone conversation with Robert Jewett (November 1993).

⁶³ Heinrich Lausberg, *Handbuch der literarischen Rhetorik: Eine Grundlegung der Literaturwissenschaft* (2 vols.; Munich: Heuber, 1960), published in English as *Handbook of Literary Rhetoric: A Foundation for Literary Study* (ed. David E. Orton and R. Dean Anderson; trans. Matthew T. Bliss, Annemiek Jansen, and David E. Orton; foreword by George A. Kennedy; Leiden: Brill, 1998).

⁶⁴ W. J. Brandt, *The Rhetoric of Argumentation* (New York: Bobbs-Merrill, 1970).

⁶⁵ In *Rhetoric and the New Testament 1992 Heidelberg Conference* (ed. Stanley E. Porter and Thomas H. Olbricht; JSNTSup 90; Sheffield: Sheffield Academic, 1993), 17.

⁶⁶ Hans Dieter Betz, *Galatians: A Commentary on Paul's Letter to the Churches in Galatia* (Hermeneia; Philadelphia: Fortress, 1979).

⁶⁷ Frank W. Hughes, *Early Christian Rhetoric and 2 Thessalonians* (JSNTSup 30; Sheffield: JSOT Press, 1989); Watson, *Invention, Arrangement and Style*.

⁶⁸ Duane F. Watson and Alan J. Hauser, eds., *Rhetorical Criticism of the Bible: A Comprehensive Bibliography with Notes on History and Method* (BIS 4; Leiden: Brill, 1994). This work includes both the Old and New Testaments. See also Thomas H. Olbricht, "An Aristotelian Rhetorical Analysis of 1 Thessalonians," in *Greeks, Romans, and Christians, Essays in Honor of Abraham J. Malherbe* (ed. David L. Balch, Everett Ferguson, and Wayne A. Meeks; Minneapolis: Fortress, 1990), 216–36.

⁶⁹ Duane F. Watson, *The Rhetoric of the New Testament: A Bibliographic Survey* (Tools for Biblical Study 8; Blandford Forum: Deo Publishing, 2006).

⁷⁰ Vernon K. Robbins, "From Heidelberg to Heidelberg: Rhetorical Interpretation of the Bible at Seven 'Pepperdine' Conferences from 1991–2002," in *Rhetoric, Ethic, and Moral Persuasion in Biblical Discourse* (ed. Thomas H. Olbricht and Anders Eriksson; ESEC 8; New York: T&T Clark International, 2005), 335–77. From the first six of these conferences have emerged published volumes: *Rhetoric and the New Testament: Essays from the 1992 Heidelberg Conference* (ed. Stanley Porter and Thomas

H. Olbricht; JSNTSup 90; Sheffield: Sheffield Academic, 1993); *Rhetoric, Scripture and Theology: Essays from the 1994 Pretoria Conference* (ed. Stanley Porter and Thomas H. Olbricht; JSNTSup 131; Sheffield: Sheffield Academic, 1996); *Rhetorical Analysis of Scripture: Essays from the 1995 London Conference* (ed. Stanley Porter and Thomas H. Olbricht; JSNTSup 146; Sheffield: Sheffield Academic, 1997); *The Rhetorical Interpretation of Scripture: Essays from the 1996 Malibu Conference* (ed. Stanley Porter and Dennis L. Stamps; JSNTSup 180; Sheffield: Sheffield Academic, 1999); *Rhetorical Criticism and the Bible: Essays from the 1998 Florence Conference* (ed. Stanley Porter and Dennis L. Stamps; JSNTSup 195; Sheffield: Sheffield Academic, 2002); *Rhetorical Argumentation in Biblical Texts: Essays from the Lund 2000 Conference* (ed. Anders Eriksson, Thomas H. Olbricht, and Walter Übelacker; ESEC 11; Harrisburg, Pa.: Trinity Press International, 2002).

CHAPTER 4

THE INFLUENCE OF GEORGE KENNEDY ON RHETORICAL CRITICISM OF THE NEW TESTAMENT

Duane F. Watson

Sharpening the focus of the preceding chapters, Duane Watson surveys the influence of Kennedy's work on broader issues of biblical interpretation as well as within each major genre of the New Testament. He finds Kennedy's influence to be pervasive and concentrated in the study of the gospels and epistles. Kennedy's brief excursion into New Testament studies has proven a major catalyst for all kinds of fresh investigations of questions old and new, many of which may find answers in socio-rhetorical analysis.

When I arrived at Duke University in 1981 as a doctoral student in religion, the program had just been modified to include a new interdisciplinary portion that required students to create a minor in an ancillary discipline. The year before, a couple of friends of mine at Duke, Jack Levison and Richard Vinson, had established a minor in classical rhetoric with Professor George Kennedy at the University of North Carolina at Chapel Hill. Several students entering the program with me decided to pursue this minor as well, including Clifton Black, Robert Hall, and Clarice Martin. At that time Professor Kennedy was working on his book *New Testament Interpretation through Rhetorical Criticism*, and we were pleased to be part of the dialogue with him, both in and out of the classroom. It is partly because of that book, that dialogue, and Kennedy's major works in classical rhetoric that many of us pursued rhetorical criticism of the New Testament. In this essay I attempt to place Kennedy's work within the flow of New Testament scholarship and to assess its influence.

KENNEDY'S PLACE IN THE RHETORICAL STUDY OF THE NEW TESTAMENT

Current rhetorical criticism of the New Testament rests on the work of many predecessors. Augustine used Cicero's *De inventione* and *Orator* to analyze the letters of Paul in his *De doctrina christiana* (book 4).[1] The eighth-century British monk the Venerable Bede analyzed figures and tropes in both the Old and New Testaments in his *De schematibus et tropis*.[2] The Reformers focused on the rhetoric of the Pauline epistles. Of particular note is Philip Melanchthon, who wrote rhetorical commentaries on Romans and Galatians utilizing classical conventions of invention, arrangement, and style.[3]

After the Reformation there were just a few works of importance until Germany became the center of rhetorical analysis of the New Testament in the late eighteenth to early twentieth centuries. Important in this stream of tradition is Karl Ludwig Bauer's massive study of Paul's use of classical rhetorical techniques, entitled *Rhetoricae Paullinae*.[4] However, this period of study left many influential scholars doubtful about the role of classical rhetoric in the New Testament. In his study *Die antike Kunstprosa vom VI. Jahrhundert vor Christus in die Zeit der Renaissance*, Eduard Norden pronounces the Pauline epistles "unhellenic."[5] It was the judgment of Adolf Deissmann that the works of the New Testament, particularly the Pauline epistles, are "non-literary."[6]

This assessment of rhetoric's relationship to the New Testament dominated most New Testament scholarship in the twentieth century. Rhetorical criticism of the New Testament became largely limited to matters of style. Only thirty-five years ago this limitation of rhetoric in New Testament studies was so complete that F. C. Grant could confidently state, "He [Paul] positively rejected the artful literary and rhetorical devices of the 'wise of this age' ... The same is true of other parts of the NT ... There are echoes of oratory and of orators here and there, but no studied imitation."[7]

In the last thirty-five years rhetorical criticism of the New Testament has experienced a revival.[8] Hans Dieter Betz's work on Galatians was a major early influence in the reintroduction of rhetorical criticism to New Testament studies, particularly his commentary on Galatians in the *Hermeneia* commentary series.[9] He argues that Paul's epistles were composed according to classical categories of invention, arrangement, and style. He interprets Galatians using Greco-Roman rhetorical and epistolary theory.

Although Betz provided the first detailed modern study of a New Testament book according to Greco-Roman rhetoric, he did not provide an accessible methodology. Kennedy was the first to provide a workable methodology for rhetorical criticism of the gospels and epistles of the New Testament in his book *New Testament Interpretation through Rhetorical Criticism*.[10] This methodology has five interrelated steps:

1. Determine the rhetorical unit.
2. Define the rhetorical situation.
3. Determine the rhetorical problem or stasis and the species of rhetoric.
4. Analyze the invention, arrangement, and style.
5. Evaluate the rhetorical effectiveness of the rhetorical unit in utilizing invention, arrangement, and style in addressing the needs of the rhetorical situation.

Since its publication in 1984, Kennedy's methodology has been extremely influential as a starting point for rhetorical analysis of the New Testament. The methodology was shown to be workable and fruitful for exegesis. The first full-scale rhetorical analysis of a New Testament book utilizing Kennedy's method was my own dissertation, *Invention, Arrangement, and Style: Rhetorical Criticism of Jude and 2 Peter*.[11] I was fortunate to have Kennedy serving on my dissertation committee and particularly appreciated his wise advice. His methodology has provided the impetus for hundreds of other contemporary studies.

SOME OVERARCHING ISSUES

Kennedy's method of rhetorical criticism of the New Testament is a historical enterprise. It utilizes a systematized and well-conceptualized discipline from the Greco-Roman era to analyze the New Testament. This approach assumes that the writers of the New Testament were familiar with rhetoric, either from formal education or from interaction with oral and written Hellenistic culture, which was permeated with rhetorical practice. This rhetoric is found in practice in school exercises, written speeches, and letters. Its conventions are encapsulated in ancient rhetorical handbooks that have come down to us. This approach to rhetorical criticism views the biblical documents as complex, interrelated wholes and recognizes their argumentative nature.[12] Kennedy's work alerted us that knowledge of ancient rhetorical conventions helps us to place the New Testament amidst its Greco-Roman oral and written culture and to appreciate the role this placement can play in interpretation.

Although he certainly did not advocate this limitation nor did his methodology necessitate it, Kennedy's approach in practice was at first almost exclusively dependent upon rhetorical theory alone. Such restrictive reliance upon the rhetorical handbooks was in part due to the simplicity of his book, which relied almost solely upon these handbooks and did not contain bibliography for primary classical works, into which many practitioners of New Testament study were uninitiated. This reliance on handbooks can lead to an imbalanced view of the New Testament documents. Ancient theory was descriptive, not prescriptive, an abstraction from previous rhetoric and its situations. Because ancient rhetoric fully recognized the need to adapt to the needs of the rhetorical situation, the ancient rhetor could, and often did, veer from conventional theory and practice. Study of the actual products of rhetorical art helps recognize this flexibility in ancient texts as well as the New Testament (especially where Jewish rhetoric may be playing a role as well).[13] The study of ancient texts has been progressively added to the practice of Kennedy's methodology.

Kennedy's book also created a needed debate about the role of modern rhetoric in rhetorical analysis. It was thought by many that restricting rhetorical analysis to Greco-Roman rhetoric denied such analysis the benefits of modern rhetoric, which is more highly conceptualized and complete.[14] One early contender was the New Rhetoric, which was a reconceptualization of Greco-Roman rhetoric with an emphasis on the historical and social situations of speech.[15] Since then a host of analyses using modern rhetoric and related disciplines has been produced.[16]

When his book was published, one aspect of Kennedy's method—his understanding of the rhetorical situation—was already enveloped by debates within philosophy and rhetoric as well as New Testament studies. He based his understanding on the seminal article by Lloyd Bitzer that assumes that the rhetorical situation is an exigence eliciting a response.[17] Within the fields of philosophy and rhetoric it was argued that the exigence of a rhetorical situation was a construction of the rhetor from the facts encountered.[18] Within the field of New Testament there was a call to move beyond the mirror-reading of texts within the historical critical paradigm.[19] I made a call at the Malibu conference to turn to understanding texts as rhetorical to explore the fact that a rhetorical response gives us insight into the rhetorical situation as the rhetor constructs it, which in turn is in some measure a reflection of the actual historical situation.[20]

What Kennedy outlines and illustrates in his book has worked to help resolve this dilemma. Once the rhetoric of the New Testament was investigated (he helped facilitate an investigation), it became apparent that it was partly within the argumentation of the New Testament books that insights into the historical and rhetorical situations were to be found. To some degree the species of rhetoric indicates the nature of the situation addressed. The explicit and implicit premises of enthymemes and syllogisms themselves reveal the assumptions that the writers are confident that they share with their audiences—that is, the ideology. The rhetorical approach of a text indicates how the writers believed they must approach their audiences in order to address the exigence.

Kennedy also helped set some of the agenda for those of us working in rhetorical criticism. He pointed out that our knowledge of ancient Jewish rhetoric itself, its relationship to Greco-Roman rhetoric, and its role in the New Testament is woefully inadequate. Early works using his method at times struggled to know what to do with elements of specifically Jewish rhetoric in a text—for example, in the Epistle of James. This struggle led Wilhelm Wuellner to call for a systematic study of Jewish rhetoric in his unpublished paper from the Malibu conference of 1996.[21]

RHETORICAL CRITICISM OF THE GOSPELS

Kennedy's method as outlined above has been applied to portions of the gospels. He himself analyzed Matthew's Sermon on the Mount, Luke's Sermon on the Plain, and John's Farewell Discourse.[22] He also provided an overview of the rhetorical features of all four gospels. He noted that Matthew uses rhetoric in the most comprehensive way, attending to invention, arrangement, style, and amplification. This is particularly attributable to the planned provision of logical proof that Jesus was the Messiah. Mark utilizes radical Christian rhetoric—that is, rhetoric characterized by claims of authority and absolute proof and a lack of logical proof. Luke relies upon *prosopopoeia*, the re-creation of speech and dialogue to suit characters and occasions. Luke most closely resembles a classical biographer. John is written in elevated style or *hypsos* (sublimity) created by great thoughts, strong emotion, figures of speech, and arrangement of words.[23]

Kennedy's analysis of the speeches in the gospels demonstrated they were constructed according to many of the principles of Greco-Roman rhetoric. His work alerted us to the possibility that, if there is Greco-Roman rhetorical finesse in the speeches, we might find Greco-Roman rhetorical finesse elsewhere in the gospels. While the overall structure of the gospels was not found to conform to Greco-Roman conventions of arrangement in their full form, their structure was shown to be rhetorically motivated nonetheless. For example, the juxtaposition of units is by rhetorical design to develop topics, compare and contrast actions, and so forth. Using this initial work on the rhetoric of the gospels and Kennedy's methodology, Black has analyzed the Olivet Discourse in Mark 13[24] and the grand style in the Farewell Discourse of John 14–17 (and 1 John).[25] He demonstrates the presence of many features of Greco-Roman rhetoric in these speeches.

Beyond these and other studies of the speeches in the gospels, studying smaller rhetorical units of the gospels using Kennedy's method has not proven to be as fruitful as it has been for the speeches. This limitation is due in part to the nature of ancient rhetoric, which does not have a theory of narrative that discusses a plot with an issue, development, and resolution of the issue. Within narrative in the Greco-Roman world, rhetorical usage was limited to smaller units in larger works and involved description and speeches.[26]

The quest to understand the rhetorical nature of the gospel narratives led scholars to the *progymnasmata*, and more specifically to the *chreiai*. A *chreia* is a saying or an action of someone that is considered useful for living. The *chreia* could be elaborated by a series of exercises outlined in handbooks called *progymnasmata*. These exercises included recitation, inflection, commentary, objection, antithesis, expansion, condensation, and refutation and/or confirmation.

The study of the ancient *chreiai* as described in the *progymnasmata* had delineated the rhetoric of the gospels with more precision, especially with regard to the teachings of Jesus as represented in the gospels.[27] The gospel writers were familiar with *chreiai* and were able to utilize the exercises of the *progymnasmata* to elaborate the *chreiai* of Jesus according to rhetorical conventions to suit their literary, theological, and polemical needs. This is especially true in the development of the pronouncement stories and the argumentation of the gospels.[28] Kennedy's own new edition of the *progymnasmata* is proving to be very helpful in this analysis by making such texts available in a critical English edition.[29]

Until recently the *chreiai* and the *progymnasmata* have been largely ignored in gospel studies. This is due in part to the negative assessment of Martin Dibelius who, because of an inadequate understanding of the *chreia* and its role in philosophy and education, did not see similarities between the *chreiai* and units of the gospels. He saw the *chreiai* functioning mainly in the biographies of philosophers.[30] However, it was Kennedy's observations about Greco-Roman rhetoric in the gospels in part that led rhetorical analysts of the gospel to look to Greco-Roman sources for assistance in their work.

Taking Kennedy's work on the gospels as his starting point, Richard Burridge outlines both the contributions and limitations of using Greco-Roman rhetoric to analyze the gospels and makes further contributions. He notes that the gospels do not exhibit the conventional elements of invention, arrangement, and style common to rhetorical speeches and handbooks. While these may be found in speeches as Kennedy has demonstrated, they are not found to influence an entire gospel. There is invention by selection of appropriate topoi and proofs, arrangement of smaller units according to the components of the *progymnasmata*, and stylistic elements, but all these are guided by the use of rhetoric in ancient biography or lives, the *bioi* or *vitae*.[31] In this biography there is rhetorical intent to persuade, but the elements of invention, arrangement, and style are different. The invention is guided by the topoi of encomium and their amplification, as well as characterization. Arrangement is guided by the births of the subjects, their arrivals in public life, their words and deeds with *chreiai* development, and their deaths as the climax of their lives. Burridge concludes, "... it is not unreasonable to study the gospels carefully for forms of rhetoric in all senses of the word, but we must be cautious about reading off a direct connection between their narrative biographical texts and the formal oratory of the law court of assembly."[32]

Kennedy's influence does not stop here. Having discussed the Sermons on the Mount and Plain, Kennedy made this intriguing statement:

> Behind the rhetoric of the two evangelists in these sermons stands their perception of the rhetoric of Jesus, and behind that perception stands the

actual rhetoric of Jesus. The last of these, first in chronological sequence, cannot be objectively determined, but it may be possible to make some suggestions about the evangelists' perception or preconceptions of the rhetoric of Jesus. They sought to give a picture of Jesus in which they believed and in which they wished others to believe.[33]

Here Kennedy raises the problem of distinguishing the rhetoric of the historical Jesus and the rhetoric of Jesus as preserved in the Jesus tradition and the gospels. He argues that they need to be analyzed separately. In his book *Rhetoric and the New Testament*, Burton Mack rightly develops separately the rhetoric of the Jesus tradition (using Q) and the rhetoric of the gospels.[34] The role of the *chreia* and its development in the *progymnasmata* underscore the necessity of these distinctions. A gospel writer is free to take a saying of Jesus and elaborate it without Jesus' necessarily having provided the content of the elaboration, or at least not on the same occasion as the saying being given.

These rhetorical developments have obvious implications for the quest for the historical Jesus; these implications are beginning to be taken seriously. A good example is the work of L. Gregory Bloomquist, who argues that while historical Jesus research may give us greater critical certainty regarding the words and deeds of the historical Jesus, these words and deeds have to be understood as the picture that the historical Jesus wanted to present. They are a picture of the rhetorical Jesus but not of the historical Jesus.[35]

RHETORICAL CRITICISM OF THE ACTS OF THE APOSTLES

In his analysis of the Acts of the Apostles, Kennedy applies his methodology to the speeches, interpreting them within the context of Hellenistic historiography as constructions of Luke.[36] His methodology, or at least the examination of the speeches from the same perspective of Greco-Roman rhetoric and historiography, has been used to interpret the speeches of Acts that comprise about a third of this book.[37] This analysis has continued to be limited primarily to the speeches and has not been applied generally to the narrative portions, the other two-thirds of Acts. Kennedy himself did not analyze the narrative portions of Acts.

The reason for this limitation in application of Kennedy's method to narrative is the same as that found in the study of the gospels:

rhetorical theory in the Greco-Roman world did not include discussion of narrative. While elements of invention, arrangement, and style common to speeches are found in narrative, their discussion in rhetorical handbooks is focused on speeches, not narrative or the use of speeches in narrative, as is the case in Acts. More specifically, within Acts the speeches interpret the narrative as they do in Hellenistic historiography, and the narrative and speech together form rhetorical units in the rhetorical scheme of Acts. However, rhetorical theory did not describe this symbiotic relationship of narrative and speeches, a problem for which New Testament scholars have been seeking a solution.[38]

Kennedy helped clarify the direction that rhetorical analysis of Acts should take. He noted that Acts was a product of Hellenistic historiography in which the author wrote speeches in character—that is, speeches to fit the character and beliefs of the character giving the speech and that are appropriate to the situation. This fact, coupled with Luke's use of *prosopopoeia* in his gospel, indicates that he probably composed the speeches in Acts. As the more creative and less similar format of the speeches indicates, he may have had firsthand notes from himself or others for the speeches of Paul in chapter 20 and following. Kennedy argues that while the rhetoric of the Paul of Acts and the Paul of the epistles is not the same, they are more similar in chapter 20 and following, and most similar in the speech to the Ephesian elders (20:18-35).[39]

Stanley Porter engages Kennedy and others in dialogue about the speeches, arguing that Paul's letters are letters and not speeches, the speeches in Acts are by Luke, and the speeches in Acts—even if by Paul—are highly abbreviated.[40] He concludes that "we cannot find Paul the ancient rhetorician in the letters, primarily because, in writing letters, Paul was a letter writer." Thus we cannot compare the speeches of Acts with the Pauline epistles to determine if the speeches in Acts give us insight into Paul the speechmaker. Bruce Winter also works with Kennedy, arguing from Roman court proceedings, in which records were kept, that Luke may have had sources for the forensic speeches of Paul in Acts 24.[41]

Kennedy's influence can also be traced to the blending of historical, literary, rhetorical, social-scientific, and social-world analysis in the recent study of Acts. This approach minimizes the significance of genre, using it as a tool to move to larger literary, rhetorical, and cultural concerns. This is a mixed genre approach that understands that these concerns are not limited to a particular genre and that formal genre analysis and classification can stifle analysis. Rhetoric plays a vital role in this analysis, especially the role of Greco-Roman rhetoric, the *progymnasmata*, declamation, *imitatio*, and socio-cultural topoi.[42]

RHETORICAL CRITICISM OF THE EPISTLES

In his book, Kennedy analyzes Romans, 2 Corinthians, Galatians, and 1 Thessalonians.[43] He assumes that these epistles were constructed with a careful use of invention, arrangement, and style. These epistles are treated as speeches with epistolary prescripts and postscripts. Kennedy's work extended the work of Betz by purposefully adding style to the rhetorical analysis of an epistle as well providing a method that opened up analysis of all the epistles of the New Testament.

THE RELATIONSHIP OF EPISTOLARY AND RHETORICAL THEORY

Kennedy's work helped ignite a vigorous debate concerning the extent to which Greco-Roman rhetorical theory influenced the epistolary genre in antiquity and the epistles of the New Testament in particular, especially those of Paul.[44] The debate is based in part upon the fact that epistolary theory and rhetorical theory were developed separately in antiquity.[45] Most ancient rhetorical handbooks rarely, if ever, discuss the role of rhetoric in epistles. When they do, they focus on stylistic matters.[46] Likewise manuals for writing epistles do not give instruction in rhetorical technique, but rather focus on the practical classification of the various types of epistles and their appropriate style.[47]

The applicability of Kennedy's method to the epistles, and the broader enterprise of looking for elements of rhetoric in the epistles, has been questioned on many points. For example, Kennedy assumes that epistles can be classified according to the three species of rhetoric: judicial, deliberative, and epideictic. In practice this classification of epistles only partially works because, as just stated, epistolary and rhetorical theory were not integrated in the first century C.E. The large variety of letters in the ancient world and, in the case of Paul, the rhetorical needs being met by letters, naturally produced some functional parallels with all three species of rhetoric.[48] However, as David Aune states, "Early Christian letters tend to resist rigid classification, either in terms of the three main types of oratory or in terms of the many categories listed by the epistolary theorists."[49]

This applicability of ancient rhetoric to epistles has been questioned for invention, arrangement, and style as well. Inventional topics in epistolary theory are determined in large part by the type of epistle needed to address a specific social context, rather than the needs of argumentation.[50] Epistolary theory did not prescribe rhetorical arrangement for epistles because formulaic traditions held a powerful sway. There are functional parallels between epistolary and rhetorical arrangement. The body opening, middle, and closing roughly parallel the *exordium, narratio-confirmatio,* and *peroratio,* respectively.[51] Style was shared by both rhetorical and epistolary theory. However, epistolary theory differentiates between style appropriate to both epistles and rhetoric (*Inst.* 9.4.19-22). Also, epistles did not consistently use rhetorical style.[52]

Obviously there are two poles in the debate. One is that the New Testament epistles are just that—epistles—and rhetoric has only a secondary influence. Rhetorical influence is mostly limited to matters of style and some invention. The other is that the New Testament epistles are speeches in epistolary form. They are essentially speeches with epistolary openings and closings. Thus, New Testament epistles can be analyzed using Greco-Roman rhetorical theory in its three main parts: invention, arrangement, and style. The truth lies somewhere in the middle. Aune argues that by the first century B.C.E. rhetoric had exerted a strong influence on epistolary composition. Letters had become "sophisticated instruments of persuasion and media for displaying literary skill."[53] Utilizing the work of J. A. Goldstein, Frank W. Hughes demonstrates that the epistles of Demosthenes were written according to rhetorical conventions in their full form.[54] He also points out that Hermann Peter argued that epistolary theory was a part of rhetorical tradition. Official letters were substitutes for speeches and, thus, epistolary theory was a part of rhetorical training.[55] Rhetorical handbooks themselves may not have discussed epistolary theory because they were dominated by the concerns of judicial rhetoric, which was rarely appropriate for letter writing. Also, their focus was upon speeches, not written works. Thus the influence of rhetoric in epistles cannot be ruled out based on the paucity of discussion of epistles in rhetorical handbooks alone.[56] As John White states, "The use of rhetorical techniques, especially in the theological body of St. Paul's letters, indicates that knowledge of these traditions is quite relevant to the study of early Christian letters."[57]

Quintilian stated that the style of letters was of a "looser texture ... except when they deal with some subject above their natural level, such as philosophy, politics or the like" (*Inst.* 9.4.19). Clearly the subject of the epistles of the New Testament can be expected to have not only a greater quality of style than epistles but also greater use of invention and arrangement. They deal with the important subject of religion, are much longer than typical epistles, and are meant to be read and enacted as speeches to their audiences. The role of rhetoric in New Testament epistles is now acknowledged with much less debate. However, the acknowledgement has been tempered. It is assumed that the epistles can be analyzed with less reliance upon classification by species of rhetoric and rigid application of arrangement, and with greater emphasis on the sophistication of their invention and the role of style.[58] The species of rhetoric in the epistles are mixed, and the overall structure of epistles does not always conform to conventions of arrangement, especially longer letters, such as 1 Corinthians, or possibly composite letters, such as 2 Corinthians. The argumentation is often a complex use of enthymemes with a sophisticated use of style supporting it. It is interesting that Kennedy's own work on the New Testament emphasized invention and style over species and arrangement long ago!

THE QUESTION OF PAUL'S FORMAL EDUCATION

Kennedy and those who followed his method created a modest debate about the educational level of Paul and other writers of the New Testament. To the point, the question was and remains, "Did, or to what extent did, these authors have rhetorical training, and did they employ rhetorical theory in a conscious manner, especially Paul?" Carl Joachim Classen argues that rhetorical features occurring in a text may originate from four sources: deliberate application of rhetorical theory, imitation of written or spoken rhetorical practice, unconscious borrowing, or a gift for effective oral and written communication. He attributes Paul's rhetorical effectiveness to unconscious borrowing from the practice of others, particularly from reading Greek works and from the rhetoric of the Old Testament.[59] Jeffrey Reed says virtually the same thing: "if rhetorical elements do appear in Paul's letters, one must allow for the possibility that Paul's usage may be functionally related to, but not formally based upon, the ancient rhetorical practices."[60] Beginning with Kennedy's many observations about Paul's rhetoric, Porter investigates the invention, arrangement, and style in Paul's epistles. He provides one of the most complete statements of the position that Paul's rhetoric has mainly functional correlations to studied rhetoric, with style being perhaps where studied rhetoric is most likely to be found.[61]

However, if Paul's epistles were to be read in the churches, a logical assumption is that they were fashioned in a way closely akin to a speech. Since the body of the ancient letter was dictated by the needs of the author, we should expect his use of rhetorical theory in his letters. Needing to communicate over vast distances, Paul has a rhetorical need to be persuasive and would be expected to have used rhetorical theory. Rhetorical analysis of entire Pauline epistles has demonstrated that this is the case.

Many scholars now affirm that Paul's usage of rhetoric is studied and formally related to ancient rhetorical practices, not just functionally related or unconsciously borrowed. Kennedy writes, "Rhetorical schools were common in the Hellenized cities of the East when Paul was a boy, and he could have attended one; certainly he was familiar with the rhetorical conventions of speeches in Roman law courts, the oral teachings of Greek philosophers, and the conventions of Greek letter-writing."[62] Kennedy's opinion and his method have greatly influenced this debate, so that we can say that many New Testament scholars are concluding that Paul had studied rhetoric in school. For example, the brilliant blend of rhetoric in 2 Corinthians 10-13 and its conformity to the principles found in Plutarch's *On Praising Oneself Inoffensively* has convinced me that this is the case and that it is arguably the best evidence of Paul's rhetorical training.[63] Ronald Hock studied Greco-Roman education, especially the tertiary level where rhetorical training is central, and compared the curriculum with portions of Paul's epistles. He concludes, "That Paul's education went beyond the secondary stage, however, is also clear, and the letters themselves are again the evidence. These letters, given their length, complexity, and power, clearly point to an author who had received sustained training in composition and rhetoric, and it was only during the tertiary curriculum that such instruction was given."[64] While working to define Paul's social location, Jerome Neyrey musters evidence of Paul's education from his letter-writing ability, rhetorical skill, use of the *progymnasmata*, and philosophy. He concludes that Paul was an educated, elite writer who would be expected to utilize rhetorical theory in his letters.[65]

THE RHETORIC OF THE BOOK OF REVELATION

Kennedy has not provided any rhetorical analysis of the Book of Revelation. Because this book is an apocalypse reporting an ecstatic vision by a Jewish-Christian prophet, Greco-Roman rhetoric does not initially seem relevant for its analysis. However, Kennedy's assumption that Greco-Roman rhetoric pervaded the ancient Mediterranean basin motivated scholars to look for it in all New Testament books, including Revelation. This rhetoric, while not as evident in Revelation as in the epistles of Paul, provides a suitable framework and vocabulary for analysis of the persuasive strategies of the text.

The species of Revelation has been identified as a complex mixture of all three rhetorical genres and their topics and purposes, especially deliberative (i.e., outlining courses of action and their consequences) and epideictic (i.e., praise and blame of cities, and God and evil forces). Regarding ethos, the author uses many strategies for increasing his own and decreasing it for the opposition. Of primary importance is the claim that the work is an apocalypse and prophecy—and the claim and repeated demonstration of the author's divine commissioning to reveal this divinely given message.[66] Little work has been done in analyzing the pathos of Revelation except by Adela Yarbro Collins. She helpfully combines exegesis and psychology to show how Revelation arouses the audience's fear toward Satan and his henchmen and resentment toward Rome. Feelings are aroused, amplified, and then released through the imagery and drama of the text.[67]

Regarding logos, Revelation does not exhibit the sustained arguments that can be found in portions of Paul's letters, but it does develop standard rhetorical topoi and use rational argumentation. For example, Stephen O'Leary identifies and elaborates three pervasive topics in Revelation—authority, time, and evil.[68] Having identified Revelation as using honor discourse throughout, David deSilva has analyzed its rationales. These include giving God honor through obedience, because God is ultimately the judge and because it is just to honor the Creator.[69] He emphasizes the deliberative strategy of considering the consequences of an action, which in Revelation is the loss of honor and safety (exposure to judgment) by participation in the imperial cult.

Revelation does not employ classical patterns of rhetorical arrangement, relying instead upon a complicated mixture comprising intercalation, interlocking series, repetitions, comparison and contrast, *inclusio*, and chiasms.[70] Revelation employs a variety of standard classical stylistic figures that support the rhetorical strategy.[71]

CONCLUSION

This chapter has shown that Kennedy's influence on rhetorical analysis of the New Testament has been pervasive across all genres: gospel, history, epistle, and apocalypse. His own demonstration of such analysis, his provision of a methodology, and his ethos as a noted classicist gave New Testament scholars the impetus they needed to renew this investigation of the rhetoric of the New Testament. The possibilities and limitations of this analysis have been explored and debated, and the end result is that rhetorical analysis is now a key tool for the interpretation of the New Testament.

One persistent problem in all this investigation has been the limitations that genre seems to place on analysis. Portions of the gospels can be analyzed with the *progymnasmata*, and the speeches of Acts are organized as true speeches, but the greater complex of gospel and history are not so easily analyzed. The epistles of Paul and others demonstrate many features of Greco-Roman and Jewish rhetoric, but not the exact form found in ancient handbooks or actual letters. The book of Revelation defies such analysis on many fronts.

The problem of finding a way to explore the many genres of the New Testament rhetorically has been greatly alleviated by socio-rhetorical analysis as created and practiced by Vernon Robbins.[72] In this interpretative approach the text as a whole is analyzed from a variety of perspectives, including inner texture, intertexture, social and cultural texture, ideological texture, and sacred texture. More specifically, this analytic examines how the text blends the six types of discourses from the Mediterranean Basin. These discourses are precreation, wisdom, priestly, prophetic, miracle, and apocalyptic. To this is added the dimension of rhetography, analyzing the images that a text evokes in the reader, which are usually indicative of the six types of discourse grounded in the images of imperial household (precreation), family household (wisdom), sacrificial temple (priestly), earthly kingdom (prophetic), body (miracle), and imperial court (apocalyptic). This multidimensional analysis is not dependent upon genre and transcends such distinctions to utilize the discourses that are woven in particular ways to create recognized genres.

As indicated by his essay in this volume, Robbins acknowledges that his thinking is rooted in part in observations that Kennedy made long ago about radical Christian rhetoric in *New Testament Interpretation through Rhetorical Criticism*. In my opinion, the work of Robbins will be the greatest catalyst for the future influence of Kennedy on New Testament rhetorical analysis.

Notes

[1] Augustine, *On Christian Doctrine* (trans. D. W. Robertson Jr.; The Library of the Liberal Arts 80; Indianapolis: Bobbs-Merrill, 1958).

[2] Gussie H. Tannenhaus, "Bede's 'De schematibus et tropis'—A Translation," *QJS* 48 (1962): 237–53; repr. in *Readings in Medieval Rhetoric* (ed. Joseph M. Miller, Michael H. Prosser, and Thomas W. Benson; Bloomington: Indiana University Press, 1973), 92–122.

[3] *Commentarii in epistolam ad Romanos hoc anno M.D.XL. recogniti et locupletati* (Argentorati: apud C. Mylium, 1540).

[4] Karl Ludwig Bauer, *Rhetoricae Paulinae* (2 vols; Halae: Impensis Ophanotrophei, 1782).

[5] Edward Norden, *Die antike Kunstprosa vom VI. Jahrhundert vor Christus in die Zeit der Renaissance* (2 vols.; Leipzig: Teubner, 1898).

[6] Adolf Deissmann, *Bible Studies* (trans. A. Grieve; Edinburgh: T&T Clark, 1901), 3–59; idem, *Paul: A Study in Social and Religious History* (2nd ed.; trans. W. Wilson; London: Hodder & Stoughton, 1926), 27–52, 144–45; and idem, *Light From the Ancient East* (trans. L. R. M. Strachan; New York: Doran, 1927), 233–51.

[7] F. C. Grant, "Rhetoric and Oratory," in *IDB* (ed. George A. Buttrick; Nashville: Abingdon, 1962), 4:76–77.

[8] For the current situation in rhetorical criticism of the New Testament, see the multitude of works in Duane F. Watson, *The Rhetoric of the New Testament: A Bibliographic Survey* (Tools for Biblical Study 8; Blandford Forum: Deo Publishing, 2006).

[9] Hans Dieter Betz, "The Literary Composition and Function of Paul's Letter to the Galatians," *NTS* 21 (1975): 353–79; repr. in *Paulinische Studien: Gesammelte Aufsätze III* (ed. Hans Dieter Betz; Tübingen: Mohr [Siebeck], 1994), 63–97; repr. in *The Galatians Debate: Contemporary Issues in Rhetorical and Historical Interpretation* (ed. Mark D. Nanos; Peabody, Mass.: Hendrickson, 2002), 3–28; idem, "In Defense of the Spirit: Paul's Letter to the Galatians as a Document of Early Christian Apologetics," in *Aspects of Religious Propaganda in Judaism and Early Christianity* (ed. Elisabeth Schüssler Fiorenza;

Notre Dame and London: University of Notre Dame Press, 1976), 99–114; repr. in *Paulinische Studien*, 98–109; idem, *Galatians: A Commentary on Paul's Letter to the Churches in Galatia* (Hermeneia; Philadelphia: Fortress, 1979).

[10] George A. Kennedy, *New Testament Interpretation through Rhetorical Criticism* (Chapel Hill: University of North Carolina Press, 1984).

[11] Duane F. Watson, *Invention, Arrangement and Style: Rhetorical Criticism of Jude and 2 Peter* (SBLDS 104; Atlanta: Scholars Press, 1988).

[12] It is not my intention to survey Greco-Roman rhetorical theory. For brief surveys, see Kennedy, *New Testament Interpretation*, 12–33; Watson, *Invention, Arrangement and Style*, 8–28; Burton L. Mack, *Rhetoric and the New Testament* (GBSNTS; Minneapolis: Fortress, 1990), 25–48. For works with detailed discussions, see those listed in Watson, *The Rhetoric of the New Testament*, 26–30.

[13] For this observation, see Margaret Mitchell, *Paul and the Rhetoric of Rhetoric of Reconciliation: An Exegetical Investigation of the Language and Composition of 1 Corinthians* (HUT 28; Tübingen: Mohr Siebeck, 1991), 8–11.

[14] Carl Joachim Classen, "St. Paul's Epistles and Ancient Greek and Roman Rhetoric," *Rhet* 10 (1992): 322, 343; Wilhelm Wuellner, "Where is Rhetorical Criticism Taking Us?" *CBQ* 49 (1987): 450–54, 460–63.

[15] Chaim Perelman and Lucie Olbrechts-Tyteca, *The New Rhetoric: A Treatise on Argumentation* (trans. John Wilkinson and Purcell Weaver; Notre Dame: University of Notre Dame Press, 1969).

[16] See Watson, *The Rhetoric of the New Testament*, 54–61.

[17] Lloyd Bitzer, "The Rhetorical Situation," *PR* 1 (1968): 1–14. Refined in his "Functional Communication: A Situational Perspective," in *Rhetoric in Transition: Studies in the Nature and Uses of Rhetoric* (ed. E. E. White; University Park: Pennsylvania State University Press, 1980), 21–38.

[18] Arthur B. Miller, "Rhetorical Exigence," *PR* 5 (1972): 111–18; Richard E. Vatz, "The Myth of the Rhetorical Situation," *PR* 6 (1973): 154–61; Scott Consigny, "Rhetoric and Its Situation," *PR* 7 (1974): 175–85; David M. Hunsaker and Craig R. Smith, "The Nature of Issues: A Constructive Approach to Situational Rhetoric," *Western Speech Communication* 40 (1976): 144–56; John H. Patton, "Causation and Creativity in Rhetorical Situations: Distinctions and Implications," *QJS* 65 (1979): 36–55; P. K. Tompkins, John H. Patton, and Lloyd F. Bitzer, "Tompkins on Patton and Bitzer, Patton on Tompkins, and Bitzer on Tompkins (and Patton)," *QJS* 66 (1980): 85–93; Alan Brinton, "Situation in the Theory of Rhetoric," *PR* 14 (1981): 234–48.

[19] George Lyons, *Pauline Autobiography: Toward a New Understanding* (SBLDS 73; Atlanta: Scholars Press, 1985); J. M. G. Barclay, "Mirror-Reading a Polemical Letter: Galatians as a Test Case," *JSNT* 31 (1987): 73–93.

[20] Duane F. Watson, "The Contribution and Limitations of Greco-Roman Rhetorical Theory for Constructing the Rhetorical and Historical Situations of a Pauline Epistle," in *The Rhetorical Interpretation of Scripture: Essays from the 1996 Malibu Conference* (ed. Stanley E. Porter and Dennis L. Stamps; JSNTSup 180; Sheffield: Sheffield Academic, 1999), 125–51.

[21] Stanley Porter and Dennis L. Stamps, eds., *The Rhetorical Interpretation of Scripture: Essays from the 1996 Malibu Conference* (JSNTSup 180; Sheffield: Sheffield Academic, 1999).

[22] Kennedy, *New Testament Interpretation*, chs. 2 and 3.

[23] Kennedy, *New Testament Interpretation*, ch. 5. This chapter is also found as "An Introduction to the Rhetoric of the Gospels," *Rhet* 1 (1983): 17–31.

[24] "An Oration at Olivet: Some Rhetorical Dimensions of Mark 13," in *Persuasive Artistry: Studies in New Testament Rhetoric in Honor of George A. Kennedy* (ed. Duane F. Watson; JSNTSup 50: Sheffield: JSOT Press, 1991), 66–92; repr. and expanded, C. Clifton Black, *The Rhetoric of the Gospel: Theological Artistry in the Gospels and Acts* (St. Louis: Chalice, 2001), 47–73.

[25] Black, *Rhetoric of the Gospel*, 75–94.

[26] Mack, *Rhetoric in the New Testament*, 79–80.

[27] Ronald F. Hock and Edward N. O'Neil, eds., *The Chreia in Ancient Rhetoric: The Progymnasmata* (Greco-Roman Religions Series 9; Atlanta: Scholars Press, 1986); idem, *The Chreia and Ancient Rhetoric: Classroom Exercises* (WGRW 3; Atlanta: Society of Biblical Literature, 2002); James R. Butts, "The Chreia in the Synoptic Gospels," *BTB* 16 (1986): 132–38; Burton Mack and Vernon K. Robbins, *Patterns of Persuasion in the Gospels. Foundations and Facets: Literary Facets* (Sonoma, Calif.: Polebridge, 1989); Burton L. Mack, *Anecdotes and Arguments: The Chreia in Antiquity and Early Christianity* (Occasional Papers 10; Claremont, Calif.: The Institute for Antiquity and Christianity, 1987); Vernon K. Robbins, "The Chreia," in *Greco-Roman Literature and the New Testament* (ed. David E. Aune; SBLSBS 21; Atlanta: Scholars Press, 1988), 1–23; Duane F. Watson, "Chreia/Aphorism," in *DJG*, 104–6.

[28] Vernon K. Robbins, ed., *The Rhetoric of Pronouncement*, Semeia 64 (1993).

[29] *Progymnasmata: Greek Textbooks of Prose Composition and Rhetoric, Translated into English, with Introductions and Notes* (WGRW 10; Atlanta and Leiden: Society of Biblical Literature/Brill, 2003).

[30] *From Tradition to Gospel* (trans. Bertram L. Woolf; New York: Charles Scribner's Sons, 1934), 152–64.

[31] Richard Burridge, "The Gospels and Acts," in *Handbook of Classical Rhetoric in the Hellenistic Period 330 B.C.–A.D. 400* (ed. Stanley E. Porter; Leiden: Brill, 2001), 507–32. See also idem, *What Are the Gospels? A Comparison with Graeco-Roman Biography* (Cambridge: Cambridge University Press, 1992; 2nd ed., Grand Rapids, Mich.: Eerdmans, 2004).

[32] Burridge, "The Gospels and Acts," 510.

[33] Kennedy, *New Testament Interpretation*, 67.

[34] Mack, *Rhetoric and the New Testament*, 49–56, 78–92.

[35] L. Gregory Bloomquist, "The Rhetoric of the Historical Jesus," in *Whose Historical Jesus?* (ed. W. E. Arnal and M. Desjardins; Studies in Christianity and Judaism 7; Waterloo, Ont.: Wilfrid Laurier University Press, 1997), 98–117. See also idem, "Rhetorical Analysis and Sociological Analysis in Historical Jesus Research," *MTSR* 9.2 (1997): 139–54.

[36] Kennedy, *New Testament Interpretation*, 114–40.

[37] E.g., Duane F. Watson, "Paul's Speech to the Ephesian Elders (Acts 20.17–38): Epideictic Rhetoric of Farewell," in *Persuasive Artistry: Studies in New Testament Rhetoric in Honor of George A. Kennedy* (ed. D. F. Watson, JSNTSup 50; Sheffield: JSOT Press, 1991), 184–208. For many such works, see Watson, *The Rhetoric of the New Testament*, 111–16.

[38] Marion L. Soards, *The Speeches in Acts: Their Content, Context, and Concerns* (Louisville, Ky.: Westminster John Knox, 1994); Todd Penner, "Civilizing Discourse: Acts, Declamation, and the Rhetoric of the Polis," in *Contextualizing Acts: Lukan Narrative and Greco-Roman Discourse* (ed. Todd Penner and Caroline Vander Stichele; SBLSymS 20; Atlanta: Society of Biblical Literature, 2003), 65–104.

[39] Kennedy, *New Testament Interpretation*, 114–40, esp. 114–16, 139–40.

[40] Stanley Porter, "Paul as Epistolographer and Rhetorician? Implications for the Study of the Paul of Acts," in his *The Paul of Acts: Essays in Literary Criticism, Rhetoric, and Theology* (WUNT 115; Tübingen: Mohr Siebeck, 1999), 125; repr., *Paul in Acts* (Peabody, Mass.: Hendrickson, 1999), 125.

[41] Bruce Winter, "The Importance of the *Captatio Benevolentiae* in the Speeches of Tertullus and Paul in Acts 24:1–21," *JTS* 42 (1991): 505–31.

[42] For fine examples, see the many essays in Penner and Vander Stichele, eds., *Contextualizing Acts*, n. 38.

[43] Kennedy, *New Testament Interpretation*, 86–96, 141–56.

[44] For an overview of the relationship between rhetorical and epistolary theory, with discussion of primary texts, see Bruce C. Johanson, *To All the Brethren: A Text-Linguistic and Rhetorical Approach to 1 Thessalonians* (ConBNT 16; Stockholm: Almqvist & Wiksell, 1987), 42–43; Frank W. Hughes, *Early Christian Rhetoric and 2 Thessalonians* (JSNTSup 30; Sheffield: JSOT Press, 1989), 24–30; G. Walter Hansen, *Abraham in Galatians: Epistolary and Rhetorical Contexts* (JSNTSup 29; Sheffield: JSOT Press, 1989), chs. 1–2; Lauri Thurén, *The Rhetorical Strategy of 1 Peter with Special Regard to Ambiguous Expressions* (Åbo: Academy, 1990), 57–64; Abraham J. Malherbe, "'Seneca' on Paul as Letter Writer" in *The Future of Early Christianity: Essays in Honor of Helmut Koester* (ed. Birger A. Pearson; Minneapolis: Fortress, 1991), 414–21; Earl Randolph Richards, *The Secretary in the Letters of Paul* (WUNT 42; Tübingen: Mohr-Siebeck, 1991), 132–36, 140–44; Carl Joachim Classen, "Paulus und die antike Rhetorik" *ZNW* 82 (1991): 1-32; idem, "St. Paul's Epistles," 319–44; Georg Strecker, *Literaturgeschichte des Neuen Testaments* (Göttingen: Vandenhoeck & Ruprecht, 1992), 86–95; Stanley E. Porter, "The Theoretical Justification for Application of Rhetorical Categories to Pauline Epistolary Literature," in *Rhetoric and the New Testament: Essays from the 1992 Heidelberg Conference* (ed. Stanley E. Porter and Thomas H. Olbricht; Sheffield: Sheffield Academic, 1993), 100–122; Jeffrey T. Reed, "Using Ancient Rhetorical Categories to Interpret Paul's Letters: A Question of Genre," in *Rhetoric and the New Testament*, 292–324; R. Dean Anderson Jr., *Ancient Rhetorical Theory and Paul* (rev. ed.; CBET 18; Leuven: Peeters, 1998), 109–27.

[45] Abraham J. Malherbe, *Ancient Epistolary Theorists* (SBLSBS 19; Atlanta: Scholars Press, 1988), 3–6; S. K. Stowers, *Letter Writing in Greco-Roman Antiquity* (LEC 5; Philadelphia: Westminster, 1986), 51–52; Classen, "St. Paul's Epistles," 269–70, 288–90.

[46] Demetrius, *On Style*, 223–35; Julius Victor, *Ars rhetorica*, 27 (*De Epistolis*) in Malherbe, *Ancient Epistolary Theorists*, 62–64; and C. Halm, ed., *Rhetores Latini Minores* (Leipzig: Teubner, 1863).

[47] Pseudo-Demetrius, *ΤΥΠΟΙ ΕΠΙΣΤΟΛΙΚΟΙ* and Pseudo-Libanius, *ΕΠΙΣΤΟΛΙΜΑΙΟΙ ΧΑΡΑΚΤΗΡΕΣ*, in Malherbe, *Ancient Epistolary Theorists*, 30–41, 66–81.

[48] Reed, "Using Ancient Rhetorical Categories," 297–301.

[49] David E. Aune, *The New Testament in Its Literary Environment* (Philadelphia: Westminster, 1987), 203.

[50] Stowers, *Letter Writing*, 53–56; Reed, "Using Ancient Rhetorical Categories," 301–4. Classen ("St. Paul's Epistles," 285) allows for some overlap of invention in rhetorical and epistolary theory.

[51] Classen, "St. Paul's Epistles," 285–90; Reed, "Using Ancient Rhetorical Categories," 304–8.

[52] Reed, "Using Ancient Rhetorical Categories," 308–11.

[53] Aune, *New Testament in Its Literary Environment*, 160.

[54] Jonathan A. Goldstein, *The Letters of Demosthenes* (New York and London: Columbia University Press, 1968); Hughes, *Early Christian Rhetoric*, 47–50.

[55] Hermann Peter, *Der Brief in der römischen Literatur: Literargeschichtliche Untersuchungen und Zusammenfassungen* (Abhandlungen der Königlichen Sächsischen Gesellschaft der Wissenschaften, philologisch-historische Classe, 20.3; Leipzig: Teubner, 1901; repr., Hildesheim: Georg Olms, 1965), 14, 19; Hughes, *Early Christian Rhetoric*, 26.

[56] Hughes, *Early Christian Rhetoric*, 28–29.

[57] John White, *Light from Ancient Letters* (FFNT; Philadelphia: Fortress, 1986), 3.

[58] Duane F. Watson, "The Three Species of Rhetoric and the Study of the Pauline Epistles," and "The Role of Style in the Pauline Epistles: From Ornamentation to Argumentative Strategies," in *Paul and Rhetoric* (ed. J. Paul Sampley and Peter Lampe; New York: Continuum, forthcoming).

[59] Classen, "St. Paul's Epistles," 268–69, 290–91.

[60] Reed, "Using Ancient Rhetorical Categories," 324; cf. 16–17.

[61] Stanley E. Porter, "Paul of Tarsus and His Letters," in *Handbook of Classical Rhetoric in the Hellenistic Period 330 B.C.–A.D. 400* (ed. Stanley E. Porter; Leiden and Boston: Brill, 2001), 533–85. See also his "The Theoretical Justification for Application of Rhetorical Criticism to Pauline Epistolary Literature," 100–122.

[62] George A. Kennedy, *Classical Rhetoric and Its Christian and Secular Tradition from Ancient to Modern Times* (Chapel Hill: University of North Carolina Press, 1980), 130; cf. *New Testament Interpretation*, 9–10.

[63] Duane F. Watson, "Paul's Boasting in 2 Corinthians 10-13 as Defense of His Honor: A Socio-Rhetorical Analysis," in *Rhetorical Argumentation in Biblical Texts: Essays from the Lund 2000 Conference* (ed. Anders Eriksson, Thomas Olbricht, and Walter Übelacker; ESEC 8; Harrisburg, Pa.: Trinity Press International, 2002), 260–75, and "Paul and Boasting," in *Paul in the Greco-Roman World: A Handbook* (ed. J. Paul Sampley; Harrisburg, Pa.: Trinity Press International, 2003), 81–95.

[64] Ronald Hock, "Paul and Greco-Roman Education," in *Paul in the Greco-Roman World: A Handbook* (ed. J. Paul Sampley; Harrisburg, Pa.: Trinity Press International, 2003), 198–227; 209; cf. 198.

[65] Jerome H. Neyrey, "The Social Location of Paul: Education as the Key," in *Fabrics of Discourse: Essays in Honor of Vernon K. Robbins* (ed. David B. Gowler, L. Gregory Bloomquist, and Duane F. Watson; Harrisburg, Pa.: Trinity Press International, 2003), 126–64.

[66] Greg Carey, "The Apocalypse and Its Ambiguous Ethos," in *Studies in the Book of Revelation* (ed. Steven Moyise; Edinburgh: T&T Clark, 2001), 163–80; idem, *Elusive Apocalypse: Reading Authority in the Revelation to John* (StABH 15; Macon, Ga.; Mercer University Press, 1999).

[67] Adela Yarbro Collins, *Crisis and Catharsis: The Power of the Apocalypse* (Philadelphia: Westminster), 1984.

⁶⁸ Stephen D. O'Leary, "A Dramatistic Theory of Apocalyptic Rhetoric," *QJS* 79 (1993): 385–426; idem, *Arguing the Apocalypse: A Theory of Millennial Rhetoric* (New York: Oxford University Press, 1994).

⁶⁹ David A. deSilva, "Honor Discourse and the Rhetorical Strategy of the Apocalypse of John," *JSNT* 71 (1998): 79–110.

⁷⁰ Bruce W. Longenecker, "'Linked Like a Chain': Rev 22.6-9 in Light of an Ancient Transition Technique," *NTS* 47 (2001): 105–17.

⁷¹ Constantin Nikolakopoulos, "Rhetorische Auslegungsaspekte der Theologie in der Johannesoffenbarung," in *"...Was ihr auf dem Weg verhandelt haben": Beiträge zur Exegese und Theologie des Neuen Testaments: Festschrift für Ferdinand Hahn zum 75. Geburtstag* (ed. C. Gerber, T. Knoppler, and P. Muller; Neukirchen-Vluyn: Neukirchener Verlag, 2001), 166–80.

⁷² Vernon K. Robbins, *Exploring the Texture of Texts: A Guide to Socio-Rhetorical Interpretation* (Valley Forge, Pa.: Trinity Press International, 1996); idem, *The Tapestry of Early Christian Discourse: Rhetoric, Society, and Ideology* (London: Routledge, 1996); idem, *The Invention of Christian Discourse*, Vol. 1: *Wisdom, Prophetic, and Apocalyptic* (Blandford Forum: Deo Publishing, 2008). For illustrations of the above method as applied to the text of Acts, see Randall C. Webber, "'Why Were the Heathen So Arrogant?' The Socio-Rhetorical Strategy of Acts 3–4," *BTB* 22 (1992): 19–25; Istvan Czachesz, "Socio-Rhetorical Exegesis of Acts 9.1-10," *CV* 37 (1995): 5–32; Milton Moreland, "The Jerusalem Commentary in Acts: Mythmaking and the Socio-Rhetorical Functions of a Lukan Setting," in *Contextualizing Acts: Lukan Narrative and Greco-Roman Discourse* (ed. Todd Penner and Caroline Vander Stichele; SBLSymS 20; Atlanta: Society of Biblical Literature, 2003), 285–310.

CHAPTER 5

KENNEDY AND THE GOSPELS
An Ambiguous Legacy, a Promising Bequest

C. Clifton Black

What follows is, up to a point, a mystery story, but of a special kind. As in Conan Doyle's tale of "the curious incident of the dog in the night-time" ("Silver Blaze," 1892), in this chapter Inspector Black notes a curious lapse of appeal by scholars of the gospels to Kennedy's method of rhetorical analysis and considers various reasons why the dog hasn't barked—at least loudly, for very long. Silence, however, is not the final word; for Professor Kennedy, like Mr. Holmes, "sees the value of imagination": the ability to envision rhetoric in a fresh way, thereby opening new paths of research. Let us proceed.

From among the thousands who attend annual meetings of the Society of Biblical Literature and similar academic conclaves, few succeed in that endeavor which motivated the builders of Babel's Tower: to make a name for themselves. Given the outcome of the project recounted in Genesis, that's probably a good thing. For good or ill, by far fewer establish themselves with scholarship that must be taken seriously by those standing outside the perimeter of their tightly circumscribed academic fields.

George Kennedy has done both, for the benefit of all. Though neither a classicist nor the son of a classicist, I find it hard to imagine any scholar who has grown more aptly into the mantle that he recounts being draped upon him during his student days at Harvard. Kennedy says that Werner Jaeger "laid his hand apostolically on [his] shoulder and said, 'I have written *Paideia*; you must write *Peitho*.'"[1] In three substantial tomes, plus numerous one-volume histories and handbooks,[2] Kennedy has accomplished that, and then some.[3] His recent, cross-cultural exercise in comparative rhetoric, to which we shall return, leads us into worlds to which even the redoubtable Jaeger never ventured. On its own terms, Kennedy's scholarship has set a standard for depth and breadth unlikely to be matched in our generation.

This volume, however, intends not merely to acknowledge Kennedy's extraordinary erudition but also to honor his scholarly hospitality: his demonstrated willingness to push beyond a specialist's comfortable boundaries to continue an extended, fruitful conversation with others in a different sector of the guild. For that, all biblical scholars stand in his debt.

To the best of my ability to survey the terrain, Kennedy has given them at least two landmark contributions. The best known is his handbook *New Testament Interpretation through Rhetorical Criticism*, which is now a standard fixture in biblical exegetes' footnotes and bibliographies. Seven years prior to its publication, however, at Trinity University, Kennedy delivered a provocative, less frequently cited paper at a Colloquy on the Relationships among the gospels, entitled "Classical and Christian Source Criticism."[4] As I consider these two contributions and their impact on subsequent research in the gospels, I confess to surprise and no little puzzlement. For it seems to me that the earlier, less well-known essay has exerted a greater, albeit subtle, impact on gospel scholarship than the later, more immediately recognizable volume. In this chapter, I articulate the nature of my confusion.

THE ROAR OF KENNEDY'S SOURCE CRITICISM

At San Antonio in 1977, Kennedy wisely resisted being drawn into controversies swirling around Q, Griesbach, and hypotheses two-source and two-gospel. Instead, he reframed the question of the gospels' interrelationships from a classicist's point of view, offering suggestions that made that colloquy's participants—particularly Wayne Meeks, the paper's respondent[5]—stop and think about the literary environment and its conventions in which the gospels arose. Of that paper's many rich suggestions, I can mention here only three.

First, the gospels had at least rough classical analogues. "One is the Socratic literature"—reminiscences of Socrates by Xenophon and Plato (and in satirical form, Aristophanes)—"which is comparable to the gospels spiritually and, like them, provides the basis for our knowledge of an outstanding personality and lays the foundation for a powerful movement."[6] In such cases, "The author had considerable freedom of treatment,"[7] on which Kennedy approvingly quoted W. K. C. Guthrie: "The justification . . . in Plato's mind for putting a doctrine into Socrates' mouth was not that the doctrine *tel quel*, in its complete form, had been taught by Socrates, but that it could appear to Plato to be based on one of Socrates' fundamental convictions, and constitute a legitimate projection, explication, and defence of it."[8] Kennedy saw in the Fourth Gospel a partial parallel of this phenomenon,[9] though one can easily descry its implications for understanding the Synoptics as well. For Kennedy, "The other [set of classical analogues] is historical, biographical, and scholarly literature, especially that written in the early Roman empire, which might indicate something about conventions of composition at that time. . . ."[10]

A second observation made on that occasion by Kennedy: In the transition from the first to the second of these analogical sets, one might contemplate an intervening use of notes, *hypomnēmata*, privately recorded at the time of a discourse or soon thereafter, which were "the raw material from which more formal publications [could] be created."[11] Such formal publications could take the form of memoirs, *apomnēmoneumata*, which of course is precisely the term Justin Martyr uses to characterize the gospels (*Apology* 1.66.3; 1.67.3). Kennedy speculates that some of the earliest witnesses of Jesus' ministry may have made and later returned to such notes, as did Plutarch, Suetonius, and other historiographers of antiquity.

Third (and for our purposes, finally): Kennedy invited his audience of biblical scholars to reconsider the potential validity of external evidence, or *testimonia*, regarding the authorship, composition, and dates of the gospels, of the sort provided by Papias of Hierapolis as cited in Eusebius's *Church History* (3.39.15–16).[12] Kennedy conceded that such external testimonies gain force by the degree to which they find corroboration within the gospels themselves. Nevertheless, against a reflexive skepticism of Papias and other patristic commentators, Kennedy wryly remarked, "[A]ncient writers sometimes meant what they said and occasionally even knew what they were talking about."[13]

While none of Kennedy's proposals in 1977 has turned research in the gospels on its ear—Whose has?—all of them, with modifications, have made an impression in subsequent scholarship. While unanimity of opinion on the gospels' genre cannot be expected this side of academic paradise, their association with ancient biography and historiography seems to me rather firm, even among those—such as Charles Talbert, David Aune, and Richard Burridge[14]—who disagree on various particulars. To be sure, Kennedy was not the first in the modern era to construe the gospels as ancient biographies: Clyde

Weber Votaw made the same proposal in 1915.[15] Kennedy, however, revisited such arguments, fortified them, and renewed their merit. The same may also be said of the *hypomnēmata* hypothesis, whose earliest expression I can verify is in Robert Grant's *The Earliest Lives of Jesus*.[16] I know of little research to date that has pressed far beyond Kennedy in this matter. I myself found his insights quite helpful some years ago, while parsing Eusebius's elliptical quotations of Papias on the origins of Mark.[17]

On a larger scale, Kennedy's proposal of *hypomnēmata* has, in my judgment, usefully complicated the question of gospel interrelationships by sensibly injecting the probability of intervening, and irrecoverable, oral and literary stages in the process of their creation. The result has been, or should be, to chasten most biblical interpreters, whatever their resolutions of the Synoptic problem or the still-disputed relationship of John with the Synoptics. Truly, I think, we remain blind judges of the elephant: Most of us have a grip on some phenomenon that is real but susceptible to misinterpretation because we cannot and shall never see the beast as a whole. Kennedy concluded, "[I]t is thus not impossible both that Matthew could have influenced Mark and that Mark could have influenced our text of Matthew."[18] I still regard Mark as probably the earliest gospel, independently used by both Matthew and Luke as one of their principal sources. Nevertheless, that hypothesis, brushed in broad strokes, does not capture all the nuances of the Synoptic problem. It is likely—as Kennedy implies and others[19] have suggested—that in the last half of the first century C.E. there was crisscross copying among various scribal editions of those three gospels, of a kind and to a degree that we shall never reconstruct with complete confidence. And while expressing reserve, still shared by most, about Kennedy's supposition of Matthew as a translation of an Aramaic gospel into Greek,[20] commentators of no less stature than W. D. Davies and Dale Allison have now concluded, "[T]he simplistic understanding of Papias that dismisses him out of hand must be questioned if not abandoned."[21] If Kennedy's earlier essay is not always cited in such matters, it is no less true that many of his judgments about the gospels, viewed from a classicist's perspective, are practically accepted by many in our guild.

THE WHISPER OF KENNEDY'S RHETORICAL CRITICISM

Turning to Kennedy's *New Testament Interpretation through Rhetorical Criticism*, I find the picture much less clear. Three of this book's eight chapters are devoted to the gospels: one, an analysis of Matthew's Sermon on the Mount and Luke's Sermon on the Plain as specimens of deliberative oratory; another on John's Farewell Discourse as an instance of epideictic rhetoric; and a third chapter summarizing Kennedy's conclusions on the rhetoric of the gospels.[22] From among the canonical evangelists, Kennedy finds Matthew the ablest in deploying rhetorical aspects; his Sermon on the Mount displays unity of thought, diversity of tone, and maintenance of audience contact through topics and stylistic devices, an authoritative ethos, and the form of logical argument.[23] Surprisingly, for those who cut their teeth on Cadbury and Dibelius,[24] Luke's Sermon on the Plain pales by comparison: for Kennedy, "[it] is not a very good speech," because it is too concise, leaves too many things unexplained, and relies almost entirely on the ethos or authority of Jesus.[25] John 13–17 manifests a complex amplification of several repetitive topics, which ultimately resolve themselves into "a kind of transcendent logic ... constructed with the help of the authoritative ethos of Jesus."[26] Like John, Mark exemplifies what Kennedy calls "radical Christian rhetoric,"

> a form of "sacred language" characterized by assertion and absolute claims of authoritative truth without evidence or logical argument.... The truth is immediate and intuitively apprehended because it is true. Some see it, others do not, but there is no point in trying to persuade the latter.[27]

In Kennedy's view, "John makes far more demands than Mark on his readers in approaching the truth they are to perceive. He uses the forms of logical argument not so much as proof, as does Matthew, but as ways of turning and reiterating the topics which are at the core of his message."[28]

Momentarily I shall return to some particulars in Kennedy's analysis, but for now I want to underscore two things that I find most intriguing when one attempts to locate Kennedy's contributions on the canvas of gospel scholarship. First, not since Amos Niven Wilder do we encounter a more intense appreciation of the gospels' power as rhetorical products. But unlike Wilder, whose 1955 SBL Presidential Address[29] and subsequent volume on *Early Christian Rhetoric*[30] made *not a single reference* to classical theorists of rhetoric, Kennedy unfolds his analysis in perpetual conversation with a dazzling array of thinkers, such as Aristotle, Cicero, Demetrius, and Menander Rhetor. I can remember leaving Kennedy's lectures at Chapel Hill marveling, "What is this? A new teaching with authority—not as one of the scribes!" (Mark 1:27a). The second thing worth underlining: In the twenty-four years since publication of *New Testament Interpretation through Rhetorical Criticism*, astonishingly few interpreters of the gospels have followed the markers laid down by Kennedy.

That last comment invites supporting evidence. In Duane Watson and Alan Hauser's comprehensive bibliography *Rhetorical Criticism of the Bible*,[31] published a decade after Kennedy's handbook (1984), I count 183 articles, essays, and monographs on the gospels. Of that number, 102 (57%) were published from 1985 on. Among that majority of entries appearing since the publication of Kennedy's book, I liberally reckon that not more than thirty (29%) demonstrate serious engagement with Kennedy's approach to rhetoric. Of that number, a half-dozen appear in the *Festschrift* for Professor Kennedy edited by Watson.[32] While the essays in that volume are serious contributions to scholarship, one naturally expects them to adopt elements of Kennedy's point of view, given their subsidiary purpose to honor his scholarship. As for the remaining seventy-two rhetorical analyses of the gospels since 1985 (71%)—though I may be badly mistaken—I can see little evidence of Kennedy's influence on them. In preparing my book *The Rhetoric of the Gospel*,[33] I tried to take into account scholarship published since the compilation of Watson and Hauser's bibliography. On a generous accounting, I judge fewer than a dozen essays, appearing between 1994 and 2000, that adopted Kennedy's approach. More recently, a research assistant and I have combed publications from 2001 to the present, again looking for traces of Kennedy's influence. We netted only a handful of titles.[34]

As with history, so with biblical scholarship: Its wheels grind slowly. Are the two-and-a-half decades that have elapsed since publication of *New Testament Interpretation through Rhetorical Criticism* time enough for its effects to have registered? Comparisons can be invidious; they may also illumine. Two comparisons may be relevant at this juncture. On the rhetorical side, the works of Wilhelm Wuellner and Vernon Robbins have spawned, within the same period, a discernible body of scholarship that considers the gospels' rhetoric from a hermeneutical[35] or socio-cultural[36] point of view. Not so with Kennedy. In the larger range of literary criticism, Alan Culpepper's *Anatomy of the Fourth Gospel*,[37] published a year before Kennedy's book, has exerted on the gospels' interpretation a profound impact, beyond all capacity to footnote. Can the same be said of Kennedy? I think not.

Why is this so?

RUMINATIONS: AN INTERLUDE

Pondering that question, I have considered possibilities that seem to me variously satisfying. Here they are, arranged in degrees of ascending plausibility.

1. *Kennedy's particular assessments of the gospels and patristic tradition are more conservative than the mainline or liberal-leaning biblical scholarship that many of us practice.* That is surely rubbish. As far as I can see, Kennedy's method is ideologically neutral, apart from its unapologetically historical bias. It can be, and has been, practiced by scholars both conservative and liberal in their orientations toward the gospels and the rest of the New Testament.

2. *Kennedy concentrates heavily on elements of the gospels that once were compelling but may now seem passé to many New Testament interpreters.* Here one thinks of Kennedy's recent translation of ancient textbooks of *progymnasmata*, whose contents resonate with earlier, form-critical studies of Dibelius and Bultmann.[38] Is the Society of Biblical Literature any longer interested in such things? Well, some must be, if the Society's own press deemed it worthy to publish Kennedy's version of these texts in a series titled "Writings from the Greco-Roman World."[39] Moreover, Kennedy's approach is far more expansive, inclusive of many more elements of ancient discourse, to be so dismissed.

3. *Kennedy's proposal is formalist, concentrating on such matters as rhetorical invention, arrangement, and style, whereas many critics are now more interested in socio-cultural and hermeneutical questions, both ancient and modern.* This is a twist on the preceding suggestion: Kennedy's approach is out of sync with current fashions, which wax and wane. Again, there may be truth in that, but it cannot be the whole truth. Even more formalist in approach than Kennedy's *New Testament Interpretation* is Culpepper's *Anatomy*, though its forms are more congruent with modern narrative theory (the old "New

Criticism"). Formalism as such has hardly stemmed the tide of recent literary criticism of the gospels.

4. *Kennedy is a classicist; most New Testament scholars have not done as good a job as he in reaching across disciplinary boundaries to avail themselves of resources available to them.* In that there may be a grain of truth, given the pluriformity of New Testament studies and historical accidents attending the ways in which we train a new generation of New Testament scholars. On the other hand, I see no evidence that such blinkered vision has prevented interpretation of the New Testament's epistles in accordance with Kennedy's method.

5. *The gospels are complex amalgams of many different genres*—bioi, *ancient history, novella, drama, aphorisms, apocalyptic, and speeches—that resist uniform analysis.* Surely that is accurate—though insufficient to account for the paucity, to date, of analysis of constitutive materials that accord with Kennedy's canons. To take but one example: such interpreters as Louis Martyn and Andrew Lincoln[40] have invited us to take seriously the heavily juridical tenor of the Fourth Gospel. Judicial rhetoric, as Kennedy reminds us, was the social location for a vast body of theory and practice of rhetoric among the ancients.[41] Why have Johannine critics so little availed themselves of its resources?

6. *Kennedy's offering is too idiosyncratic or recondite to be easily appropriated.* That is a tricky proposition, patient of multiple ripostes. The study of New Testament rhetoric is hardly eccentric; it boasts a venerable heritage that extends, in the modern era, at least as far back as C. G. Wilke.[42] Kennedy's presentation is, furthermore, crystalline in its clarity. If investigators of the gospels can swallow Derrida, Kennedy is a slice of coconut angel food.

On the other hand, in order to practice Kennedy's species of rhetorical criticism, one does have to master a considerable body of ancient literature that speaks in terms distant from us in space and time. Kennedy is, I believe, every bit as clear as Culpepper. I am not at all certain the same may be said of Quintilian and Seymour Chatman. Kennedy's method lives in a world in which such concepts as *ekphrasis* and *enthymemes*[43] were common coins of its intellectual realm. Chatman's *Story and Discourse*, and Culpepper following Chatman,[44] breathes the atmosphere of plot, characterization, readers and audiences implied—all of which are more immediately recognizable for those whose literary sensibilities are now shaped by novels, motion pictures, and television.

7. *The gospels are narratives; Kennedy's rhetorical criticism, based on ancient handbooks that detail the proper construction of speeches, is less well suited for the exegetical task.* Here, I believe, we draw even nearer to the problem's nub. Whether exegetes have been wise to interpret New Testament epistles as though they were speeches remains, for me, an open question.[45] In the case of a document like Hebrews, perhaps the longest sustained argument in the New Testament, I can see pertinence in Kennedy's method. "It was the intent of the evangelists," he claims, "to present speeches, and early Christian audiences, listening to the gospels read, heard these chapters as speeches."[46] That is assumption, not fact. In point of fact, the gospels are *not* speeches, though all of them *contain* speeches.[47] This is especially true of the Fourth Gospel, which, unlike the Synoptics, presents Jesus as delivering a succession of extended, highly stylized discourses. Even in John, however, those speeches are embedded in an indelibly narrative structure that may not be immediately amenable to Kennedy's form of criticism. As my colleague George Parsenios has suggested to me in conversation, to practice Kennedy's method with the gospels requires a somewhat oblique approach and intellectual suppleness on the interpreter's part.

8. *Kennedy's method subliminally gives pride of place to logos, or logical argument, whereas the gospels tend more obviously towards ethos, the power of Jesus' authority.* This is a debatable point, but a point I think worth debating. Kennedy esteems the rhetoric of the Sermon on the Mount over that of the Sermon on the Plain on the grounds of logical force: "The Beatitudes [in Matthew] take enthymematic, and thus syllogistic form, and are *formally* valid."[48] "[Matthew's Sermon] repeatedly utilizes the form of logical argument with premises based on nature and experiences well known to the audience."[49] By contrast, for Kennedy, "What persuasive power Luke's speech has inheres almost solely in the ethos, or authority of Jesus. In Matthew too ethos is primary, *but more attempt is made to couch statements in logical form*, and greater pathos is achieved."[50] Kennedy approves the divine messenger who appears to Joseph in Matthew's infancy narrative as "a *logical* angel who wants Joseph to understand and is not content simply to make authoritative announcements."[51] Kennedy says nothing of Gabriel's logic in Luke 1. The real question, however, is whether logic is as important to any of the evangelists as Kennedy's treatment would lead one to expect. As I read the gospels, all, with different inflections, lay greater stress upon Jesus' inspired authority, not on his logic. In that regard, they seem

to me more exemplary of sophistic rhetoric than of its technical or philosophical versions. And sophistry in this technical sense, as Kennedy himself notes, "is not necessarily depraved, decadent, or in poor taste. It is that natural aspect of rhetoric which emphasizes the role of the speaker . . . where allowance is made for genius and inspiration."[52] In Matthew (to take but one example), disciples should attend to what Jesus says, not because it is logical—often it seems contrary to logic— but because Jesus is Immanuel, God-With-Us (1:23).

9. *Kennedy's method assumes that the evangelists intend to persuade. Is that a valid, or adequate, assumption?* Kennedy himself seems to evince ambivalence at this point. On the one hand, "[the gospels] are rhetorical works in the sense that their intention is to persuade the readers that the Christian message is true or to deepen their understanding of this message."[53] Luke's prologue (1:1-4) and the apparently original ending of John (20:30-31) confirm Kennedy's estimate. On the other hand, Kennedy also argues, "Christian preaching is thus not persuasion but proclamation, and is based on authority and grace, not on proof." Accordingly, "the basis of Jesus' [rhetoric] did not lie in rational proof and his rhetoric is much like that . . . found in the Old Testament," namely "truth known from revelation."[54] If we accept Willi Marxsen's dictum that the gospels function as sermons ("Christian preaching"),[55] then their rhetoric across the board—not just in Mark—may be more radical than Kennedy's method is designed to measure and evaluate.

This seems to me especially the case with the parables. Contrary to Kennedy's assessment that they "could have been useful to Jesus in avoiding confrontation with the Pharisees,"[56] in all of the Synoptics they have the practical effect of solidifying resistance to Jesus among those so predisposed. Mark's famous hardening theory (in 4:10-12) is only the most blatant expression of their effect and intent throughout. To put the matter more generally: Granting that the gospels intend to fortify the faith of Jesus' disciples, would their rhetoric persuade anyone to whom God had not already revealed the identity and authority of his Son? In John, just the reverse is the case: Jesus' deeds and words convict when they do not convince, exposing those who live in darkness and those who live in light (John 3:17-21; 9:38-41). Broadly speaking, the same is true of the Synoptics as well.

Or so it appears to me. Biblical scholars have good reason to honor Kennedy, who among us has abundantly modeled the virtue of Chaucer's cleric, who "would glad learn, and gladly teach" (*The*

Canterbury Tales Prologue, 308). Yet the promise of his rhetorical criticism, articulated in 1984, has not yet been fulfilled for the gospels, even in those areas—such as the five great discourses in Matthew, the oratoria in Luke's infancy narrative, the forensic cut-and-thrust of the Johannine Jesus—where the fields look ripe for the harvest. There may also be built into Kennedy's mode of criticism assumptions that the gospels themselves resist for literary, theological, and other reasons. In any case, Kennedy's legacy for understanding the gospels seems, to this point, ambiguous at best.

NEW HORIZONS: COMPARATIVE RHETORIC

That, however, is not the story's end. A conspicuous feature of Kennedy's lifetime of scholarship has been not only his thorough mastery of a field—as though that were not achievement enough in one lifetime—but also his relentless inquisitiveness and intellectual courage. As Margaret Zulick reminds us in her contribution to the present volume, Kennedy put rhetorical study on the map of classicists and theorists in speech communication at a time when its consideration was regarded by many academicians as at best recherché. Later he ventured into biblical and especially New Testament studies, a complex field in which he was not trained as a specialist. His doing so sprang not from arrogance, as though he claimed to hold the key that would unlock scriptural interpretation, but rather from an intelligent curiosity that encouraged him to move from his own academically safe quarters into a related area of inquiry in which his own learning and that of his readers might be extended with profit and delight.

That pioneering spirit—always questioning, ever learning, never satisfied to guard terrain freshly cleared—is evident, in spades, in Kennedy's most recent monograph to date, *Comparative Rhetoric* (1998).[57] Greek and Roman rhetoricians had claimed that the phenomena they were describing and categorizing were universal. In effect, Kennedy's latest work is an exercise in testing the validity of that proposition across an extraordinary range of cultures: not only in the ancient literate societies of Mesopotamia and Egypt, China, and India, but also in such nonliterate cultures as aboriginal Australians, the Ethiopian Mursi, Philippine Ilongots, and North American Indians. Perhaps most fascinating of all is this volume's first chapter, in which Kennedy explores rhetoric among nonhuman, social animals: various quadrupeds like deer and elk, birds, and primates. Kennedy is too wise and too generous a scholar to fall into the trap of imposing Western biases upon such a range of cultures. "Indeed," he affirms, "my objective is rather the opposite: to modify Western notions by comparison with other traditions in the interests of coming to an understanding of rhetoric as a more general phenomenon of human [and animal] life."[58] Needless to say, in the hands of an inept dilettante, the outcome of such an exercise could be pure bosh. From Kennedy's hand, who has clearly done his homework in such daunting disciplines as biogenetics, zoology, and comparative anthropology, the result is altogether educational and provocative. Experts in those fields must speak to the cogency of those aspects of his investigation. As one New Testament specialist, I want to underline only a few dimensions of Kennedy's *Comparative Rhetoric* that might send readers of the gospels back to those and other biblical texts with renewed vision.

1. Kennedy's investigation of traditional Australian "Dreamtime" as a font from which tropes, metaphors, and poetry have sprung offers a fresh approach to the rhetoric of dreams and visions that pervades the New Testament.[59] Traditionally the interpretation of such passages as Joseph's dreams in Matthew (1:18-25; 2:13-15, 19-23) has been somewhat constrained by the (doubtless correct) notation of parallels with another Joseph: son of Jacob (himself a dreamer: Gen 28:10-17; 31:11-16), a dreamer (37:5-11), and interpreter of others' dreams (40:1-19; 41:14-36). Comparable to such dreams in the New Testament (note Acts 2:17, following Joel 2:28) are the angelic visions of Zechariah (Luke 1:8-23), Mary (Luke 1:26-38), Simon Peter (Acts 10:1-16), and Paul (2 Cor 12:1-10). Adopting Kennedy's earlier method of rhetorical criticism, modern interpreters could analyze the invention, arrangement, and style of such texts (though few have done so). By contrast, in his later consideration of "kaleidoscopic visualization in the ancient 'Dreamtime,'"[60] Kennedy invites us to move beyond strictly logical analysis to the "proto-metaphorical" power of dreams and visions as *expressions of rhetoric* in their own right. It is at once ironic and fitting that Kennedy, who has arguably done more than anyone to encourage New Testament exegetes to repair to rhetorical handbooks for interpretive strategies, should so convincingly invite us to take steps beyond them—more accurately, backward from them—to re-envision New Testament rhetoric in a more comprehensive way.

2. Following the lead of Jane Atkinson, Kennedy observes the phenomenon among the Indonesian Wana of conventional *kyori*, "wrapped words," that (in Atkinson's words) "encapsulate a state of affairs in a fitting image, express opinions or sentiments, pose questions, or propose a course of action."[61] In such discourse, Kennedy notes, "Speakers disguise their meaning, however, and say something indirectly"—often of a millenialist nature—"in an elegant way to one who understands."[62] The same kind of rhetoric can be documented among Native Americans, especially as they were forced to respond to European occupation of their territories.[63] One cannot help but be reminded of Jesus' parables of the kingdom of God: all are eschatological in tenor, oblique in their referents, and implicitly subversive of many first-century political and religious mores. At the very least, Kennedy's recent research offers us yet another entrée into Jesus' characteristic discourse, whose home was in an ancient, largely non-literate environment.

3. Finally, we should note that Kennedy's latest adventure has prompted him, upon return to his "native land," to reconsider some of its working assumptions. "Classical rhetorical theory," he concludes, "turns out to have some universal features, some features unique to Greek and Roman culture—especially its focus on judicial oratory—and a number of central concepts, including epideictic and ethos, that require some redefinition if they are to describe rhetoric in general."[64] That deduction implies a modification in one's definition of rhetoric itself, which in this book Kennedy explicitly tenders. Rhetoric may be better conceived as something more than an art of persuasive speech or writing. Now viewed through a lens wider than that offered by Greek and Roman theorists, "Rhetoric is apparently a form of energy that drives and is imparted to communication," and as a natural phenomenon "rhetoric is prior logically and historically to human speech."[65]

Grant that, and the implications for interpreting a text like the prologue of the Fourth Gospel, which creatively extends the creation account in Genesis 1:1–2:3, are illuminating in various ways:

> In the beginning was the word [λόγος], and the word was alongside God, and what God was the word was. This one was in the beginning beside God. Everything came to be through him, and apart from him there was nothing. What came to be in him was life, and the life was the light of mortals. . . . And the word came to be flesh and dwelled among us; and

we beheld his glory, glory as the only-begotten of the Father, full of grace and truth (John 1:1-4, 14; author's translation).

Regarding this passage, the student of comparative religions is better positioned to recognize the truth in Kennedy's comment: "Exclusively oral societies [like those among the audience of P, the Pentateuchal source, and many among John the Evangelist's readers] usually think in specific terms and feel little need to erect systems of abstract thought. Their religion too is primarily mythological, not philosophical."[66] The historian of Hellenistic-Jewish religions, including early Christianity, can see in the Fourth Gospel's prelude a development beyond Genesis, influenced by the Old Testament's sapiential tradition (Prov 8:22-31; Sir 1:4; 24:1-12) and such thinkers as Philo of Alexandria (*De Opificio Mundi* 20; *De Somniis* 1.229-30), in which a myth of origins has been enriched by reflection on the activity of personified σοφία or λόγος. Thanks to Kennedy, the biblical theologian may recognize something else at work in this passage: the evangelist's stunning assertion that the "energy" at work before creation, prior to all human speech or animal communication of any kind, not only exerted its power in creation but became one with it in a particularized human form "that dwelled among us." To move Kennedy's reconsidered definition of rhetoric down a theological path he has not taken: God is— among other things—an inherently rhetorical power, whose creation by speech, whose renewal of that creation by λόγος, is a manifestation of the Creator's desire to communicate with his creation and to remain in eternal companionship with it. When, probably building upon the Fourth Gospel, the author of 1 John identifies God as love (1 John 4:16b), that ἀγαπή is more than a sentiment or affection: it is the very nature of God's rhetorical power, which fans out among creatures begotten of and dependent on that God's energizing love (1 John 3:16; 4:7-12).

AN OPEN-ENDED CONCLUSION

For as long as Kennedy continues to open new frontiers in the study of rhetoric, it will be impossible to take the full measure of his scholarship's impact on the study of the gospels. This chapter, therefore, can serve only as an interim report, which has attempted to chart some peaks and valleys as the terrain appears to one surveyor. Of one thing I am reasonably confident: however little or much New Testament interpreters avail themselves of the prolific fruit of this erudite, gracious scholar's research, Kennedy will probably stay several steps ahead of most of us, who struggle to keep up with him. It is then that we recognize we are following a master whose work is somehow never masterful but always masterly, and whose interest never comes to rest in cultivating a method or attracting disciples as mere gardeners. Kennedy's vast erudition and expansive humanism are, as they have always been, concentrated on a continuously deeper understanding of human beings as communicative creatures who seek to understand and to be understood by how they speak and what they write.

Notes

[1] George A. Kennedy, *Greek Rhetoric under Christian Emperors* (Princeton: Princeton University Press, 1983), xvi.

[2] Kennedy's magisterial "History of Rhetoric" comprises *The Art of Persuasion in Greece* (Princeton: Princeton University Press, 1963), *The Art of Rhetoric in the Roman World: 300 B.C.–A.D. 300* (Princeton: Princeton University Press, 1972), and the volume cited in the preceding note. Among many others handbooks: George A. Kennedy, *Classical Rhetoric and Its Christian and Secular Tradition from Ancient to Modern Times* (Chapel Hill: University of North Carolina Press, 1980); and *A New History of Classical Rhetoric* (Princeton: Princeton University Press, 1994).

[3] *Comparative Rhetoric: An Historical and Cross-Cultural Introduction* (New York: Oxford University Press, 1997 [1998]).

[4] In *The Relationship among the Gospels: An Interdisciplinary Dialogue* (ed. William O. Walker Jr.; Trinity University Monograph Series in Religion 5; San Antonio: Trinity University Press, 1983), 125–55.

[5] Wayne A. Meeks, "*Hypomnēmata* from an Untamed Sceptic: A Response to George Kennedy," in Walker, ed., *The Relationship among the Gospels*, 157–72.

[6] Kennedy, "Classical and Christian Source Criticism," 129.

[7] Kennedy, "Classical and Christian Source Criticism," 136.

[8] Kennedy, "Classical and Christian Source Criticism," 133, citing W. K. C. Guthrie, *A History of Greek Philosophy*, Vol. 3: *The Fifth-Century Enlightenment* (Cambridge: Cambridge University Press, 1969), 353.

[9] Kennedy, "Classical and Christian Source Criticism," 130.

[10] Kennedy, "Classical and Christian Source Criticism," 129.

[11] Kennedy, "Classical and Christian Source Criticism," 136.

[12] Kennedy, "Classical and Christian Source Criticism," 147–52.

[13] Kennedy, "Classical and Christian Source Criticism," 126.

[14] Charles H. Talbert, *What Is a Gospel? The Genre of the Canonical Gospels* (Philadelphia: Fortress, 1977); David E. Aune, *The New Testament in Its Literary Environment*

(Philadelphia: Westminster, 1987); Richard Burridge, *What Are the Gospels? A Comparison with Graeco-Roman Biography* (2nd ed.; Grand Rapids, Mich.: Eerdmans, 2004).

[15] C. W. Votaw, "The Gospels and Contemporary Biographies," *AJT* 19 (1915): 45–73, 217–49.

[16] Robert M. Grant, *The Earliest Lives of Jesus* (New York: Harper & Brothers, 1961), 18.

[17] C. Clifton Black, *Mark: Images of an Apostolic Interpreter* (Columbia: University of South Carolina Press, 1994; repr., Minneapolis and Edinburgh: Fortress/T&T Clark, 2001), 92–94.

[18] Kennedy, "Classical and Christian Source Criticism," 153.

[19] For a well-balanced analysis, see E. P. Sanders and Margaret Davies, *Studying the Synoptic Gospels* (London and Philadelphia: SCM/Trinity Press International, 1989), 19–119.

[20] Kennedy, "Classical and Christian Source Criticism," 143–44.

[21] W. D. Davies and Dale C. Allison Jr., *A Critical and Exegetical Commentary on the Gospel According to Saint Matthew* (ICC; vol. 1; Edinburgh: T&T Clark, 1988), 16.

[22] Kennedy, *New Testament Interpretation*, 39–72 (on Sermon on Mount), 73–85 (on Sermon on the Plain), 97–113 (on rhetoric).

[23] Kennedy, *New Testament Interpretation*, 101–4, 163.

[24] Henry Joel Cadbury, *The Style and Literary Method of Luke*, Vol. 1: *The Diction of Luke and Acts* (Cambridge and London: Harvard University Press/Oxford University Press, 1920); Martin Dibelius, *Aufsätze zur Apostelgeschichte* (Göttingen: Vandenhoeck & Ruprecht, 1951).

[25] Kennedy, *New Testament Interpretation*, 63–67 (quotation, 67).

[26] Kennedy, *New Testament Interpretation*, 73–85 (quotation, 85).

[27] Kennedy, *New Testament Interpretation*, 104–5.

[28] Kennedy, *New Testament Interpretation*, 113.

[29] Amos N. Wilder, "Scholars, Theologians, and Ancient Rhetoric," *JBL* 75 (1956): 1–11.

[30] Amos N. Wilder, *The Language of the Gospel: Early Christian Rhetoric* (London and New York: SCM/Harper & Row, 1964; repr., Cambridge: Harvard University Press, 1994).

[31] Duane F. Watson and Alan J. Hauser, eds., *Rhetorical Criticism of the Bible: A Comprehensive Bibliography with Notes on History and Method* (Leiden: Brill, 1994).

[32] Duane F. Watson, ed., *Persuasive Artistry: Studies in New Testament Rhetoric in Honor of George A. Kennedy* (JSNTSup 50; Sheffield: JSOT Press, 1991), esp. 41–183.

[33] C. Clifton Black, *The Rhetoric of the Gospel: Theological Artistry in the Gospels and Acts* (St. Louis: Chalice, 2001).

[34] The following are representative of the best research in aspects of the gospels lately influenced by Kennedy's scholarship: Evelyn R. Thibeaux, "'Known to Be a Sinner': The Narrative Rhetoric of Luke 7:36-50," *BTB* 23 (1993): 151–60; Jaroslav Pelikan, *Divine Rhetoric: The Sermon on the Mount as Message and as Model in Augustine, Chrysostom, and Luther* (Crestwood, N.Y.: St. Vladimir's Press, 2001); Harold W. Attridge, "Argumentation in John 5," in *Rhetorical Argumentation in Biblical Texts: Essays from the Lund 2000 Conference* (ed. Anders Eriksson, Thomas H. Olbricht, and Walter Übelacker; Harrisburg, Pa.: Trinity Press International, 2002), 188–99. A striking contrast

is presented by Carl Joachim Classen, *Rhetorical Criticism of the New Testament* (Tübingen: Mohr [Siebeck], 2000), in whose 177 pages Kennedy's work is mentioned only thrice and *never* in conjunction with the gospels (see esp. 69–98).

35 An exemplary specimen is James D. Hester and J. David Hester (Amador), eds., *Rhetorics and Hermeneutics: Wilhelm Wuellner and His Influence* (New York: T&T Clark International, 2004).

36 See, for instance, Vernon K. Robbins, *The Tapestry of Early Christian Discourse: Rhetoric, Society, and Ideology* (London: Routledge, 1996).

37 R. Alan Culpepper, *Anatomy of the Fourth Gospel: A Study in Literary Design* (Philadelphia: Fortress, 1983).

38 George A. Kennedy, *Progymnasamata: Greek Textbooks of Prose Composition and Rhetoric, Translated into English, with Introductions and Notes* (WGRW 10; Atlanta and Leiden: Society of Biblical Literature/Brill, 2003); Martin Dibelius, *Die Formgeschichte des Evangeliums* (Tübingen: Mohr, 1919); Rudolf Bultmann, *Die Geschichte der synoptischen Tradition* (Göttingen: Vandenhoeck, 1921).

39 In the same series, see also Ronald F. Hock and Edward N. O'Neil, eds., *The Chreia and Ancient Rhetoric: Classroom Exercises* (Atlanta: Society of Biblical Literature, 2002), and George A. Kennedy, *Invention and Method: Two Rhetorical Treatises from the Hermogenic Corpus* (WGRW 15; Atlanta and Leiden: Society of Biblical Literature, 2005/Brill, 2006). At this writing, Kennedy's deepest impression on gospel scholarship appears *umweltlich*: encouraging translations into English of ancient classical texts whose subject matter intersects with some of the gospels' subgenres.

40 J. Louis Martyn, *History and Theology in the Fourth Gospel* (3rd ed.; NTL; Louisville, Ky.: Westminster John Knox, 2003); Andrew T. Lincoln, *Truth on Trial: The Lawsuit Motif in the Fourth Gospel* (Peabody, Mass.: Hendrickson, 2000).

41 Kennedy, *New Testament Interpretation*, 86–96.

42 C. G. Wilke, *Die neutestamentliche Rhetorik: Ein Seitenstück zur Grammatik des neutestamentlichen Sprachidioms* (Dresden and Leipzig: Arnold Christian Gottlob, 1843).

43 *Ekphrasis*: vivid description intending to excite the listeners' emotions (*Rhet. Her.* 4.38.51); *enthymeme*: a rhetorical syllogism, or statement with a supporting reason, which may or may not be formally valid (Aristotle, *Ars Rhet.* 1.2.8–22; 2.22–25).

44 Seymour Chatman, *Story and Discourse: Narrative Structure in Fiction and Film* (Ithaca: Cornell University Press, 1980); Culpepper, *Anatomy of the Fourth Gospel*, esp. 3–49, 101–9, 205–11.

45 Expressing reasoned skepticism are, among others, Stanley E. Porter, "The Theoretical Justification for Application of Rhetorical Categories to Pauline Epistolary Literature," in *Rhetoric and the New Testament: Essays from the 1992 Heidelberg Conference* (ed. Stanley E. Porter and Thomas H. Olbricht; Sheffield: Sheffield Academic, 1993), 100–122, and R. Dean Anderson Jr., *Ancient Rhetorical Theory and Paul* (Kampen: Kok Pharos, 1996; rev. ed., CBET 18; Leuven: Peeters, 1998).

46 Kennedy, *New Testament Interpretation*, 39.

47 In *The Rhetoric of the Gospel* (47–94), I have employed Kennedy's method for interpretation of Mark 13 and John 14–17, with a sidelong glance at the style of 1 John.

48 Kennedy, *New Testament Interpretation*, 49.

49 Kennedy, *New Testament Interpretation*, 63.

50 Kennedy, *New Testament Interpretation*, 67 (emphasis added).

[51] Kennedy, *New Testament Interpretation*, 103 (emphasis added).
[52] Kennedy, *Classical Rhetoric and Its Christian and Secular Tradition*, 39–40.
[53] Kennedy, "Classical and Christian Source Criticism," 137.
[54] Kennedy, *Classical Rhetoric and Its Christian and Secular Tradition*, 121–27.
[55] Willi Marxsen, *Der Evangelist Markus: Studien zur Redaktionsgeschichte des Evangeliums* (Göttingen: Vandenhoeck & Ruprecht, 1956).
[56] Kennedy, *New Testament Interpretation*, 71.
[57] For bibliographical details, see above, n. 3.
[58] Kennedy, *Comparative Rhetoric*, 217.
[59] Kennedy, *Comparative Rhetoric*, 58–59.
[60] Kennedy, *Comparative Rhetoric*, 60.
[61] Jane M. Atkinson, "'Wrapped Words': Poetry and Politics among the Wana of Central Sulawesi, Indonesia," in *Dangerous Words: Language and Politics in the Pacific* (ed. Donald Brennis and Fred R. Meyers; Prospect Heights, Ill.: Waveland, 1984), 34–68 (quotation, 40).
[62] Kennedy, *Comparative Rhetoric*, 71.
[63] Kennedy, *Comparative Rhetoric*, 89–108.
[64] Kennedy, *Comparative Rhetoric*, 230.
[65] Kennedy, *Comparative Rhetoric*, 215, 216.
[66] Kennedy, *Comparative Rhetoric*, 218.

Chapter 6

RHETOGRAPHY
A New Way of Seeing the Familiar Text

Vernon K. Robbins

Vernon Robbins takes us on a journey from Kennedy's observations about radical Christian rhetoric in the New Testament to Robbins' own socio-rhetorical interpretation. That journey begins in the courthouse, political assembly, and civil ceremonies with their judicial, deliberative, and epideictic rhetoric, respectively. It leads us to the new locations of early Christian discourse: the imperial court, the kingdom of God on earth, the imperial household, the body, the family household, and the sacrificial temple. These are the locations of apocalyptic, prophetic, precreation, miracle, wisdom, and priestly rhetoric, respectively. Robbins opens up new vistas that make for a rewarding journey.

The process of writing this essay has reminded me that "There is nothing new under the sun."[1] It also has renewed my conviction that all things humans perceive to be new are reconfigurations of that which is old and commonplace. The topic of this essay is *rhetography*, a term of importance for scholars investigating the "Rhetoric of Religious Antiquity."[2] Rhetography refers to the graphic images people create in their minds as a result of the visual texture of a text.[3] Rhetography communicates a context of meaning to a hearer or reader. A speaker or writer composes, intentionally or unintentionally, a context of communication through statements or signs that conjure visual images in the mind which, in turn, evoke "familiar" contexts that provide meaning for a hearer or reader.

The term rhetography emerges from blending both the linguistic and the pictorial turns that are occurring at the beginning of the twenty-first century.[4] The term has an important relation to the ancient progymnastic rhetorical exercise of *ekphrasis* in ancient Greek literature, which is "descriptive language, bringing what is shown clearly before the eyes."[5] It has a direct relation to Erwin Panofsky's "Iconography and Iconology" and his dialogue with Karl Mannheim on interpretation.[6] In addition, Roland Barthes' "The Imagination of the Sign" and "Literature and Signification" are important for understanding this essay.[7] W. J. T. Mitchell's *Picture Theory*, appearing in 1994, was a landmark moment in the discussion, and the three chapters in the section entitled "Textual Pictures" have a special relation to this essay.[8] In this broader context, this chapter emerges at the interface of "icon" and "logos,"[9] namely in a discussion of the interactive relation of rhetography (pictorial narration)[10] and *rhetology* (argumentative narration) in discourse.[11] In the study of religion, this essay is especially informed by Harvey Whitehouse's work on arguments and icons, the work of Robert N. McCauley and E. Thomas Lawson on "bringing ritual to mind," and Laurie L. Patton's work on the history of images in the religious literature of early India that people used for the attainment of mental and verbal ability.[12]

The importance of rhetography in rhetorical analysis has emerged as a result of extended socio-rhetorical analysis of classical rhetoric and its function in interpretation of texts. Classical rhetoric developed its rhetorical system by picturing the rhetorical dynamics in three locations in the city-state: courtroom (judicial or forensic); political assembly (deliberative or symbouleutic [advisory]), and civil ceremony (epideictic or demonstrative). Classical rhetoric understands the purposes, goals, and procedures of each kind of rhetoric by picturing in the mind the speaker (ethos), speech (logos), and audience (pathos) in these three different locations.

Traditional interpretation influenced by classical rhetoric has placed primary emphasis on speech (logos) in texts. From the perspective of socio-rhetorical interpretation, this approach has given primary attention to rhetology at the expense of rhetography in literature. In New Testament studies, the emphasis on "rhetology" has produced extensive investigation of the Sermon on the Mount in Matthew; substantive analysis of the speeches of Stephen, Peter, and Paul in the Acts of the Apostles; and many other insightful studies of other portions of narrative and speech in the gospels and Acts.[13] It also has focused on epistles as speeches or conversations.[14] The absence of attention to "rhetography" has left a gap in rhetorical interpretation, namely a widespread consensus that it is not possible to formulate a systematic rhetorical approach to narrative portions of the gospels and Acts, apocalyptic portions of early Christian literature, and other aspects of early Christian rhetoric in which rhetography plays a major role in the rhetoric. In private conversations with some well-known New Testament scholars, I have been informed that: (1) the Revelation to John contains no rhetorical argumentation, (2) classical rhetoric never analyzed stories, and (3) it is not possible to perform rhetorical analysis of all the writings in the New Testament. A major reason for these assertions by otherwise well-informed people has been a rhetorical focus on the rhetology of texts, which is a natural heritage from classical rhetorical interpretation, rather than a focus on the blending of rhetology and rhetography in texts.

A doorway into rhetography in texts, and subsequently into analysis and interpretation of the rhetoric of rhetography in texts, begins to open when one focuses on the speakers, who evoke ethos, and the audiences, who respond with pathos, in classical rhetoric. In the context of composing or analyzing a speech (logos), a speaker/writer or interpreter is asked to envision attributes of the speakers and characteristics of the audiences where a speech occurs. This "envisioning" introduces dynamics of rhetography into classical rhetoric. Cognitive picturing of the context for the speaker and the audience guides writers, speakers, and interpreters in understanding the meaning of the communication. Classical rhetoricians distinguished three major types of rhetoric by differentiating between the role of (1) prosecutors and defenders in the context of judges and juries; (2) political leaders in the context of a political assembly; and (3) a civil orator in the context of a funeral, the dedication of a harbor or ship, the founding of a city, or the like. By picturing three different kinds of speakers and audiences, classical rhetoricians described three different kinds of rhetoric. As the tradition of classical rhetoric has unfolded throughout subsequent centuries, rhetorical interpreters have decontextualized judicial, deliberative, and epideictic rhetoric from the classical city-state; namely, they have placed the rhetography of the three modes of rhetoric so far in the background as to effectively remove it. The result has been the development of more and more abstract forms of rhetorical interpretation in the tradition of classical rhetoric that focus attention so completely on the "rhetology" of the discourse that it ignores substantive sequences and movements in the "rhetography" of the discourse.

The focus in the present essay is on the work of George A. Kennedy, because he observed a blending of what he called "worldly" rhetoric in New Testament texts, which from our perspective is guided by a focus on the rhetology of New Testament texts, and what he called "radical" rhetoric, which our investigation has found to be rhetoric in which the rhetography of New Testament discourse presupposes contexts in God's created and uncreated world rather than contexts in the classical city-state. The approach in the present essay is to show how "radical" rhetography in the midst of texts Kennedy analyzes from the perspective of "worldly" rhetology creates rhetorical modes of discourse that require terminology beyond deliberative, judicial, and epideictic. Our argument is that Kennedy's systematic rhetorical analysis of New Testament texts produces data supporting the socio-rhetorical view that first-century Christians produced at least six rhetorical modes of discourse that blend worldly and radical rhetoric: prophetic, apocalyptic, miracle, wisdom, precreation, and priestly. Our goal is to show that Kennedy's work should not be taken as a final statement about the nature of New Testament rhetoric in relation to classical rhetoric but as an investigation that exhibits blends of worldly and radical rhetorics that New Testament rhetorical interpreters need to analyze and interpret carefully and systematically within a conceptual framework that moves beyond the categories of deliberative, judicial, and epideictic rhetoric.

EARLY CHRISTIAN DISCOURSE AS A BLEND OF RADICAL AND WORLDLY RHETORIC

The present essay demonstrates how current socio-rhetorical interpretation is building on Kennedy's investigation during the 1980s of rhetoric in the New Testament. Of special importance for socio-rhetorical interpretation is Kennedy's conclusion that early Christian discourse contains a mixture of worldly and radical rhetoric. In his words:

> A striking result of the present study is recognition of the extent to which forms of logical argument are used in the New Testament. Though sacred language stands behind this, inherent in many of the utterances of Jesus, and though a tradition of radical, nonlogical discourse survived in the Church and still exists in modern existentialism and fundamentalism, even in the first century a process was underway of recasting expressions in enthymematic form, thus making sacred language into premises which are supported, at least in a formal sense, by human reasoning. The workings of the human mind significantly changed in the centuries preceding

the Christian era because of the conceptualization of thought in Greece and the spread of Greek culture throughout the East. The New Testament lies not only at the cusp of Judaism and Hellenism, but at a cusp in Jewish and Hellenic culture where thought in myths confronts thought in logical forms. Some modern philosophers, or antiphilosophers, regard logical analysis and exegesis as a negative factor in civilization which has vitiated human efforts to comprehend reality. But "those things which can be learned from men should be learned without pride," Augustine argues in the Prologue to *On Christian Doctrine*. "The condition of man would be lowered if God had not wished to have men supply his word to men." It is rhetoric that supplies word to men, as Augustine well knew, and it is conceptualized rhetoric that describes that process.[15]

Kennedy observes that New Testament writings contain a mixture of worldly rhetoric (rational argumentation) and radical rhetoric (sacred rhetoric of authority). In his investigation of New Testament literature, he defines worldly rhetoric as "an understanding of the forms of logical argument and refutation, . . . deliberate arrangement of material, and . . . careful choice and composition of words."[16] A beginning point for Kennedy was an assertion that most New Testament writings contain enthymemes, which are "*forms* of logical argument, but the *validity* of their arguments is entirely dependent on their assumptions, which cannot be logically and objectively proved."[17]

Accepting Kennedy's focus on enthymemes as important for understanding the rhetorical nature of New Testament discourse, I introduced the word *rhetórolect* (emphasis on the antepenult) in 1994 to describe multiple enthymematic kinds of reasoning in first-century Christian discourse.[18] The essay describes a rhetorolect as "a form of language variety or discourse identifiable on the basis of a distinctive configuration of themes, topics, reasonings, and argumentations."[19] The presupposition underlying the definition was twofold: (1) early Christians spoke in ways that were significantly "understandable" among Greek-speaking people in the Mediterranean world; and (2) even though their discourse was in many ways understandable, it was highly unusual, in the manner in which a dialect is unusual. The essay displays enthymematic reasoning in the form of a thesis followed by a rationale and sometimes a summarizing conclusion for six rhetorolects: wisdom, miracle, apocalyptic, opposition, death-resurrection, and cosmic.[20] The implication of the essay, from the perspective of Kennedy's analysis, was that early Christian rhetoric contained at least six modes of rhetoric that used "worldly" reasoning in their argumentation, not simply three: deliberative, judicial, and epideictic.

An essay for the Lund Rhetoric Conference in 2000 entitled "Argumentative Textures in Socio-Rhetorical Argumentation"[21] provided an opportunity to analyze larger portions of New Testament literature to show how each of the six early Christian rhetorolects produced enthymematic rhetorical elaborations.[22] This was an exercise in moving beyond exploration of enthymemes in the six rhetorolects into the "deliberate arrangement of material" in the "worldly" rhetoric in the rhetorolects.[23] The analysis was not limited to speeches and letters in the New Testament, but it focused on the twenty-seven books in the New Testament in their broader context. Then, in research on the Coptic *Gospel of Thomas* after 2000, I became aware that pictorial narration was essential to early Christian rhetoric and therefore central to enthymematic argumentation.[24] Analysis of pictorial narration, namely the rhetography of each rhetorolect, gradually led to a delineation of the social-cultural-ideological location that gave each first-century Christian rhetorolect its contextual meaning in Mediterranean antiquity. After the "worldly" rhetorical nature of each of the six major early Christian rhetorolects had come into view, a careful review of Kennedy's rhetorical investigation of New Testament literature called attention to the distinctive blending of "radical" rhetoric with "worldly" rhetoric in each of the rhetorolects. This meant that the challenge must be to develop a "conceptualized rhetoric"[25] that reflects the manner in which "thought in myth" (radical rhetoric) confronts "thought in logical forms" (worldly rhetoric) in early Christian discourse. The result was an awareness that what Kennedy called radical rhetoric emerged from the rhetography of early Christian discourse in the context of the rhetology of the discourse, which Kennedy called "worldly rhetoric."

GEORGE KENNEDY'S CONCLUSIONS AND RHETOGRAPHY IN EARLY CHRISTIAN DISCOURSE

Kennedy's definition of "radical rhetoric" as "a form of 'sacred language' characterized by assertion and absolute claims of authoritative truth without evidence or logical argument"[26] provided a beginning point for socio-rhetorical exploration of the contexts of meaning in early Christian discourse that Kennedy himself did not explore. These contexts, available to us through the rhetography of the discourse, provide the cultural frames for understanding and negotiating the meanings in early Christian argumentation. In other words, every form of Christian rhetoric contains a radical dimension, namely a sacred rhetoric of authority, but every form also contains a worldly dimension, namely a kind of rational argumentation. These blends of worldly and radical rhetoric result from the multiple contexts of meaning in God's created and uncreated world that early Christians embedded in the rhetography of their discourse, instead of the primary contexts of meaning in the classical city-state that first-century Hellenistic-Roman rhetoricians embedded in the rhetography of their discourse.

To view the emergence of six major early Christian rhetorolects from the perspective of classical rhetoric, it is helpful to begin with the rhetography in the three classical forms of rhetoric as Kennedy analyzed them in New Testament texts: deliberative, judicial, and epideictic rhetoric. Kennedy's analysis reveals that early Christian discourse blended deliberative rhetoric from the political assembly in the city-state with assemblies in which prophets confronted leaders and participants in the kingdom of God on earth (prophetic rhetoric). Also, it blended judicial rhetoric from the courtroom in the city-state with a future imperial apocalyptic court over which either God in heaven or the Son of Man on earth would preside (apocalyptic rhetoric). In addition, it blended epideictic rhetoric from civil ceremonies in the city-state with public events featuring miraculous renewal of human bodies (miracle rhetoric).

It is important to recognize that the "radical" rhetorics of first-century Christianity blended the "worldly" rhetorics of the first-century Mediterranean world into their rhetorics rather than simply developing new forms of rhetoric. The process produced not only prophetic, apocalyptic, and miracle discourse through the use of rhetorics of reasoning and argumentation associated with the contexts of earthly kingdom, imperial court, and body, but also the family household (wisdom rhetoric), imperial household (precreation rhetoric), and sacrificial temple (priestly rhetoric). Then by the fourth century, when Christian leaders began to enjoy alliances with Roman emperors, they used the context of the imperially sanctioned city council to produce creedal (doctrinal) rhetoric.

The thesis underlying this essay, then, is that first-century Christians created at least six forms of radicalized worldly rhetoric—apocalyptic, prophetic, miracle, wisdom, precreation, and priestly—and by the fourth century they successfully launched creedal rhetoric, which became an even more distinctive form of radicalized worldly rhetoric in Western culture. This thesis is so large that it will take a generation of scholarship to work out its implications. The present essay is a midpoint of exploration and refinement of the thesis through deeper engagement with Kennedy's rhetorical analysis of New Testament writings. Since the socio-rhetorical thesis was launched in its initial form in 1996, partially modified and more fully developed in 2000, and is undergoing fuller explication at present,[27] this essay is not designed to persuade the reader of the underlying thesis. Rather, in the midst of an ongoing process of socio-rhetorical testing and refinement of the thesis, the present essay explores the relation of the six first-century "rhetorolectic" forms of Christian discourse to Kennedy's investigation of "mixtures" of worldly rhetoric and radical rhetoric in the New Testament.

PROPHETIC DISCOURSE AND THE RHETOGRAPHY OF GOD'S EARTHLY KINGDOM

In Kennedy's chapter on deliberative rhetoric, he analyzes the Sermon on the Mount, Sermon on the Plain, and some additional sayings of Jesus that exhibit deliberative rhetoric.[28] Then in a later context he analyzes 1 Thessalonians and Galatians as instances of deliberative rhetoric.[29] Kennedy's analysis is, as one would expect, deeply informed by his knowledge of classical rhetoric and highly instructive for New Testament interpreters. It will only be possible briefly to discuss aspects of his interpretation of Matthew's Sermon on the Mount in this essay.

It is noticeable in Kennedy's discussion of the Sermon on the Mount that he never mentions the reconfiguration of the rhetography of the speaker, speech, and audience in these texts from a political assembly, such as one found in the city-state, to an assembly where people are being informed about the earthly kingdom of God.[30] Instead of reference to benefit for a particular city-state, Kennedy refers to "self-interest and the expedient" as an abstract "focus of argument in deliberative rhetoric."[31] There are eight references to the kingdom of heaven in the Sermon on the Mount and four references to prophets.[32] Kennedy observes that "radical" rhetoric comes into play in the logic of the verses that refer to the kingdom, but he does not correlate the reconfiguration of the context in the rhetography of the discourse with the "radical" reasoning in the rhetoric. In his excellent analysis of the Beatitudes as enthymemes, he observes that the value of the minor premises ("The poor in spirit will obtain the kingdom of heaven," and so forth) to Jesus' audience "is dependent on all three factors in the speech situation: speaker, speech, and audience. Jesus speaks with external authority, based on the miracles he has performed, strengthened by his general reputation, his role as rabbi and perhaps Messiah, and the support of his disciples."[33]

Most of all, perhaps, it is noticeable that Kennedy does not mention the prophetic nature of Jesus' speech in the context of the multiple references to prophets in the Sermon on the Mount. The context of Jesus' speech is not that of a leader in a city-state appealing to his fellow citizens to act in an expedient manner. Rather, the rhetography of the discourse shows that Jesus functions with the external authority of a prophet who knows the inner nature and responsibilities of living in God's kingdom on earth. In other words, the rhetorical context of the speaker, speech, and audience evokes the dynamics of the conventional call and activities of a prophet in the context of an earthly kingdom over which God rules. In an unexpected context, God confronts a person, calls the person to a prophetic task, and provides the person with a "word of God" that must be pronounced before the king, groups of official leaders, and assemblies of the people in the kingdom. Kennedy actually shows an awareness of this in this assertion toward the end of his analysis: "Few orators could have delivered the sermon successfully, but the warnings of the Hebrew prophets did constitute some precedent for Jesus, and his teaching therefore did not fall into a genre with which his audience was entirely unfamiliar."[34] Yet Kennedy does not correlate his observations about the mixture of worldly and radical rhetoric in the Sermon on the Mount with a reconfiguration in the rhetography of the discourse from a leader in a political assembly in a city-state to a prophetic speaker engaged in deliberative rhetoric with people who are already blessed in God's kingdom on earth and aspire to inherit the kingdom of heaven. An explication of the nature of the blending of "worldly" deliberative rhetoric and "radical" prophetic rhetoric in the Sermon on the Mount remains for socio-rhetorical interpreters to achieve.

The rhetography of prophetic rhetoric evokes a picture of God calling and sending a prophet to perform a specific set of tasks associated with a kingdom over which God rules both on earth and in heaven. Biblical prophetic discourse evokes the context of a kingdom of God with specific boundaries on earth. God chose a special region of land, arranged for anointed kings to rule over it, and called prophets to confront the leaders and the people when they were not living according to God's covenantal guidelines.[35] In early Christian speech and writing, the regional boundaries of God's kingdom expand beyond the land of Israel to an area that spans from Rome (Acts 28:16) to Ethiopia (Acts 8:27-39), with a plan of expanding from Rome to Spain (Rom 15:24, 28). In this context, early Christian prophetic rhetoric reconfigures God's promise of land to God's promise of "an inheritance" (*klēronomos*).[36] The power of early Christian prophetic argumentation resides as fully in the authoritative picture it evokes of God's calling of the speaker as it does in the deliberative reasons, rationales, analogies, precedents, and arguments from contraries and opposites in the discourse itself.

APOCALYPTIC DISCOURSE AND THE RHETOGRAPHY OF IMPERIAL DIVINE COURTROOM

Kennedy's discussion of judicial rhetoric in 2 Corinthians illustrates work that needs yet to be done to blend "worldly" judicial rhetoric with the "radical" imperial courtroom rhetoric of apocalyptic in the New Testament. Kennedy considers 2 Corinthians to provide "the most extended piece of judicial rhetoric in the New Testament."[37] Again, his analysis is excellent and very important for New Testament interpreters. There is, however, once again an absence of interpretation of the rhetography in the discourse that exhibits the "radical" reconfiguration of its context of argumentation. In short, Paul makes clear that his defense is before the imperial courtroom of God rather than before a courtroom of humans, but Kennedy does not discuss this aspect of the rhetoric. As a result, Kennedy only partially exhibits to the reader the blend of radical and worldly rhetoric in 2 Corinthians.

Kennedy skillfully observes that 2 Corinthians 1:3-8 is a proem that introduces a narration in 1:8–2:13. Then, after the narration, there is a proposition followed by a partition in 2:14-17 containing three headings that will provide the proof: (1) as men of sincerity; (2) as commissioned by God, and (3) in the sight of God we speak in Christ. In the analysis and interpretation that follows, Kennedy adroitly interprets the headings "as men of sincerity" and "as commissioned by God." When interpreting the third heading, however, he drops the "in sight of God," interpreting only "we speak in Christ."[38] This results in an omission of the "radical" role of first-century Christian imperial apocalyptic rhetorolect that is blended into the "worldly" judicial rhetoric in 2 Corinthians.

Kennedy's omission begins with no mention of Paul's assertion in the narration that the Corinthians will be able to be proud of Paul and his companions, and they will be able to be proud of them "on the day of the Lord Jesus" (1:14). Paul's addition of reference to the apocalyptic day of the Lord Jesus in the rhetography of the discourse already reconfigures the judicial context from a courtroom in the city-state to an imperial heavenly courtroom on the day of judgment. This external appeal introduces a radical dimension, which Kennedy does not discuss, into the worldly judicial rhetoric. After Paul's reference to the day of the Lord Jesus, he continues the topic of the day of judgment: first through the phrase "in the presence of Christ" in 2:10, and then through the phrase "in the sight of God" in the partition in 2:17. Paul's defense of himself in 2 Corinthians, then, is before the imperial courtroom of Christ and God, not really before the Corinthians as judge and jury in a particular city on earth.

As Kennedy's excellent discussion of the sections on "as men of sincerity" and "as commissioned by God" in 2 Corinthians 3:4-5:10 unfolds,[39] he fails to observe that Paul concludes the section with an explicit and detailed reference to the imperial divine courtroom of apocalyptic rhetoric: "For we must all appear before the judgment seat of Christ, so that each one may receive good or evil, according to what he has done in the body" (5:10 RSV). Kennedy's failure to notice this leads to an interpretation of the worldly rhetoric in the last section without including the radical apocalyptic rhetography of the imperial divine courtroom as Paul starts the elaboration of the third heading: "Therefore, knowing the fear of the Lord, we persuade men; but what we are is known to God, and I hope it is known also to your conscience" (5:11). Here the fear of the Lord, known to God, concerns God and the Lord Jesus as judges of guilt or innocence on the Day of the Lord. Kennedy's failure to observe this causes him to drop the phrase "in the sight of God" in the final heading, referring to it only as "we speak in Christ" as he begins an interpretation of the final section.[40] This leads, in turn, to Kennedy's omission of Paul's reference to "the sight of God" in Paul's recapitulation of his defense in 7:12 and to Paul's summary of the context of his defense in 12:19. When Paul summarizes the judicial context for his defense, the radical rhetography of the discourse is explicitly clear: "Have you been thinking all along that we have been defending ourselves before you? It is in the sight of God that we have been speaking in Christ, and all for your upbuilding, beloved" (12:19). Here the blending of Paul's "worldly" judicial defense with the rhetography of Paul's "radical" imperial apocalyptic context of interpretation is fully evident. In the context of Kennedy's skillful explication of the worldly judicial rhetoric in Paul's argumentation, then, there is an absence of a full explication of the blending of the radical judicial rhetoric in the rhetography that moves the contextual picture beyond a courtroom in a city-state to the imperial divine courtroom of apocalyptic rhetoric. Once again, the stage for interpretation of the blending of worldly and radical in judicial rhetoric in early Christian discourse has been skillfully set by Kennedy, but careful analysis and interpretation awaits the tools and strategies of the socio-rhetorical interpreter who works carefully with the rhetography of the discourse.

MIRACLE DISCOURSE AND THE RHETOGRAPHY OF BODY

When Kennedy discusses epideictic rhetoric in chapter 3, he refers to various New Testament texts but analyzes and interprets only the "topical" configuration of John 13–17.[41] While this is an informative discussion in the context of the expansion of epideictic rhetoric by the time of Menander Rhetor in 300 C.E., it bypasses the "praise" orientation that lies at the basis of epideictic rhetoric. As Kennedy himself observes, the initial focus of epideictic rhetoric was on praise in panegyrics and funeral orations.[42] One of the most central epideictic features of first-century Christian epideictic rhetoric is its miracle discourse. Kennedy discusses at a number of points the "radical" nature of miraculous healing in the New Testament, but nowhere does he pursue the epideictic nature of this rhetoric. This aspect of Kennedy's analysis and interpretation will require some of the most serious socio-rhetorical reformulations of the function of first-century Christian epideictic rhetoric in the future.[43] Various places in Kennedy's book, however, represent an important inroad into the epideictic nature of miracle discourse in the New Testament. For example, Kennedy identifies the importance of miracle discourse in the Gospel of Mark as he talks about the "radicality" of its rhetoric:

> "Immediately" is one of Mark's favorite words and gives a forward movement to his account. The truth is immediately and intuitively apprehended because it is true. Some see it, others do not, but there is no point in trying to persuade the latter. This is the most radical form of Christian rhetoric. When Jesus performs his first miracle, the witnesses are "amazed" (1:27); they recognize truth but do not comprehend it rationally. The miracle is a sign of authority, as the crowd at once admits.[44]

To understand how miracle discourse functions as radical epideictic rhetoric in Mark, one needs to analyze how the narration depicts Jesus repeatedly performing miracles in Mark 1–10 in a manner that brings forth praise from public audiences. As Aristotle says in *Ars Rhetorica* 1.9.32: "Since praise is based on actions and to act in accordance with deliberate purpose is characteristic of a worthy person, one should try to show him acting in accordance with deliberate purpose. It is useful for him to be seen to have so acted often."[45] While miraculous healing of the body regularly leads to sanctuaries of healing in the Mediterranean world, in early Christian discourse it presupposes interaction between Jesus' body and the malfunctioning body of an ill, diseased, or otherwise afflicted person that evokes praise and amazement in public contexts. In other words, in early Christian discourse a major context for understanding the function of praise emerges from miraculous recoveries of illness, ailment, or death in the body itself. The geophysical context for early Christian miracle discourse is the body itself in relation to the body of the healer. An excellent example is the healing story just after the verse to which Kennedy refers:

> Now Simon's mother-in-law was in bed with a fever, and they told him about her at once. He came and took her by the hand and lifted her up. Then the fever left her, and she began to serve them. (Mark 1:30-31)

With this act, Jesus' deeds of healing begin to become commonplace in Markan characterization of Jesus. At sunset, Jesus heals all kinds of ill people, with "the whole city gathered around the door" (1:33). Then Jesus heals a leper, a paralyzed man, and a man with a withered hand in the ensuing narration, leading to a summary of Jesus' healings and exorcisms, which cause the unclean spirits to shout out, "You are the Son of God" (3:11). This is first-century Christian epideictic miracle narration, so central to early Christian discourse that it occurs repetitively in all the New Testament gospels and Acts.

Once Kennedy has observed the radical function of miracle rhetoric in the Gospel of Mark, he does not show the reader how to analyze it as early Christian epideictic rhetoric. The important thing is the presence of Jesus' body in relation to the body of those who are ill. In early Christian discourse, the hand of the healer is often central, but it need not be. The essential context for the discourse is a relationship between the body of the healer and the body of the person who is ill or otherwise afflicted. The healing can occur in a house, alongside a road, by the sea, on a mountain, or anywhere. Early Christian epideictic miracle rhetoric regularly occurs in the form of a story that features an extraordinary transformation of a malfunctioning person into a healthy and well-ordered social being or in a summary of Jesus' healing of a large number of people. This is radical rhetoric containing epideictic dimensions, which is well understood through the actions of Elijah and Elisha in biblical tradition and through the healings of Asklepios in Mediterranean tradition.[46] First-century Christians gave it a prominent place in their epideictic discourse. Since its rhetography, rather than its rhetology, is so central to its epideictic rhetorical function, it remains for socio-rhetorical interpreters to show the blends of worldly and radical rhetoric that make it a prominent aspect of early Christian discourse in the Mediterranean world.

WISDOM DISCOURSE AND THE RHETOGRAPHY OF FAMILY HOUSEHOLD

Kennedy observes argumentation that evokes radical worldly wisdom discourse. Early Christian wisdom rhetoric naturally unfolds according to patterns and principles Kennedy assigns to rationally oriented, worldly rhetoric in his study of New Testament literature. The rhetography in this rhetoric blends the household and its members with God's created world and the vegetative productivity in it. As a result, virtually everything in a household and in God's created world function by analogy in relation to one another. God the Father of the created world is like the father in a household, and people in the world are children of God, like the little people in a household are children of the parents. In addition, people may be like animals (sheep, wolves, doves, serpents) or like trees that bear good or bad fruit. This is a primary form of deliberative rhetoric in early Christian discourse. Nevertheless, much of this, as Kennedy says, is radical rhetoric.

In the context of the strategies of worldly rhetoric, as Kennedy calls it, careful investigation of early Christian wisdom discourse reveals that imagery of the family household lies at the base. The ideal teacher is a father figure who teaches his children how to live, because he cares for them. This imagery blends with a concept of God as Father over the created world, making it into a household where God provides food, shelter, and clothing for all who live in it, like a father provides for the needs of his family. In early Christian discourse, the function of God as father finds its beginnings in God's creation of the universe and provision of light as a means for productivity in it. In this conceptual domain, the light of God is God's wisdom, which guides people to live generously and harmoniously with their neighbors. Luke 11:33-36 is a very interesting passage in this regard, evoking many aspects of the picturing central to early Christian wisdom discourse:

> No one after lighting a lamp puts it in a cellar, but on the lampstand so that those who enter may see the light. Your eye is the lamp of your body. If your eye is healthy, your whole body is full of light; but if it is not healthy, your body is full of darkness. Therefore consider whether the light in you is not darkness. If then your whole body is full of light, with no part of it in darkness, it will be as full of light as when a lamp gives you light with its rays.

This wisdom discourse evokes the context of a family household. The imagery of the lighting of a lamp and the placing of the lamp in the household brings to mind the location where parents teach their children wisdom in the context of caring for their bodies from early childhood. The goal is to bring the light of God's wisdom into their bodies, so they may function like the good, productive world God created at the beginning of time. This is didactic, rather than political, deliberative rhetoric. The eye is the special vehicle for the knowledge that will lead the hearer or reader to the right decision and action. Learning to see in the visible world the light of God's goodness and learning allows the eye to shine this light into the body and create a person who is able to produce goodness and righteousness in the world.[47] This is radical wisdom discourse that functions internally in most of the "worldly" rhetoric in the New Testament. A basic challenge for socio-rhetorical interpreters is to identify, analyze, and describe how this "radical" worldly rhetoric pervades most of early Christian discourse and exhibits inner reasonings of wisdom that make it immediately accessible to the understanding of the hearers and readers.

PRECREATION DISCOURSE AND THE RHETOGRAPHY OF IMPERIAL HOUSEHOLD

Kennedy makes statements that lead an interpreter to the nature of precreation rhetoric in early Christian discourse:

> John's gospel is radical Christian rhetoric in its demand for immediate and direct response to the truth, but John makes far more demands than Mark on his readers in approaching the truth they are to perceive. He uses the forms of logical argument not so much as proof, as does Matthew, but as ways of turning and reiterating the topics which are at the core of his message.[48]

Kennedy's insights lead a person to precreation rhetoric, a kind of radical epideictic rhetoric that presupposes that Jesus' knowledge is in Jesus as a result of the intimate relation he, as the only begotten Son of God, has had with God since before creation. The experiential base of this was knowledge about the imperial household, which for most early Christians was far away and never seen by them. Blending the imperial household with the household of God, the Gospel of John evokes an imperial primordial household outside of time and space with an intimate relation between the imperial father and his son. The father sends his son out into his empire to distribute the benefits of his eternal wealth to those who profess unconditional loyalty and friendship to the son. By this means, friendship with the son enacts a relationship with the father that yields benefits from the realm of eternal peace, salvation, and life.[49]

The Gospel of John, then, evokes the context of an imperial realm with a son of the emperor who goes throughout the empire to distribute primordial benefits that only an emperor can bestow. Everything Jesus does and says is primordial wisdom and action. God's creation of the world only made God's wisdom partially visible to human beings. Jesus' action and speech present the unfathomable wisdom of God to humans in terms that are comprehensible only with truly exceptional insight into the nature of God. In this instance, then, the radical rhetoric evokes a picture of Jesus with God before the creation of the world. Jesus, as the only begotten Son who listened carefully to everything God the Father said to him, and who watched carefully everything his Father did, uses extraordinary images and arguments, regularly in the form of logical argument, to communicate the extraordinary knowledge available to him from God's primordial sphere. When God sends Jesus to earth to speak to people, Jesus uses unusual images and performs extraordinary signs among them. In early Christian discourse, this is epideictic precreation wisdom that gains plausibility for the hearer through blending with the scope of divine powers and benefits inherent in the emperor and his household.

PRIESTLY DISCOURSE AND THE RHETOGRAPHY OF SACRIFICIAL TEMPLE

Kennedy leads us incidentally to a sixth major kind of radical rhetoric in early Christian discourse when he discusses "topics," topoi or *loci*, which are "the 'places' where [the speaker] looks for something to say about his subject."[50] He presents the following example of "past fact leading to the topic of degree":

> "While we were yet sinners Christ died for us. Since, therefore, we are now justified by his blood, much more shall we be saved by him from the wrath of God" (Rom 5:8-9). This type of *a fortiori* argument is commonly known as "the more and the less."[51]

With this example, Kennedy incidentally introduces early Christian priestly rhetoric blended with apocalyptic rhetoric. The statement about being justified by Christ's blood when he died evokes epideictic priestly reasoning associated with a temple containing a sacrificial altar. Then the statement about being saved from the wrath of God evokes apocalyptic reasoning associated with the power of an emperor to destroy rebellious, "impure" people with legions of his imperial army. In this conceptual domain, the impurity of the people is regularly a result of an unwillingness to participate in ritual worship of the emperor and the emissaries the emperor sends out to perform certain tasks in his empire.

The picturesque nature of early Christian priestly discourse reaches its fullest form in a passage from Hebrews:

> But when Christ came as a high priest of the good things that have come, then through the greater and more perfect tent (not made with hands, that is, not of this creation), he entered once for all into the Holy Place, not with the blood of goats and calves, but with his own blood, thus obtaining eternal redemption. (9:11-12 NRSV)

This discourse evokes the context of a sacrificial temple and blends this context with the conceptual realm of God in the heavens. Jesus is the high priest in God's temple in the heavens who offers himself as the perfect sacrifice. This is radical reasoning, but it is reasoning based on Mediterranean understanding of the process and benefits of offerings on an altar in a temple designed for sacrificial ritual.[52] The image of the context in the mind of the hearer enacts a conceptual domain in which the assertions can be understood as reasonable. The blend of radicality and reasonableness in it again is a rhetorical characteristic Kennedy identifies both appropriately and skillfully.

CONCLUSION

From the perspective of socio-rhetorical interpretation, Kennedy's approach to radical rhetoric is a key for understanding the nature of the rhetoric in the New Testament writings. Kennedy's approach does not move us fully into rhetorical analysis of early Christian rhetoric, however, because it brings a system of "rational rhetoric" to the New Testament writings and describes the "nonrational rhetorical" aspects of the New Testament in terms that are oppositional to "real rhetoric," which he calls "worldly rhetoric." In contrast to an approach that uses worldly rhetoric as a normative standard for real rhetoric, the goal of a rhetorical interpreter must be to use the insight that the New Testament writings blend rational and nonrational rhetoric, worldly and radical rhetoric, rhetology and rhetography, together. Careful analysis of the relation of the rhetography to the rhetology in the discourse can lead us to the multiple kinds of rhetoric in early Christian discourse.

Since 2002, the theories of critical spatiality and conceptual blending have provided a means to identify the inner nature and boundaries of each rhetorolect more clearly.[53] A special result has been an awareness of the rhetography characteristic of each rhetorolect and the relation of that rhetography to its argumentative texture. In the present understanding of socio-rhetorical interpreters, now influenced by conceptual integration (blending) and critical spatiality theory, a rhetorolect is an idealized cognitive model. This means there are four aspects to a rhetorolect: (1) argumentative-enthymematic patterning (rhetology), (2) image-descriptive patterning (rhetography), (3) metaphoric mappings, and (4) metonymic mappings.[54] The present essay has focused on the image-descriptive patterning, namely the rhetography, in six basic rhetorolects in early Christian discourse. Focusing on the rhetography leads us to rhetorolects as cultural frames that contain an argumentative texture that blends rhetography and rhetology in a manner that evokes a conventional context of understanding for negotiating its reasonings and meanings. The argumentative texture of each rhetorolect is a result of the interaction of its particular rhetography with its particular rhetology. This means that an early Christian rhetorolect is a network of significations and meanings associated with social-cultural-ideological places and spaces familiar to people in a certain geophysical region. In terms that combine insights from Kennedy's analysis and from Gilles Fauconnier and Mark Turner's conceptual integration theory, a rhetorolect is a blending of radical and worldly rhetoric in a cultural frame that functions as an environment of emergent structure.[55] Rhetography is an essential ingredient in a rhetorolect, since rhetography is the means by which people envision a speaker and audience as a context that gives meaning to its rhetoric.

An early Christian rhetorolect achieves its status as a cultural frame that functions as an environment of emergent structure by means of a blending of what Kennedy calls worldly and radical rhetoric. In other words, every rhetorolect is radical from the perspective of worldly rhetoric, yet every major type of radical rhetoric in early Christian discourse has actual or imitative worldly rhetoric in it. Identifying the central cultural rhetography in a rhetorolect and correlating it with its particular cultural rhetology enables an interpreter to establish and interpret both the inner rhetorical workings and the boundaries of a particular rhetorolect. The reasoning in a rhetorolect emerges from social-cultural-ideological experiences in specific geophysical locations.

Therefore the rhetography provides the primary cultural clue to the logic of the discourse.

The rhetography in a rhetorolect—in other words, the pervasive pictorial narration in it—evokes the conventional context of meaning for the texture of its argumentation. Picturing a kingdom of God in which God calls, authorizes, informs, and commands prophets to confront the leaders and people in the kingdom to enact God's principles of justice and righteousness in the region evokes the reasoning internal to early Christian deliberative prophetic rhetorolect. Picturing an empire with an emperor who rules through an imperial court evokes judicial reasoning about divine action that judges and destroys evil to create contexts of peace and salvation internal to early Christian apocalyptic rhetorolect. Picturing a malfunctioning body miraculously healed through the presence of the body of a healer evokes epideictic reasoning internal to early Christian miracle rhetorolect. Picturing a household in which parents teach their children wisdom, then employ teachers outside the family to take them further into adult wisdom, evokes deliberative logics internal to early Christian wisdom rhetorolect. Picturing an emperor who has an intimate relationship with his son outside of time evokes epideictic reasoning about the sending of a special son to distribute the benefits of special divine resources to the loyal subjects of his empire internal to precreation rhetorolect. Picturing a priest at an altar evokes epideictic reasoning about the actions and results described and asserted in early Christian priestly rhetorolect.

After the attributes of the six major rhetorolects that emerged by 100 C.E. have been more fully explored and explained,[56] the next challenge will be to explore the rhetorolects that participate in the movement of Christian discourse beyond its first-century rhetorical modes into the creedal rhetorolect that became central to it during the fourth century. By the fourth century C.E., fully developed creedal rhetorolect emerged that was based on the imperial political structures that convened church councils in particular cities in the Roman Empire. The beginnings of this seventh rhetorolect lie in those parts of New Testament literature characterized by Kennedy as "when a doctrine is purely proclaimed and not couched in enthymemes."[57]

While the six basic first-century Christian rhetorolects had their beginnings prior to earliest Christianity, creedal rhetorolect had its decisive beginnings in the interfaces among Jewish, Christian, and

Hellenistic-Roman discourse during the first and second centuries C.E. Lewis Ayres' *Nicaea and Its Legacy*[58] skillfully describes the dynamics that created the context for creedal rhetorolect to emerge as a major force within fourth-century Christian discourse. One of the major strengths of his account lies in its preservation of the multiplicities, tensions, counter-valences, and unresolved issues as pro-Nicene forces gained a stronghold over a large sector of the Christian church.

At the center of the Christian creedal rhetorolect that emerged during the fourth century stands the Nicene-Cosmopolitan creed.[59] Within an overall frame that blends Christian wisdom and priestly rhetorolect, this creed features God as Father, Jesus as the only Son, the Holy Spirit as "worshipped and glorified like the Father and the Son," and Mary as the mother of Jesus. In this context, the creed foregrounds precreation and apocalyptic rhetorolect rather than elaborating priestly imagery that would make Christ an atoning, substitutionary, or expiational sacrifice. In addition, the creed pushes prophetic and miracle rhetorolect almost entirely into the background. Philosophical debate reconfigures the "authority, power, and illumination" of prophetic rhetorolect into a reference to the Holy Spirit, "who spoke through the prophets." In turn, it redirects the "amazement" of miracle rhetorolect into creedal conviction in the amazing story of "the one Lord Jesus Christ" who came down from heaven, was incarnate, became human, rose on the third day, ascended to heaven, sits on the right hand of the Father, and will come again in glory to judge the living and the dead. In other words, the overall Christographical story line becomes the miracle rhetorolect in the context of the creedal rhetorolect. The result was creedal rhetorolect that asserted

> that God was one power, nature, and activity; that there could be no degrees in divinity; that the divine persons were irreducible although all share in the divine being without any ontological hierarchy; that human beings would always fail to comprehend God and that one could only make progress towards knowledge and love of God through entering a discipline and practice that would reshape the imagination.[60]

Philosophy, mystery, and institutional structure blended together in Christian creedal rhetorolect, providing a cultural frame that has functioned as an emergent structure for sixteen centuries. At a time when Christianity faces a special need to enter into productive conversation with Muslims, Buddhists, and Hindus, some scholars are calling for Christian theology to return to a more creedal base of discourse. In turn, other scholars are calling for Christian theology to renew itself by discovering and reclaiming the inner dynamics of its multiple discourses in contexts of interaction with the discourses of other religions in the world. Perhaps an awareness of the rhetography in New Testament discourse that leads to six major first-century Christian rhetorolects can help to create more healthy and productive interaction not only among biblical interpreters but also between biblical interpreters and interpreters of sacred texts in other religious traditions.[61]

Notes

[1] Ecclesiastes 1:9. I am grateful in particular to my Emory colleagues Gordon D. Newby, Devin Stewart, Laurie L. Patton, John D. Dunne, Robert von Thaden, Bart B. Bruehler, Juan Hernandez, and William K. Gilders; and my Rhetoric of Religious Antiquity colleagues L. Gregory Bloomquist, Roy R. Jeal, Duane F. Watson, David A. deSilva, Fred J. Long, Priscilla Geisterfer, and Robert L. Webb for contributing to specific aspects of this essay. In addition, I am deeply indebted to my son Rick A. Robbins, a figurative abstract and color-field artist in the area of neo-abstract expressionism, whose efforts to bring art into words has informed my attempt to describe how words evoke images in the mind; see his "Statement" at http://home.comcast.net/~rick1216/.

[2] See http://www.deopublishing.com/rhetoricofreligiousantiquity.htm. A search on Google for the word rhetography, after a basic search with more conventional scholarly tools produced no findings, led to an announcement of the section of the SBL in November 2006 for which this paper was written; my May 1, 2004, essay on "Beginnings and Developments in Socio-Rhetorical Interpretation"; my paper entitled "Conceptual Blending and Early Christian Imagination" for the 2005 conference in Helsinki on "Body, Mind, and Society in Early Christianity"; and an essay by my Rhetoric of Religious Antiquity colleague Roy R. Jeal on "Clothes Make the (Wo)man," at www.ars-rhetorica.net/Queen/VolumeSpecialIssue5/Articles/Jeal.pdf. Also, see p. 175 in Vernon K. Robbins, "Enthymeme and Picture in the Gospel of Thomas," in *Thomasine Traditions in Antiquity: The Social and Cultural World of the Gospel of Thomas* (ed. J. Ma Asgeirsson, A. D. DeConick, and R. Uro; NHMS 59; Leiden: Brill, 2006), 175–207; Roy R. Jeal, "Blending Two Arts: Rhetorical Words, Rhetorical Pictures and Social Formation in the Letter to Philemon," at http://rhetjournal.net/Jeal.pdf.

[3] Visual texture is an aspect of sensory-aesthetic texture, which exhibits the range of senses the text evokes or embodies (thought, emotion, sight, sound, touch, smell): Vernon K. Robbins, *Exploring the Texture of Texts: A Guide to Socio-Rhetorical Interpretation* (Valley Forge, Pa.: Trinity Press International, 1996), 29–36; idem, *The Tapestry of Early Christian Discourse: Rhetoric, Society, and Ideology* (London: Routledge, 1996), 64–65,

89–91. Roy R. Jeal describes these senses as visual, oral, aural, olfactory, tactile, gustatory, textual, prosaic, poetic, and intellectual: "Writing Socio-Rhetorical Commentary: Colossians 1:15-20" (paper presented at the SBL, RRA Seminar, Washington, D.C., November 17, 2006), 12.

[4] For the linguistic turn in New Testament studies, see Anthony C. Thiselton, *The Two Horizons: New Testament Hermeneutics and Philosophical Description with Special Reference to Heidegger, Bultmann, Gadamer, and Wittgenstein* (Grand Rapids, Mich.: Eerdmans, 1980), 117–39; idem, *New Horizons in Hermeneutics: The Theory and Practice of Transforming Biblical Reading* (Grand Rapids, Mich.: Zondervan, 1992). For the pictorial turn in the study of literature and art, see W. J. T. Mitchell, *Picture Theory: Essays on Verbal and Visual Representation* (Chicago and London: University of Chicago Press, 1994), esp. 11–34. After using the term rhetography, I discovered a reference to "theography" in Jack Miles, *God: A Biography* (New York: Vintage Books, 1996), 12; see my reference to it in Robbins, "Enthymeme and Picture," 175, n. 2. See now the extensive use of the term rhetography alongside theology on the Internet.

[5] Aphthonius, *Progymnasmata* [46 Spengel/37–38 Rabe]; see George A. Kennedy, *Progymnasmata: Greek Textbooks of Prose Composition and Rhetoric, Translated into English, with Introductions and Notes* (WGRW 10; Atlanta and Leiden: Society of Biblical Literature/Brill, 2003), 117. Also see Douglas J. Stewart, "On Ekphrasis: A Communication," *Arion* 5 (1966): 554–56; W. J. T. Mitchell, "Ekphrasis and the Other," in Mitchell, *Picture Theory*, 151–81.

[6] Erwin Panofsky, *Studies in Iconology: Humanistic Themes in the Art of the Renaissance* (New York: Oxford University Press, 1939), 3–31; Karl Mannheim, "Erwin Panofsky and Karl Mannheim: A Dialogue on Interpretation," *Critical Inquiry* 19 (1993): 534–66; see Mitchell, *Picture Theory*, 16–34.

[7] Roland Barthes, "The Imagination of the Sign," in *Critical Essays* (trans. Richard Howard; Evanston, Ill.: Northwestern University Press, 1972), 205–11, 261–79.

[8] Mitchell, *Picture Theory*: "Visible Language: Blake's Art of Writing" (111–50); "Ekphrasis and the Other" (151–80); and "Narrative, Memory, and Slavery" (183–207).

[9] Mitchell, *Picture Theory*, 24.

[10] In Mitchell's words, the "iconology of the text" (*Picture Theory*, 112).

[11] A central feature of argumentative rhetorical reasoning is the *enthymeme*: see George A. Kennedy, *New Testament Interpretation through Rhetorical Criticism* (Chapel Hill: University of North Carolina Press, 1984), 16–17, 49–61 et passim; cf. Vernon K. Robbins, "From Enthymeme to Theology in Luke 11:1-13," in *Literary Studies in Luke-Acts: A Collection of Essays in Honor of Joseph B. Tyson* (ed. R. P. Thompson and T. E. Phillips; Macon, Ga.: Mercer University Press, 1998), 191–214. Online: http://www.religion.emory.edu/faculty/robbins/Theology/theology191.html.

[12] Harvey Whitehouse, *Arguments and Icons: Divergent Modes of Religiosity* (Oxford: Oxford University Press, 2000); Robert N. McCauley and E. Thomas Lawson, *Rethinking Religion: Connecting Cognition and Culture* (Cambridge: Cambridge University Press, 1990); idem, *Bringing Ritual to Mind: Psychological Foundations of Cultural Forms* (Cambridge: Cambridge University Press, 2002); Laurie L. Patton, "A History of the Quest for Mental Power," in her *Bringing the Gods to Mind: Mantra and Ritual in Early Indian Sacrifice* (Berkeley and London: University of California Press, 2005), 142–51.

[13] On Sermon on the Mount: Hans Dieter Betz, *The Sermon on the Mount* (Hermeneia; Minneapolis: Augsburg Fortress Press, 1995); on speeches in Acts: e.g., the bibliography in Todd Penner, *In Praise of Christian Origins: Stephen and the Hellenists in Lukan Apologetic Historiography* (ESEC 10; New York and London: T&T Clark, 2004), and Duane F. Watson, "Paul's Speech to the Ephesian Elders (Acts 20.17-38): Epideictic Rhetoric of Farewell," in *Persuasive Artistry: Studies in New Testament Rhetoric in Honor of George A. Kennedy* (ed. D. F. Watson; JSNTSup 50; Sheffield: JSOT Press, 1991), 184–208; on narrative and speech in gospels and Acts: Duane F. Watson, *The Rhetoric of the New Testament: A Bibliographic Survey* (Tools for Biblical Study 8; Blandford Forum: Deo Publishing, 2006), 93–120.

[14] Hans Dieter Betz, *Galatians: A Commentary on Paul's Letters to the Churches in Galatia* (Hermeneia; Philadelphia: Fortress, 1979); Calvin J. Roetzel, *The Letters of Paul: Conversations in Context* (4th ed.; Louisville, Ky.: Westminster John Knox, 1998); Watson, *The Rhetoric of the New Testament*, 121–80.

[15] Kennedy, *New Testament Interpretation*, 159.

[16] Kennedy, *New Testament Interpretation*, 96.

[17] Kennedy, *New Testament Interpretation*, 17–18 (emphasis in original).

[18] Vernon K. Robbins, "The Dialectical Nature of Early Christian Discourse," *Scriptura* 59 (1996): 353–62; online at http://www.religion.emory.edu/faculty/robbins/dialect/dialect353.html. The linguist Benjamin H. Hary, Emory University, encouraged me to contract the two words *rhetorical dialect* into *rhetorolect* by analogy to his use of the term *sociolect* in his research: Benjamin H. Hary, *Multiglossia in Judeo-Arabic* (Leiden: Brill, 1992); idem, "Judeo-Arabic in Its Socio-Linguistic Setting," *IOS* 15 (1995): 73–99; idem, "Adaptations of Hebrew Script," in *The World's Writing Systems* (ed. P. T. Daniels and W. Bright; New York: Oxford University Press, 1996), 727–34, 741–42.

[19] Robbins, "The Dialectical Nature of Early Christian Discourse," 356.

[20] Robbins, "The Dialectical Nature of Early Christian Discourse," 357–61. In the ensuing years, three of the names for the rhetorolects stayed the same (wisdom, miracle, apocalyptic) and three of them changed (opposition to prophetic, death/resurrection to priestly, and cosmic to precreation).

[21] Vernon K. Robbins, "Argumentative Textures in Socio-Rhetorical Interpretation," in *Rhetorical Argumentation in Biblical Texts: Essays from the Lund 2000 Conference* (ed. A. Eriksson, T. H. Olbricht, and W. Übelacker, ESEC 8; Harrisburg, Pa.: Trinity Press International, 2002), 27–65; online at http://www.religion.emory.edu/faculty/robbins/Pdfs/LundArgument.pdf.

[22] In Robbins, "Argumentative Textures," 31–63, the six rhetorolects were called wisdom, miracle, prophetic, suffering-death, apocalyptic, and pre-creation.

[23] Cf. Kennedy, *New Testament Interpretation*, 96.

[24] Vernon K. Robbins, "Enthymeme and Picture in the Gospel of Thomas," in *Thomasine Traditions in Antiquity: The Social and Cultural World of the Gospel of Thomas* (ed. J. Ma Asgeirsson, A. D. DeConick, and R. Uro; NHMS 59; Leiden: Brill, 2006), 175–207.

[25] Kennedy's term in *New Testament Interpretation*, 159.

[26] Kennedy, *New Testament Interpretation*, 104; see also 7, 93, 96, 104–6, 113, 159.

[27] Robbins, "The Dialectical Nature of Early Christian Discourse"; idem, "Argumentative Textures"; idem, *The Invention of Christian Discourse*, Vol. 1: *Wisdom, Prophetic, and Apocalyptic* (Blandford Forum: Deo Publishing, 2008).

[28] Kennedy, *New Testament Interpretation*, 39–72.

[29] Kennedy, *New Testament Interpretation*, 141–52.

[30] Kennedy, *New Testament Interpretation*, 39–63.

[31] Kennedy, *New Testament Interpretation*, 46.

[32] Kingdom: Matt 5:3, 10, 19(2), 20; 6:10, 13, 33; 7:21; prophets: Matt 5:12, 17; 7:12, 15.

[33] Kennedy, *New Testament Interpretation*, 50.

[34] Kennedy, *New Testament Interpretation*, 62.

[35] For an excellent example of analysis of biblical prophetic discourse that provides rich data for understanding the nature of early Christian prophetic rhetoric, see Mark Roncace, *Jeremiah, Zedekiah, and the Fall of Jerusalem* (Library of Hebrew Bible/Old Testament Studies; JSOTSup 423; New York and London: T&T Clark, 2005), esp. 5–25, 146–73.

[36] E.g., Rom 4:13, 14; 8:17; 1 Cor 6:9-10; 15:50; Gal 3:18, 29; 4:1, 7, 30; 5:21.

[37] Kennedy, *New Testament Interpretation*, 86.

[38] Kennedy, *New Testament Interpretation*, 87–88, 89–90, 90–96.

[39] Kennedy, *New Testament Interpretation*, 88–90.

[40] Kennedy, *New Testament Interpretation*, 90.

[41] Kennedy, *New Testament Interpretation*, 73–85.

[42] Kennedy summarizes the initial focus on praise in *New Testament Interpretation*, 73–75, but moves away from this emphasis to the third/fourth-century C.E. handbooks on epideictic rhetoric on pp. 75–77 to establish the context for interpreting John 13–17.

[43] A major start on socio-rhetorical interpretation of miracle discourse in the New Testament will appear in *The Role of Miracle Discourse in the Argumentation of the New Testament* (ed. D. F. Watson; SBLSymS; Atlanta: Society of Biblical Literature and Leiden: Brill, forthcoming).

[44] Kennedy, *New Testament Interpretation*, 105.

[45] Aristotle, *On Rhetoric: A Theory of Civic Discourse* (trans. with intro., notes, and appendices by George A. Kennedy; Oxford: Oxford University Press, 1991), 84.

[46] Vernon K. Robbins, "Socio-Rhetorical Interpretation of Miracle Discourse in the Synoptic Gospels," forthcoming in *The Role of Miracle Discourse*.

[47] John H. Elliott, "The Evil Eye and the Sermon on the Mount: Contours of a Pervasive Belief in Social Scientific Perspective," *BibInt* 2 (1994): 51–84; John J. Pilch and Bruce J. Malina, eds., *Handbook of Biblical Social Values* (Peabody, Mass.: Hendrickson, 1998), 68–72.

[48] Kennedy, *New Testament Interpretation*, 113.

[49] For an initial exploration of the imperial nature of the discourse in the Gospel of John, see Gerhard van den Heever, "Finding Data in Unexpected Places (Or: From Text Linguistics to Socio-Rhetoric): A Socio-Rhetorical Reading of John's Gospel," in *SBLSP* 37 (2 vols.; Atlanta: Scholars Press, 1998), 2:629–76.

[50] Kennedy, *New Testament Interpretation*, 20.

[51] Kennedy, *New Testament Interpretation*, 20.

[52] For an excellent analysis of biblical priestly discourse that provides rich data for analysis of early Christian priestly rhetoric, see William K. Gilders, *Blood Ritual in the Hebrew Bible: Meaning and Power* (Baltimore: The Johns Hopkins University Press, 2004).

[53] On critical partiality: David M. Gunn and Paula M. McNutt, eds., *'Imagining' Biblical Worlds: Studies in Spatial, Social and Historical Constructs in Honor of James W. Flanagan* (JSOTSup 359; Sheffield: Sheffield Academic, 2002); on conceptual blending: Gilles Fauconnier and Mark Turner, *The Way We Think: Conceptual Blending and the Mind's Hidden Complexities* (New York: Basic Books, 2002).

[54] George Lakoff, *Women, Fire, and Dangerous Things: What Categories Reveal about the Mind* (Chicago and London: University of Chicago Press, 1987), 68–76, esp. 68.

[55] The definition has been refined especially through insights from Robert von Thaden, "The Wisdom of Fleeing *Porneia*: Conceptual Blending in 1 Corinthians 6:12–7:7" (Ph.D. diss., Emory University, 2006); and the Ph.D. work of Priscilla Geisterfer at St. Paul University, Ottawa. Also, see the discussion of framing in Patton, *Bringing the Gods to Mind*, 46–47.

[56] Vernon K. Robbins, *The Invention of Christian Discourse* (2 vols.; Blandford Forum: Deo Publishing, 2008).

[57] Kennedy, *New Testament Interpretation*, 7.

[58] L. Ayres, *Nicaea and Its Legacy: An Approach to Fourth-Century Trinitarian Theology* (Oxford: Oxford University Press, 2006).

[59] J. N. D. Kelly, *Early Christian Creeds* (London, New York, and Toronto: Longmans, Green, 1952), 344–67; cf. Luke Timothy Johnson, *The Creed: What Christians Believe and Why It Matters* (New York: Doubleday, 2003), 32–38.

[60] Ayres, *Nicaea and Its Legacy*, 434.

[61] E.g., Bart B. Bruehler, "Karma Yoga and Christian Ethics: Reading Bhagavad Gita 3 in Light of Ephesians 4–6," in *Song Divine: Christian Commentaries on the Bhagavad Gita* (ed. Catherine Cornille; Leuven: Peeters Press, 2006), 23–48.

CHAPTER 7

GEORGE KENNEDY'S INFLUENCE ON RHETORICAL INTERPRETATION OF THE ACTS OF THE APOSTLES

Blake Shipp

George Kennedy's method has been used to interpret every book of the New Testament. However, its use in understanding the Acts of the Apostles has been limited. Blake Shipp traces the role of Kennedy's approach in the interpretation of Acts and offers some intriguing insights into why that role has been limited. The interplay of narrative and speeches stands front and center. Shipp raises many questions about the future rhetorical analysis of Acts and how Kennedy's methodology—expanded in an even more thoroughly, classically informed vein—might still play a role.

My introduction to the work of George Kennedy came as what one might term "fortuitous happenstance." As a new doctoral student in my first seminar on the theology of the New Testament, I sat in rapt attention listening to my professor, recently returned from a sabbatical leave spent studying communication theory, discuss the possibilities of using the canons of rhetoric as a tool for interpreting the biblical text. Intrigued, I soon was scouring the stacks of the library looking for guidance and a seminar topic involving the use of rhetoric as an interpretive tool. In my search I came across a slim, unassuming volume entitled *New Testament Interpretation through Rhetorical Criticism* by Kennedy.[1] Thinking the volume might be of some assistance, I added it to the stack of works to check out. What I found within the pages of that modest tome was a priceless treasure. Kennedy introduced me to the power of speech and how speech might be arranged to carry persuasive effect. I was hooked. Kennedy's words built within my mind an interpretive framework, a new world in which my companions became Quintilian, Aristotle, and Cicero. Soon, additional acquaintances were made with the likes of Livy, Sallust, Thucydides, Plutarch, Theon of Alexandria, and others. Lazy New Orleans afternoons would be spent with my new friends, pondering their words and how the world that molded their thoughts might have shaped the thoughts and words of the New Testament authors. The work of Kennedy has forever changed how I view and interpret the writings of the New Testament. For this I am in his debt, the recipient of a foundation upon which I continue to build. It is therefore a great honor to offer the following reflections about Kennedy's influence on the rhetorical interpretation of Acts.

KENNEDY'S IMPACT ON THE STUDY OF THE RHETORIC OF ACTS

The influence of Kennedy and his methodological framework upon the interpretation of Christian Scripture in general seems hard to overestimate. Certainly, he was not the first to propose or practice such an interpretation of the writings of the New Testament. His distinctive contribution lies in providing a focus for New Testament studies—the first programmatic definition of and outline for rhetorical criticism of that portion of Christian Scripture. Aware of the lack of methodological consistency and the total absence of a formal method for using rhetoric in New Testament studies, Kennedy sought to provide methodological cohesion with his *New Testament Interpretation through Rhetorical Criticism*. Scholars quickly noticed the importance of Kennedy's work for rhetorical criticism. In now oft-quoted words, Wilhelm Wuellner epitomizes the massive impact Kennedy had made upon the field: "With Kennedy's proposal for New Testament interpretation through rhetorical criticism, publications with rhetoric in their titles will likely reach tidal-wave proportions."[2] The tidal wave of publications did rise, supporting volumes of publications about various New Testament texts, especially the Pauline Epistles.[3] That wave, however, gave us comparatively few publications about Acts.

APPROACHES TO THE RHETORICAL ANALYSIS OF ACTS

The application of the principles and forms of rhetoric to the text of Acts as an interpretive tool is a recent phenomenon attempted by only a few scholars. The works of those interpreters who have utilized rhetoric may be subsumed under four broad categories: comparative studies, studies providing formal rhetorical analysis, works utilizing socio-rhetorical criticism, and investigations using recent, eclectic rhetorical approaches. Although overlapping at various points and not to be sharply divided, each of these four approaches reveals enough difference in emphasis that they may be differentiated for heuristic purposes.

The Comparative Approach

The earliest attempts to use the principles of rhetoric in interpreting Acts were comparative analyses.[4] In these studies scholars correlate features of textual units in Acts with the principles and guidelines for constructing speeches in the rhetorical handbooks.[5] The interpreter's basic objective is to demonstrate the rhetorical competence of the biblical author. In this effort, interpreters often utilize three basic steps. First, they identify the ancient rhetorical tradition to which they are referring. The guidelines for specific rhetorical structures are detailed from both the handbook tradition and from ancient practice.[6] Second, the interpreter turns to the text of Acts, seeking to determine the rhetorical structure of the pericope in view. Third, the guidelines for rhetorical structures are compared with structures identified within the text of Acts, and a conclusion is drawn concerning Luke's rhetorical competence or incompetence. The presiding questions seem to be, Was the author familiar with the ancient rhetorical tradition in view, and how might that familiarity be demonstrated?[7]

The purposes for such an approach range from discovering rhetorical patterns within Acts to identifying the genre of the book. In these studies scholars argue about the appropriateness of employing canons of rhetoric in investigating the text of Acts. While these analyses provide solid ground for further rhetorical study of Acts, they provide little understanding of the rhetorical movement of the text as a whole. Little effort is made to draw a unified view of the author's rhetorical intent or of how an ancient audience might have perceived that intent. In other words, those that utilize the comparative approach have little interest in using rhetoric as a tool for interpretation. The principal objective is a second-order exhibition of Luke's rhetorical competence. Therefore, this approach, while rhetorical in nature, has a rather different agenda than Kennedy's brand of rhetorical criticism. Accordingly, such studies typically demonstrate little influence of Kennedy's methodology.

Formal Rhetorical Analysis

A second approach to the use of rhetoric in the study of Acts is the formal rhetorical analysis of portions of the text. This approach involves analyzing various units in light of commonly accepted principles and rules for constructing speeches and narratives, most often found within rhetorical handbooks. This approach, only a little over twenty years old, has grown primarily out of the influential works of Kennedy and Hans Dieter Betz.[8] The basic aim of these investigations is to determine the rhetorical dynamics and persuasive patterns within the text of Acts. They are especially interested in discovering the potential persuasiveness of an individual speech in view of the textual movement the speech creates within its larger context.[9]

However, within the realm of the investigation of the literary world of Luke-Acts, the principles outlined by Kennedy in his *New Testament Interpretation through Rhetorical Criticism* have provided less direct guidance than one might expect. Duane Watson's investigation of Paul's speech at Miletus (Acts 20:17-38) stands as one of the few examples of a formal rhetorical analysis strictly governed by Kennedy's methodology.[10] All other published approaches are akin, however, to Kennedy's principles in their overarching objective of discovering the persuasive movement of the text under consideration.[11]

Socio-Rhetorical Analysis

The third application of rhetoric to the text of Acts might be described as socio-rhetorical analysis. This method, associated primarily with Vernon Robbins, is actually the melding of numerous methodologies: social-scientific criticism, rhetorical criticism, postmodern criticism, and historical-theological approaches.[12] As an approach representing the confluence of various methodologies, some drastically different from what I have typed as comparative or formalist approaches, socio-rhetorical investigations demonstrate little in common with the principles outlined by Kennedy in his seminal volume of 1984. While such investigations are concerned, as is Kennedy, with the rhetorical structure and persuasiveness of speeches and narratives, they differ from "purely" rhetorical approaches in that they determine this structure and effect through lenses other than those of ancient rhetorical theory and practice. In those rare instances when authors of these socio-rhetorical studies employ Kennedy's method, they do so by noting his rhetorical insights concerning individual biblical texts found in *New Testament Interpretation through Rhetorical Criticism*. What they do not do is actually engage his methodology.[13]

Eclectic Rhetorical Analysis

The final rhetorical approach to the text of Acts is one that is currently under development and has yet to assume a firm shape. The general direction of this approach seems to be an endeavor to interpret the text from within the parameters of a larger rhetorical worldview rather than limiting one's interpretive foundation to the Greco-Roman handbook tradition. Like the socio-rhetorical analysis just described, the eclectic approach draws from an array of auxiliary disciplines; like formal analyses, it tends to operate in conjunction with primarily literary or communication theories. This approach can entail, as in my own study and in that of Todd Penner, an expansion of one's primary literature to include the *progymnasmata* and other rhetorically influenced works; the inclusion of modern rhetorical and narrative canons, as in the work of Mark Given; or the incorporation of modern communication and linguistic theories, as in the study by Michael Enyinwa Okoronkwo.[14] These works are recent attempts to refine rhetorical criticism by answering criticisms of previous, rhetorically driven endeavors. Of these works, however, only my own demonstrates an overt connection to the methodology of Kennedy. All the others represent significant departures from Kennedy's approach, or (as in the case of Okoronkwo) a complete neglect of it.

A Preliminary Assessment

What is noteworthy in the preceding survey of rhetorical approaches to Acts is the general lack of influence by, or dependence upon, the work of Kennedy. Watson's analysis of Paul's Miletus speech is the rare published example of an approach to Acts that follows Kennedy's proposals in a strict fashion.[15] My own investigation of the Damascus Road narratives in Acts (9:1-22; 22:3-21; 26:2-33) is among the most recent examples of an approach heavily influenced by Kennedy. However, I have employed his work in a heavily modified manner, constructing a distinctive rhetorical approach that I defined as "literary-rhetorical criticism": the enhancement of the handbook tradition with greater attention to classical stasis theory and the guidelines provided by the tradition of ancient *progymnasmata*.[16] In light of the evidence, one must conclude that Kennedy's methodological approach, which over a period of years has offered some cohesion to the general field of New Testament rhetorical criticism, has had little effect upon most rhetorical interpretations of Acts. Such a conclusion is surprising. Not only have Kennedy's proposals exerted relatively little influence; recent investigations fail to interact with Kennedy on any level.[17] What small influence he has exercised has not yet demonstrated an enduring influence.[18]

REASONS FOR KENNEDY'S LIMITED IMPACT ON RHETORICAL STUDY OF ACTS

While the reasons for the paucity of publications on the rhetoric of Acts within the "tidal-wave" predicted for Kennedy's proposals are somewhat unclear, the reality of this phenomenon is nonetheless unfortunate. Kennedy's methodology hinges upon the understanding that, although the Bible is a literary collection, these texts can be interpreted as oral speeches because the biblical books were presented orally in their first-century setting.[19] Kennedy concludes that the Bible should display oral qualities, designed as such by New Testament authors for oral reading. Because the Bible was oral in origin, he posits that the canons of Greco-Roman rhetoric were an appropriate resource for interpreting New Testament documents, even if the authors of the New Testament had not received formal training in classical rhetoric. Matters of invention were, in his estimation, universal, and the pervasive influence of rhetoric in the first century would have been impossible to avoid, even by those unschooled in rhetoric.[20]

Of all New Testament texts, Acts would seem to be fertile ground for rhetorical investigations in a mode reflecting Kennedy's proposals, for that text demonstrates an acute awareness of the rhetorical milieu of the ancient world and bears a high oral quality.[21] Depending on one's reckoning, almost one-third of Acts is made up of speeches, with many of them conforming to the Greco-Roman framework found in the handbook tradition.[22] Further, Kennedy's approach offers a way out of the source- and tradition-critical maze that has constituted a large part of the study of Acts. In other words, a formal rhetorical analysis takes the text as it is, suggesting that one might discover the author's or editor's persuasive intent and how the author's audience would have perceived such intent.[23] Finally, Kennedy's approach provides one of the best means of understanding Acts, a rhetorically influenced book, within its own historical context by drawing upon oral and literary principles that were accessible and known—in whatever manner—to the author. One is further perplexed by the absence of Kennedy's influence on the interpretation of Acts when one considers the great influence he has had upon the investigation of the New Testament epistles, especially the Pauline Epistles.[24]

Why has Kennedy's method failed to catch the attention of scholars interpreting Acts? The reasons are unclear, in part because no formal debate or discussion concerning the appropriateness of Kennedy's approach within the literary world of Acts has yet occurred. This is not to say, however, that scholars have neglected Kennedy because of simple oversight. The neglect appears almost purposeful. Three broad reasons might be proposed for the almost complete disregard of Kennedy's proposals in the study of Acts.

The Nature of the Text of Acts

Perhaps the primary reason lies not within Kennedy's proposals but within the nature of the text of Acts itself. This document stands at an amazing confluence of literary streams, a blending of multiple narrative and generic threads that often baffles scholars who attempt to solve the enigma of its author's purpose. One of the greatest literary realities complicating the examination of Acts is its mixture of speech and narrative. The literary world of Acts is neither speech nor narrative, but an amalgamation of both primary and secondary rhetoric—that is, narration and direct speech—with no clear authorial guidance for how the two function collaboratively. That the speeches embedded within the text bear narrative meaning is clear, as is the reality that the surrounding narrative interprets and is interpreted by the embedded speeches. Obviously the two function persuasively and rhetorically, but on different levels—the narratives functioning more subtly and less blatantly than, say, a forensic speech.[25] Interpreting a speech and its surrounding narrative is akin to cutting a Gordian knot, often forcing interpreters to focus on one to the exclusion of the other.[26] Such may be one of the primary reasons why so few rhetorically oriented studies of Acts have been published. Understanding the speech is of little value if one's method makes little headway in interpreting the narrative in which the speech is embedded.[27]

Kennedy himself makes no attempt to deal with the mixture of speech and narrative that Acts comprises. In *New Testament Interpretation*'s treatment of Acts, Kennedy discusses the speeches but does not tackle the narrative as a whole or discuss how the speeches relate to the narrative, nor does he provide his audience with guidance in applying his method in this polymorphous setting. He does note that the "speeches in Acts often occur at important points in the action or in unusual and interesting situations."[28] What he does not discuss is how the speech and action of the narrative work together in achieving the author's persuasive intent. The lack of discussion concerning the integration of narrative and speech is a key weakness, not only in Kennedy's methodology, but arguably in rhetorical criticism generally. One of the chief claims made for the benefit of rhetorical criticism is its consideration of the individual unit under investigation within the persuasive context as a whole.[29] In such a text as Acts, the inability to move from speech to narrative and back again in the interpretive process stymies the very goal for which the interpreter works.

The Nature of Kennedy's Method and Its Practice

A second reason for the lack of Kennedy's influence may lie within the nature of his method and its practice by himself and others. Kennedy's method was immediately popularized because of its apparent simplicity. However, he achieved this simplicity by incorporating a level of ambiguity into his delineation of rhetorical criticism, an obscurity that left interpreters ill prepared to employ principles found in *New Testament Interpretation through Rhetorical Criticism*. R. Dean Anderson has insightfully noted this deficiency: "Such a method seems virtually self-explanatory, but one thing is startlingly lacking. There appears to be no distinction made between the study of the rhetoric or argumentation of the unit in general, and the relationship or contribution of *ancient* rhetoric to the unit."[30]

Anderson's critique is on target. At no point does Kennedy instruct his readers how ancient rhetoric informed and influenced the construction of the New Testament texts by their authors. Such an omission may have been purposeful. That Kennedy assumes such influence is clear in his statements about reading the Bible as speech and the pervasive influence of Greco-Roman rhetoric in first-century society. Yet to what extent were the authors actually affected by this influence? Should one limit the influence to matters of style, or should one extend the influence to the use of stasis, genre, and formal rhetorical divisions? The disarming simplicity of Kennedy's method has left scholars with few guideposts in applying Greco-Roman rhetoric to interpret such rhetorically influenced texts as Acts.

Kennedy's chapter on Acts is of little help in solving the ambiguity created by his method. In the preface to this chapter he states, "The following discussion consists of notes on some rhetorical features of discourses in Acts consisting of four or more verses."[31] Kennedy then proceeds to an overview of twenty-five speeches in Acts. In this survey he supplies his readers with important rhetorical markers and elements—remarks about exigence, stasis, species, and the like—with some incidental notes on the structure of various speeches.[32] These notes provide an invaluable guide to the important rhetorical landmarks in the speeches of Acts. What Kennedy does not offer is a systematic application of his method to the text of Acts as a whole. As a result, Kennedy's chapter leaves the reader aware of traces of rhetoric in Acts but uncertain of how to use his method to interpret such rhetoric in the discovery of Luke's persuasive intent.

With little formal guidance from Kennedy, many interpreters have approached the task of describing the author's persuasive intent by classifying the formal rhetorical structure of a text in Acts. Determining the supposed rhetorical structure was then equated with such persuasive intent.[33] Equating structure with intent is immediately suspect, however, especially in a text like Acts, for such an approach does not address how the author utilized the rhetorical structure and movement of the individual unit to advance the overall persuasive flow of the book, nor does this approach adequately permit the persuasive movement of the context to influence the classification of the rhetorical structure of the text in view. The result is an interpretation of Acts within a kind of literary vacuum unlikely to have existed in the author's creative agenda.

Moreover, the equation of rhetorical structure with persuasive intent has led to the application of rhetorical criticism to texts that defy such an approach. Actually, the prime example of such an approach may be witnessed in some forms of rhetorical criticism applied to the letters of Paul. Following the trend begun by Betz, many scholars have applied rhetorical criticism to New Testament epistles, focusing primarily on the Pauline Epistles. The basic approach, imitating Betz, is to separate the epistolary opening and closing of these letters from the body of the letter. The body of the letter is then divided in accordance with the standard canons of rhetorical arrangement, based on the understanding that Paul's letters were really speeches sandwiched within an epistolary framework. The result of such assumptions is the subsuming of epistolary features under rhetorical categories. In response, epistolary theorists have cried foul, questioning the systematic application of formal rhetorical categories to the construction of epistles in the ancient world.[34] Such misapplications of Kennedy's brand of rhetorical criticism thus led to a decline in further attempts to use his method, even in the interpretation of a different genre, such as Acts represents. Perhaps thinking that Kennedy's methodological ship had sunk on its maiden voyage, few have attempted to apply his principles to texts outside of the epistles.[35]

In short, left with little formal guidance, interpreters' (minimal) applications of Kennedy's approach to Acts have varied widely. One might expect that such diversity would lead to a serious discussion of the refinement of those principles. Instead, the result has been silence and an almost chilling effect on rhetorical criticism of Acts, at least along Kennedy's lines.

THE RISE OF NEW RHETORICAL APPROACHES

A final reason for the lack of influence of Kennedy's methodological approach in the study of Acts may lie with the rise in popularity and application of other, more recent approaches deemed "rhetorical" in nature. The strongest challenger, effectively supplanting Kennedy's mode of criticism in the realm of rhetorical interpretation, is Robbins' socio-rhetorical criticism. Robbins published his first thoughts and an application of his method the same year that Kennedy published his *New Testament Interpretation through Rhetorical Criticism*.[36] The formal explanation of his theory followed in later years.[37] Robbins saw his approach as an opportunity and "challenge to integrate major strategies of the new movements and methods through a rhetorical approach that focuses on literary, social, cultural and ideological issues in the texts."[38] The outcome—deserved or otherwise—of drawing in a selective fashion from numerous approaches is that socio-rhetorical criticism is plagued with none of the criticism that seems to have overwhelmed Kennedy's approach. As a result scholars have readily adopted Robbins' socio-rhetorical criticism as the predominate expression of rhetorical criticism. A scholarly minority has widened their understanding of the "rhetorical" interpretation of Scripture, noting a distinction between rhetoric and argumentation and seeking to identify an author's persuasive intent through the use of logic and dialectic.[39] The shifts in methodological approaches, coupled with the harsh criticism of previous applications, have eventuated in the current, virtual absence of Kennedy's mode of rhetorical criticism in the interpretation of Acts.

KENNEDY AND THE FUTURE OF RHETORIC IN ACTS

In spite of early predictions of its dramatic influence, Kennedy's rhetorical approach to the New Testament, particularly to the Acts of the Apostles, has proven underutilized to date. The field of rhetorical criticism has shifted to the point that many of the insights and principles set forth by Kennedy have been abandoned by those still attempting to interpret texts rhetorically. Unless we concede that Robbins' socio-rhetorical analysis has practically commandeered the field, the result of such abandonment is that rhetorical study is returning to the state of unbounded methodological flux that reigned prior to Kennedy. One is left wondering whether any life remains at all in the rhetorical approach as classically articulated. Has the rhetorical approach to Scripture become an interpretive dinosaur whose time has quickly come and gone, only to be replaced by more evolved, better-adapted methodologies? Certainly, Kennedy's method has its flaws, and these coupled with the misapplication of his approach have had, perhaps justifiably, a chilling effect on the employment of his brand of rhetorical criticism. However, its outright rejection, with no attempts to correct the flaws and misapplication, is unwarranted. The possibility exists of retaining and modifying Kennedy's methodological framework. By filling lacunae and providing firm guidelines for the method's application, a new form of rhetorical criticism might be proposed, a form that maintains Kennedy's proposal as a touchstone while providing methodological cohesion once again to the field of rhetorical criticism.

Though my own, more eclectic approach is doubtless subject to criticism at various points, I have proposed (for instance) that Luke embeds in the narrative of Acts various accounts of the Damascus Road episode in order to construct a *Paulusbild* that demonstrates an oscillating pattern of resistance to God's will, which eventuates in God's restraint, and obedience to God's will, whose consequence is empowerment.[40] Thus, Acts 9:1-26a depicts God's overcoming of a murderous Saul (vv. 1-9) and a resistant Ananias (vv. 10-16), culminating in Saul's partial restoration (vv. 17-19a) and empowered witness (vv. 19b-26a).[41] In Acts 21:33–22:24a Paul's humiliation is emphasized, his subjugation intensified (21:33-40; 22:2, 22-24a), as his forensic rehearsal of his earlier persecution of the Way (22:1, 3-16) culminates in his still resistant witness (vv. 17-21). At this point, however, his resistance to God is not expressed in persecution of followers of the Way, but rather a refusal to leave Jerusalem in fulfillment of God's specific directions to go bearing witness to the Gentiles.[42] Paul's forensic defense before Festus and Agrippa (25:23–26:32) yields an ambivalent portrait: The Saul of Paul's speech (transformed and empowered), anticipated by "the vision of grace" in 23:11, stands in tension with the depiction of Paul, at this point in Luke's narrative, as an overpowered prisoner who is partially transformed.[43] It may be Luke's intention to complete the transformation of Paul as he travels to Rome, so that when the apostle arrives he can powerfully and effectively bear witness. That seems to be the projected narrative trajectory in Acts, even though Luke does not resolve a certain tension in Paul's character.[44] The stasis of each of these three Damascus Road tableaux can be articulated without Kennedy's introduction of Lloyd Bitzer's modern statement of the "exigence" in a "rhetorical situation."[45] Moreover, as I have demonstrated elsewhere,[46] Theon's six prescriptions for a properly constructed narrative—clearly identifying an episode's character(s), action(s), setting, time, manner, and reason—repeatedly illuminate Luke's narrative *and* discourse in the book of Acts.

Mine, however, is only one proposal. Other trajectories for more effective rhetorical analysis of Acts are yet to be determined. As Kennedy himself reminds us, promising insights are being gleaned from the *progymnasmata*, the foundational exercises that lay behind the Greco-Roman rhetorical world.[47] Future refinement of rhetorical study may also lie in principles drawn from narrative and dialogical models, which describe how primary and secondary rhetoric function cooperatively. What becomes of Kennedy's rhetorical criticism remains to be seen, for those willing to struggle in clearing a new way.

Notes

[1] George A. Kennedy, *New Testament Interpretation through Rhetorical Criticism* (Chapel Hill: University of North Carolina Press, 1984).

[2] Wilhelm Wuellner, "Where Is Rhetorical Criticism Taking Us?" *CBQ* 49 (1987): 448–63.

[3] The following is a broad—but by no means complete—sampling of published works that employ the methodology proposed by George Kennedy. See Duane F. Watson, *Invention, Arrangement, and Style: Rhetorical Criticism of Jude and 2 Peter* (SBLDS 104; Atlanta: Scholars Press, 1988); idem, "James 2 in Light of Greco-Roman Schemes of Argumentation," *NTS* 39 (1993): 94–121; Rollin Grams, "The Temple Conflict Scene: A Rhetorical Analysis of Matthew 21–23," in *Persuasive Artistry: Studies in New Testament Rhetoric in Honor of George A. Kennedy* (ed. Duane F. Watson; JSNTSup 50; Sheffield: Sheffield Academic, 1991), 41–65; Marty L. Reid, "A Rhetorical Analysis of Romans 1:1–5:21 with Attention Given to the Rhetorical Function of 5:1-21," *PRS* 19 (1992): 255–72; idem, "Paul's Rhetoric of Mutuality: A Rhetorical Reading of Romans," in *SBLSP* 34 (Atlanta: Scholars Press, 1995), 117–39; J. Ian H. McDonald, "Rhetorical Issue and Rhetorical Strategy in Luke 10:25-37," in *Rhetoric and the New Testament: Essays from the 1992 Heidelberg Conference* (ed. Stanley E. Porter and Thomas H. Olbricht; JSNTSup 90; Sheffield: Sheffield Academic, 1993), 59–73; and Johann D. Kim, *God, Israel, and the Gentiles: Rhetoric and Situation in Romans 9–11* (SBLDS 176; Atlanta: Society of Biblical Literature, 2000).

[4] The comparative was the first rhetorically driven approach employed by scholars with the text of Acts, and it continues to provide the foundation for a significant number of recent rhetorical interpretations of Acts. For example, see Derek Hogan, "Paul's Defense: A Comparison of the Forensic Speeches in Acts, Callirhoe, and Leucippe and Clitophon," *PRS* 29 (2002): 73–87; and Bruce W. Longenecker, *Rhetoric at the Boundaries: The Art and Theology of New Testament Chain-Link Transitions* (Waco, Tex.: Baylor University Press, 2005).

[5] The following represents a broad selection of the types of comparative studies published to date: Stephen Lösch, "Die Dankesrede des Tertullus, APG 24.1-4," *ThQ* 112 (1931): 295–319; Charles H. Talbert, *Literary Patterns, Theological Themes and the Genre of Luke-Acts* (SBLMS 20; Missoula: Scholars Press, 1974), 125–40; Fred Veltman, "The Defense Speeches of Paul in Acts," in *Perspectives on Luke-Acts* (ed. Charles H. Talbert, PRS 5; Edinburgh: T&T Clark, 1978), 243–56; William Kurz, "Hellenistic Rhetoric in the Christological Proof of Luke-Acts," *CBQ* 42 (1980): 171–95; Lawrence Wills, "The Form of the Sermon in Hellenistic Judaism and Early Christianity," *HTR* 77 (1984): 277–99; Dean Zweck, "The *Exordium* of the Areopagus Speech, Acts 17.22, 23," *NTS* 35 (1989): 94–103; Vernon K. Robbins, "Narrative in Ancient Rhetoric and Rhetoric in Ancient Narrative," in *SBLSP* 35 (Atlanta: Scholars Press, 1996), 368–84; Daryl D. Schmidt, "Rhetorical Influences and Genre: Luke's Preface and the Rhetoric of Hellenistic Historiography," in *Jesus and the Heritage of Israel* (ed. David P. Moessner and David L. Tiede; vol. 1 of *Luke the Interpreter of Israel*; Harrisburg, Pa.: Trinity Press International, 1999), 27–60; Hogan, "Paul's Defense," 73–87; Bruce W. Longenecker, "Lukan Aversion to Humps and Hollows: The Case of Acts 11.27–12.25," *NTS* 50 (2004): 185–204; idem, *Rhetoric at the Boundaries*. See also the

following chapters in *The Book of Acts in Its Ancient Literary Setting* (ed. Bruce W. Winter and Andrew D. Clarke; vol. 1 of *The Book of Acts and Its First-Century Setting*; Grand Rapids, Mich.: Eerdmans, 1993): Conrad Gempf, "Public Speaking and Published Accounts," 259–303; Philip Satterthwaite, "Acts Against the Background of Classical Rhetoric," 337–79; and Bruce Winter, "Official Proceedings and the Forensic Speeches in Acts 24–26," 306–36.

[6] It is important to remember in the study of ancient rhetoric that what ancient rhetoricians did in practice is often more important, and more revealing, than what the ancient handbook traditions prescribed ought to happen in the speech-event.

[7] See Longenecker, *Rhetoric at the Boundaries*; Hogan, "Paul's Defense," 73–87; Zweck, "The Exordium," 94–103; and Satterthwaite, "Acts Against the Background," 337–79, as recent examples of this approach.

[8] See Jacques Dupont, "La structure oratoire du discourse d'Étienne," *Bib* 66 (1985): 153–67; C. Clifton Black, "The Rhetorical Form of the Hellenistic Jewish and Early Christian Sermon: A Response to Lawrence Wills," *HTR* 81 (1988): 1–18; Burton L. Mack, *Rhetoric and the New Testament* (GBSNTS; Minneapolis: Fortress, 1990), 88–92; Karl Olav Sandness, "Paul and Socrates: The Aim of Paul's Areopagus Speech," *JSNT* 50 (1993): 13–26; Frank Crouch, "The Persuasive Moment: Rhetorical Resolutions in Paul's Defense before Agrippa," in *SBLSP* 35 (Atlanta: Scholars Press, 1996), 333–41; Ira J. Jolivet, "The Lukan Account of Paul's Conversion and Hermagorean Stasis Theory," in *The Rhetorical Interpretation of Scripture: Essays from the 1996 Malibu Conference* (ed. Stanley E. Porter and Dennis L. Stamps; JSNTSup 180; Sheffield: Sheffield Academic, 1999), 210–20.

[9] See, for instance, Black, "The Rhetorical Form," 1–18; Sandness, "Paul and Socrates," 13–26; and Crouch, "The Persuasive Movement," 333–42.

[10] Duane F. Watson, "Paul's Speech to the Ephesian Elders (Acts 20.17–38): Epideictic Rhetoric of Farewell," in *Persuasive Artistry: Studies in New Testament Rhetoric in Honor of George A. Kennedy* (ed. D. F. Watson, JSNTSup 50; Sheffield: JSOT Press, 1991), 184–208.

[11] These studies demonstrate fundamental differences on almost every level, differing even in such basic areas as which rhetorical traditions are used and how these traditions are manipulated for the study of Acts. For example, Ira Jolivet ("The Lukan Account," 210–20) utilizes Hermagorean stasis theory to interpret the triple accounts of Paul's conversion in Acts, while Clifton Black ("The Rhetorical Form," 1–18) places Paul's "word of exhortation" at Pisidian Antioch against the larger backdrop of classical rhetoric to determine the persuasive patterns found in the text.

[12] For an overview of socio-rhetorical criticism as outlined by Robbins, see his *Exploring the Texture of Texts: A Guide to Socio-Rhetorical Interpretation* (Valley Forge, Pa.: Trinity Press International, 1996), 2; and *The Tapestry of Early Christian Discourse: Rhetoric, Society, and Ideology* (London: Routledge, 1996), 1–43. For illustrations of this method as applied to the text of Acts, see Istvan Czachesz, "Socio-Rhetorical Exegesis of Acts 9.1-10," *CV* 37 (1995): 5–32; Randall C. Webber, "'Why Were the Heathen So Arrogant?' The Socio-Rhetorical Strategy of Acts 3–4," *BTB* 22 (1992): 19–25; and Ben Witherington III, *The Acts of the Apostles: A Socio-Rhetorical Commentary* (Grand Rapids, Mich.: Eerdmans, 1998). Some questions exist in my own mind as to whether to consider this approach to the biblical text as truly rhetorical, for much of this method

has little in common with other rhetorical approaches. I continue to group this methodology within the larger universe of literary-rhetorical approaches in line with recent scholarly convention. In my own estimation, however, socio-rhetorical criticism is a methodology in its own right, separate from but influenced by rhetorical criticism.

[13] See Witherington, *Acts*, 115, 691, 704–5, and 751. Witherington relies upon Kennedy, as do most socio-rhetorical exegetes, for his insights concerning rhetorical structure, species, and issues of stasis. There is little evidence, however, of any methodological influence.

[14] Mark D. Given, *Paul's True Rhetoric: Ambiguity, Cunning, and Deception in Greece and Rome* (ESEC 7; Harrisburg, Pa.: Trinity Press International, 2001); Michael Enyinwa Okoronkwo, *The Jerusalem Compromise as a Conflict-Resolution Model: A Rhetoric-Communicative Analysis of Acts 15 in the Light of Modern Linguistics* (AI 1; Bonn: Borengässer, 2001); Todd Penner, *In Praise of Christian Origins: Stephen and the Hellenists in Lukan Apologetic Historiography* (ESEC 10; New York and London: T&T Clark, 2004); Blake Shipp, *Paul the Reluctant Witness: Power and Weakness in Luke's Portrayal* (Eugene, Oreg.: Cascade, 2005). Mikeal Parsons has demonstrated this same methodological shift in considering the wider literary world of Luke-Acts: "Luke and the Progymnasmata: A Preliminary Investigation into the Preliminary Exercises," in *Contextualizing Acts: Lukan Narrative and Greco-Roman Discourse* (ed. Todd Penner and Caroline Vander Stichele; SBLSymS 20; Atlanta: Society of Biblical Literature, 2003), 43–63. These investigations represent, in my estimation, the future of rhetorical criticism. However, identifying these studies as exemplary of "the new rhetorical criticism" is somewhat tenuous, as they demonstrate tendencies toward other established methodologies. For instance, Penner's work has much in common with the socio-rhetorical approach, while my own work demonstrates the influence of narrative criticism.

[15] Watson, "Paul's Speech," 184–208. The claim that no other published example exists is issued with some hesitancy. I have thoroughly investigated the rhetorical approaches to Acts over the last several years and have yet to discover another specimen as clear as that of Watson. A few unpublished dissertations do maintain Kennedy's approach; a recent example is Petrus Maryono, "Luke's Use of Biblical History and Promise in Acts 13.16-41" (Ph.D. diss., Dallas Theological Seminary, 2001). Other published analyses, of which I am unaware, may follow Kennedy's methodology in a strict fashion.

[16] Shipp, *Paul the Reluctant Witness*, 156–58.

[17] See Jolivet, "The Lukan Account"; and Okoronkwo, *Jerusalem Compromise*. Judging from his monograph's bibliography, Okoronkwo seems completely unaware of Kennedy.

[18] It appears that my own investigation remains the lone recent published study that utilizes Kennedy's methodology in any form with the text of Acts.

[19] Kennedy, *New Testament Interpretation*, 5.

[20] Kennedy, *New Testament Interpretation*, 6–8.

[21] One might equally be amazed with the apparent dearth of rhetorically generated investigations within the literary realm of Luke-Acts. While beyond the scope of this investigation, a great lacuna in the interpretation of Luke-Acts lies in the use of rhetoric to understand the literary movement and agenda of the author.

[22] Satterthwaite, "Acts Against the Background," 337–79; and Hogan, "Paul's Defense," 73–87.

[23] Kennedy, *New Testament Interpretation*, 4.

[24] See above, n. 3.

[25] See William Kurz, "Narrative Models for Imitation in Luke-Acts," in *Greeks, Romans, and Christians: Essays in Honor of Abraham J. Malherbe* (ed. David L. Balch, Everettt Ferguson, and Wayne A. Meeks; Minneapolis: Fortress, 1990), 171–98; and Frank Witt Hughes, "The Parable of the Rich Man and Lazarus (Luke 16:19-31) and "Graeco-Roman Rhetoric," in *Rhetoric and the New Testament: Essays from the 1992 Heidelberg Conference* (ed. Porter and Olbricht), 29–41.

[26] The impressive work of Marion L. Soards, *The Speeches in Acts: Their Content, Context, and Concerns* (Louisville, Ky.: Westminster John Knox, 1994), is a prime example of this difficulty. Soards has provided one of the best studies on the speeches of Acts. Soards attempts to view Acts as a rhetorical whole by seeking themes across its speeches. Yet his attempt makes little headway in tying together narrative and speech elements. Brief comments on narrative settings are coupled with his analyses of the speeches, but often these are not factored into his interpretation as a whole.

[27] Todd Penner has noted that, in general, the approach to the speeches of Acts is somewhat disconnected from the study of the narrative portions and argues that the two should be viewed in tandem. See his essay, "Civilizing Discourse: Acts, Declamation, and the Rhetoric of the Polis," in *Contextualizing Acts* (ed. Penner and Vander Stichele), 80–81.

[28] Kennedy, *New Testament Interpretation*, 114–40; quotation,115.

[29] Kennedy, *New Testament Interpretation*, 3–4.

[30] R. Dean Anderson Jr., *Ancient Rhetorical Theory and Paul* (emphasis in original; rev. ed.; CBET 18; Leuven: Peters, 1998), 28.

[31] Kennedy, *New Testament Interpretation*, 116.

[32] Kennedy, *New Testament Interpretation*, 116–40.

[33] Watson's lone investigation exemplifies such an approach ("Paul's Speech to the Ephesian Elders," 208).

[34] Stanley E. Porter, "The Theoretical Justification for Application of Rhetorical Categories to Pauline Epistolary Literature," in *Rhetoric and the New Testament* (ed. Porter and Olbricht), 100–122.

[35] A pervading distrust of applying Kennedy's methodology remains. Serving as the third reader of my own dissertation ("A Literary-Rhetorical Analysis of the Damascus Road Accounts in Acts"; New Orleans Baptist Theological Seminary, 2003)—which utilizes a heavily modified form of Kennedy's rhetorical criticism—Stanley Porter questioned the viability of such an approach because of its association with Kennedy's methodology.

[36] Vernon K. Robbins, *Jesus the Teacher: A Socio-Rhetorical Interpretation of Mark* (Philadelphia: Fortress, 1984).

[37] Robbins, *Exploring the Texture of Texts*, 1–4; and idem, *The Tapestry of Early Christian Discourse*, 1–41.

[38] Robbins, *The Tapestry of Early Christian Discourse*, 1.

[39] See Lauri Thúren, "Is There Biblical Argumentation?" in *Rhetorical Argumentation in Biblical Tests: Essays from the Lund 2000 Conference* (ed. Anders Eriksson, Thomas H. Olbricht, and Walter Übelacker; Harrisburg, Pa.: Trinity Press International, 2002), 77–92; and Okoronkwo, *Jerusalem Compromise*.

[40] Shipp, *Paul the Reluctant Witness*, 114–20.
[41] Shipp, *Paul the Reluctant Witness*, 27–61.
[42] Shipp, *Paul the Reluctant Witness*, 62–92.
[43] Shipp, *Paul the Reluctant Witness*, 93–113.
[44] Shipp, *Paul the Reluctant Witness*, 112, 117–18.
[45] Lloyd F. Bitzer. "The Rhetorical Situation," *PR* 1 (1968): 1–14.
[46] Shipp, *Paul the Reluctant Witness*, tables 1–13 (for page listings, see ix).
[47] See George A. Kennedy, *Progymnasmata: Greek Textbooks of Prose Composition and Rhetoric, Translated into English, with Introductions and Notes* (WGRW 10; Atlanta and Leiden: Society of Biblical Literature/Brill, 2003).

CHAPTER 8

GEORGE KENNEDY'S CONTRIBUTION TO RHETORICAL CRITICISM OF THE PAULINE LETTERS

Frank W. Hughes

Frank Hughes gives us an eyewitness account from the earliest discussions in the 1980s about Greco-Roman rhetoric and its relationship to the New Testament to current analysis of the Pauline Epistles. He outlines Kennedy's contribution in bringing rhetorical study of Paul back into mainstream Pauline studies, the resistance to rhetoric's reemergence among theologians, and the fresh perspective that rhetorical analysis has ultimately created.

I am often asked what's new in the study of the Pauline Letters. I often respond that there are five breaths of fresh air in the study of Paul. These are the development of rhetorical criticism of the letters of the Pauline corpus, the development of criticism based on social-scientific models, the renewed study of Paul in connection with Judaism, the renewed study of Paul in connection with Greco-Roman philosophy, and the renewed study of Pauline theology. Of these, it seems to me, rhetorical criticism is the most important. The contribution that rhetorical criticism has made to the historical and literary interpretation of the Bible has been significant, and it has been well chronicled by two rhetorical critics in recent years.[1] In this chapter I want to highlight the important contribution that George A. Kennedy has made to rhetorical criticism of the Pauline Letters.

NEW TESTAMENT INTERPRETATION THROUGH RHETORICAL CRITICISM

Most New Testament scholars are aware of Kennedy's small book, *New Testament Interpretation through Rhetorical Criticism*, published in 1984.[2] This book gives an introduction to Greek and Roman rhetoric; provides access to Greek and Roman rhetoric through the rhetorical handbooks; and offers a brief analysis of several Pauline Letters, some speeches in the Acts of the Apostles, and the rhetoric of the gospels. In particular, there is an excellent chapter on the three *genera* of rhetoric (judicial, epideictic, and deliberative) and the arrangement of speeches.[3] Kennedy's book was the first book to challenge Hans Dieter Betz's identification of the rhetoric of Galatians as judicial, as found in his Hermeneia commentary appearing in 1979.[4]

Kennedy's 1984 monograph was an important event in the rhetorical analysis of Pauline Letters. In his gentlemanly way, Kennedy encouraged students of the New Testament to become familiar with the rich and complex tradition of Greek and Roman rhetoric, both in theory (the handbooks) and in practice (actual speeches). Of great importance is the fact that Kennedy's monograph includes a method for doing a rhetorical analysis of text, which has been briefly summarized by Duane Watson.[5] It includes the determination of the rhetorical unit; the definition of the rhetorical situation; the determination of the rhetorical problem or main question at issue and the *genus* of rhetoric (whether judicial, epideictic, or deliberative); the analysis of the invention, arrangement, and style of the rhetorical unit; and the evaluation of the rhetorical effectiveness of the rhetorical unit in utilizing invention, arrangement, and style.[6]

The decade of the 1980s was a very exciting time in the rhetorical criticism of Pauline Letters. I remember the early 1980s well, when there was no published analysis of the rhetoric of several Pauline Letters, including 1 or 2 Thessalonians. Wilhelm Wuellner's highly influential early article on Romans had appeared in 1976, as well as F. Forrester Church's excellent rhetorical analysis of Philemon which was published in 1978. Wuellner's article on three passages in 1 Corinthians had also appeared in 1979.[7] Perhaps one good thing about that era of scholarship is that we did not have to wade through the large amount of secondary literature of rhetorical criticism of Pauline Letters that we and other scholars have produced in the last twenty years. However, we did have the works of Demosthenes, Aristotle, Cicero, the *Rhetorica ad Herennium*, Quintilian, and Menander Rhetor.

In the 1980s rhetorical criticism was being developed in several centers of graduate study of the New Testament, most notably the University of Chicago, Garrett-Evangelical Theological Seminary/ Northwestern University, Pacific School of Religion, Wycliffe College, and Emory University. Such scholars as Betz, Robert Jewett, Richard

N. Longenecker, Wuellner, and Vernon Robbins were exploring Greek and Roman rhetoric for themselves and were guiding some of their graduate students in the development of rhetorical criticism based on Greco-Roman rhetoric. This was also taking place among graduate students at Duke University who traveled over to the University of North Carolina at Chapel Hill to participate in classes with George A. Kennedy. Similarly, graduate students at the University of Chicago turned to Elizabeth Asmis for help with classical rhetoric, and graduate students at Garrett-Evangelical turned to Thomas B. Farrell, Leland Griffin, and Michael C. Leff at Northwestern in their explorations of classical as well as modern rhetoric.

When I went to Göttingen for a year in 1986–1987, my presentation of rhetorical criticism, both its methodology and my application of it to 1 Thessalonians, got fairly mixed reactions among New Testament scholars and doctoral students, although Gerd Luedemann, Georg Strecker, and Johannes Schoon-Janßen were certainly open to it.[8] Carl Joachim Classen, a distinguished classical scholar and specialist in rhetoric, became interested in the rhetoric of the New Testament, though he remained generally critical of the application of the canons of rhetorical arrangement to Paul's letters.[9] During that year Bruce C. Johanson defended and published his dissertation on 1 Thessalonians, combining an analysis based on Greco-Roman rhetoric with the text-linguistic method that was certainly in full swing in Uppsala, under the direction of Lars Hartmann and Birger Olsson.[10] In 1987 at the general meeting of Studiorum Novi Testamenti Societas in Göttingen, Wuellner delivered a seminar paper, "Reading Romans in Context," on the rhetoric of that letter. The next year at the Colloquium Biblicum Lovaniense, Wuellner delivered another paper on the rhetoric of 1 Thessalonians.[11]

Rhetorical criticism of Pauline Letters based on Greco-Roman rhetoric was a logical way to go beyond the form criticism of letters pioneered by Paul Schubert's justly famous dissertation.[12] Since many rhetorical critics of Pauline Letters had cut their teeth on form criticism of letters, it is not surprising that most Pauline rhetorical critics focused more on arrangement than on other matters, at that time. I used to tell my students that form critics could tell you "*that* a letter was structured a certain way, but rhetorical criticism could tell you *why* it was structured that way." In other words, where form critics of Pauline Letters could quite correctly repeat Schubert's famous dictum that the thanksgiving prayer was where the "vital theme" of the letter was stated,[13] rhetorical critics could show that the thanksgiving prayer did what it did because it was the major part of the *exordium* of the letter. Aristotle had pointed out that the *exordia* of speeches

> provide a sample of the subject, in order that the hearers may know beforehand what it is about . . . so that he who puts the beginning, so to say, into the hearer's hand enables him, if he holds fast to it, to follow the story. . . . So then the most essential and special function of the exordium is to make clear what is the end or purpose of the speech. (*Ars Rhet.* 3.14.6)

Thus there appeared to be an excellent correlation between the function of the thanksgiving prayer of letters and the function of the exordium of a speech. Other points of contact could be noted: the function of the acquisition of good will at the beginning of letters and what has sometimes been called the *captatio benevolentiae* (i.e., the exordium) of a speech. Cicero reminds us, "An *exordium* is a passage which brings the mind of the auditor into a proper condition to receive the rest of the speech. This will be accomplished if he [the auditor] becomes well-disposed, attentive, and receptive" (*Inv.* 1.20). Since the exordium comes at the beginning of a speech and the thanksgiving prayer comes at almost the beginning of a Hellenistic letter, it is appropriate to note the correlation between the functions of the thanksgiving prayer and of the exordium.

The influence of Kennedy was strong, especially on the next generation of scholars. Kennedy himself was involved in a number of dissertations, particularly at Duke University. Watson published his dissertation on 2 Peter and Jude in 1988,[14] followed by the appearance of many other articles on rhetorical aspects of Pauline Letters. The year before, Jewett published a monograph on 1 and 2 Thessalonians, using both rhetorical and social-scientific criticism.[15] Jewett directed four Northwestern University dissertations on the rhetoric of Pauline Letters, including those on Romans 9 by David E. Mesner, 1 Corinthians 8 and 10 by K. K. Yeo, 2 Corinthians by Jeffrey A. Crafton, and my own on 1 Thessalonians.[16] At the University of Chicago Glenn S. Holland wrote a dissertation on the rhetorical and historical analysis of 2 Thessalonians, and Margaret M. Mitchell completed her dissertation on 1 Corinthians, directed by Betz.[17] At Wycliffe College in the University of Toronto, in the 1980s as well, Longenecker was engaged in the rhetorical analysis of Galatians, culminating both in his Word commentary on that letter and his direction of G. Walter Hansen's dissertation on Abraham in Galatians. Another of Longenecker's students, L. Gregory Bloomquist, completed a dissertation on Philippians that combined form criticism with rhetorical criticism.[18]

Kennedy's influence could be felt quite directly in the case of Watson's dissertation, as well as in other dissertations from the 1980s, but his indirect influence was considerably more pervasive in the guild of New Testament scholars. Kennedy's encyclopedic knowledge of the history of Greek and Roman rhetoric and his critique of Betz's commentary on Galatians were both duly noted. The newer generation of New Testament rhetorical critics was generally well trained in Greek and Roman rhetoric. They relied less on Heinrich Lausberg's *Handbuch der literarischen Rhetorik*[19] and more on the ancient sources to which Lausberg and all historians and systematicians of ancient rhetoric must refer. They were rather more critical of Lausberg's systematization of rhetoric, because they were better informed about the complexities of the history of Greek and Roman rhetoric. This generation of rhetorical critics was generally North American, and they were completely inclined to learn from those who had a greater knowledge of the Greco-Roman world than most theologians do. I cannot fail to mention that such rhetoricians as Kennedy, Farrell, Griffin, and Leff, to mention a few, were extremely forthcoming with the help that New Testament graduate students wanted and needed. The multidisciplinary character of most graduate study in the United States and Canada contrasted with the way theology is usually studied in most of Europe. Hence the welcome that rhetorical criticism was given in North American circles of New Testament study was sooner and generally more positive than in comparable European settings.

An example of this welcome can be found in "mainstream" New Testament scholars such as Karl Paul Donfried, who, relatively late in their teaching careers, discovered and promoted rhetorical criticism of Pauline Letters in their own publications. For example, in his part of *The Theology of the Shorter Pauline Letters*, Donfried begins his chapter entitled "The Setting of 1 Thessalonians" with a five-page section entitled "The Rhetorical Structure." Similarly his chapter "The Setting of 2 Thessalonians" begins with a two-page section, also entitled "The Rhetorical Structure."[20] These sections include, right up front, rhetorical analyses of both Thessalonian letters. Not long after that, during the Studiorum Novi Testamenti Societas general meeting of 1995 in Prague, Donfried and Johannes Beutler convened the first meeting of a seminar that ran for four years, entitled "The Thessalonian Correspondence," at which papers were delivered by Schoon-Janßen, Edgar Krentz, Raymond F. Collins, Charles A. Wanamaker, and me concerning rhetorical criticism of 1 Thessalonians, in comparison with epistolary analysis of that letter. In 1996 Donfried contributed a paper, "The Epistolary and Rhetorical Context of 1 Thessalonians 2:1-12."[21] Many of us are looking forward to Donfried's new commentary on 1 and 2 Thessalonians, to appear in the venerable International Critical Commentary series, a commentary that will doubtless contain much material dealing with the persuasive character of both 1 and 2 Thessalonians.

J. Paul Sampley's commentaries on 1 and 2 Corinthians, in *The New Interpreter's Bible*, deal quite extensively with Paul's rhetoric in that letter.[22] The year 2002 saw the first Studiorum Novi Testamenti Societas seminar entitled "Paul and Rhetoric," convened by Sampley and Peter Lampe, with its inaugural meeting at the general meeting in Durham, England, followed by further meetings of the seminar at Bonn in 2003 and Barcelona in 2004. In 2006 Jewett's long-awaited Hermeneia commentary on Romans appeared. A major component of this new commentary on Romans is Jewett's own rhetorical analysis of that highly persuasive letter, together with significant analyses of the social situation of the Roman Christians to whom Paul was writing.[23] The existence of the seminar "Paul and Rhetoric" as part of Studiorum Novi Testamenti Societas general meetings, together with the appearance of works by Donfried, Sampley, Jewett, and Betz, would seem to indicate that rhetorical criticism has made it into the "mainstream" of Pauline scholarship, especially when we consider that these commentaries are appearing in highly respected series such as the Hermeneia, the International Critical Commentary, and *The New Interpreter's Bible*.

It now seems like a long time since, at the 1984 annual meeting of the Society of Biblical Literature at the Palmer House in Chicago, I commented to Robbins that we should not have to talk about our work in the halls and the coffee shop at SBL; we should rather be presenting and discussing our work in real seminars. Not least due to Robbins' tireless efforts in beginning the SBL section "Rhetoric and the New Testament," in 1991, followed by similarly dedicated work by conveners Watson and Bloomquist, rhetorical criticism of the New Testament made its way out of the hallways and coffee shops and into seminar rooms at SBL meetings. The several meetings principally sponsored by Pepperdine University, starting in 1992 in Heidelberg and continuing in Pretoria, London, Malibu, and Florence, organized by the distinguished rhetorician Thomas H. Olbricht,[24] also brought rhetorical critics of the New Testament together in a unique and international way.

WHAT RHETORICAL CRITICISM IMPLIES ABOUT PAUL

At the beginning of this article I mentioned that rhetorical criticism was one of five breaths of fresh air in the study of Paul. This fresh air is welcomed in Pauline studies for several reasons. First of all, the study of Paul's theology and/or Pauline theology had dominated the study of Paul for a very long time. To a large extent this was because of the importance of Paul's thought in the Reformation of the sixteenth-century Western church. The rediscovery of Holy Scripture by the Protestant reformers on the continent of Europe and in England and Scotland made possible the restructurings of both the church and theology itself. Martin Luther and such British reformers as Thomas Cranmer read Paul in such a way that his theology of justification was the most important aspect of Paul to be studied and appropriated for and by the church. If Paul's theology of justification not only dominated Paul but also dominated the New Testament and the Bible as a whole, then no effort should be spared to understand Paul's theology as fully and as well as possible. Few if any biblical scholars were interested in the letters of Paul without being rather more interested in the theology of Paul. This generalization holds true even when we look at the works of Ferdinand Christian Baur, the father of modern Pauline studies. The lack of Paul's theology and language of justification in 1 and 2 Thessalonians caused Baur, for example, to declare both letters to the Thessalonians to be pseudonymous.[25] So, as Jewett put it, the study of Pauline Letters had been held in the "hammerlock of the Reformation." The development of form criticism of letters and various types of literary criticism and historical criticism has been a change from the usual theological interpretation, and this change was important for those who were neither interested in ordination nor in the study of Christian theology, as well as for those interested in

Christian theology who wished to have a fuller understanding of the structure of Paul's letters.

The development of religious studies courses and departments in colleges and universities outside of schools of theology, a development that one has seen most strongly in the United States, also contributed to the importance of the new ways of reading Paul. In America, theology cannot be taught in state universities and colleges, but religion or religious studies can be. Religious studies departments grew in the United States in the 1970s, even if the enrollments in courses taught in those departments in the 1980s and 1990s did not always seem to justify their existence. Yet in these departments and courses, if one is going to study Christianity responsibly, it is clearly necessary to study the New Testament—not for doctrine's sake but for the sake of contributing to an accurate picture of the phenomena that have shaped our Western and American cultures. Whether or not we are fond of Paul or his theology (and many scholars of religion appear not to be), we at least should study the problems of which letters attributed to him he really wrote, what he was arguing in those letters, and how he was making his argument persuasive. If we can study Demosthenes' or Cicero's argumentation in their speeches and letters, why not also study the rhetoric of the speeches of Acts and of Paul's letters?

Rhetorical criticism of Paul's letters can fit very well into a religious studies model of the study of Paul, as well as theological models of Pauline study. Ultimately the sources of authority upon which Paul drew were religious ones: God, God's revelation in Jesus Christ, and God's revelation in Scripture. It is not hard, however, to see how the topics of advantage, honor, good, evil, blame, and praise can be given special Christian twists by early Christian writers, such as Paul.

It is hard to see why some theologically oriented New Testament scholars have as many objections to rhetorical criticism of Paul's letters as they sometimes do. They will grant that Paul makes use of the traditions of letter-writing, and that he not only adopts but also adapts these traditions. They will grant that Paul is able to appropriate various bits and pieces of rhetorical style, such as the rhetorical figure of *praeteritio* in 1 Thessalonians 1:8 and 5:1. They will grant that Paul quite intentionally uses the topics of praise and blame (the standard topics for epideictic rhetoric), such as in the first few chapters of 1 Thessalonians. They will also grant that the arrangement of Paul's letters at times reflects rhetorical practice in speeches. At this point, they have granted that Paul uses all three parts of written rhetoric, these three being style, invention (perhaps better translated: "the use of topics" or "the finding of topics"), and arrangement. Only memory and delivery are lacking out of the familiar five parts of rhetoric taught in antiquity. If a scholar were to argue that Paul is using rhetorical style and rhetorical topics (albeit with several Christian twists) and then also was structuring his letters with rhetorical arrangements as major contributors to the structure, then that scholar has identified all three of the elements of written rhetoric and has come close to saying that Paul is not only *using* quite a few bits and pieces of rhetoric, but is actually *doing* rhetoric. It is ironic that patristic scholars had been working with the rhetoric of Tertullian and St. Augustine and St. John Chrysostom for a long time, and yet when we see some of the same rhetorical techniques and phenomena in the Bible itself—as St. Augustine himself did in *De doctrina christiana*—for some reason it is thought that we biblical scholars are supposed to look the other way and talk about matters other than rhetoric.

This identification of rhetorical strategies and techniques in the letters of Paul has some real consequences for the study of Paul and for our overall understanding of Christian theology. This would mean that Paul's letters employ the tradition and methods of persuasion that the pagan Isocrates or the pagan Aristotle and the pagan Cicero and the pagan Quintilian wrote about or taught (never mind the fact that such Christians as Tertullian, St. Clement of Alexandria, St. John Chrysostom, and St. Augustine of Hippo used them as well). Because rhetoric had such a checkered (not to say bad) reputation on most college and university campuses for such a long time, it is not surprising that many New Testament scholars would be more than a little hesitant to identify any of the sources of Paul's theology or writing as the tradition of Greek rhetoric.

Paul himself had been aware of rhetoric's bad reputation. Quite understandably, he did not wish to be identified as a traveling sophist, a person who came to town and made some impressive speeches, only to leave shortly after he had separated people interested in his message from some of their money. This must have been the reason that, at least in 1 Corinthians 2:1-5, he ostensibly distances his ministry during his prior visit to Corinth from the tradition of rhetoric, quite ironically so because of the rhetorical skill he demonstrates, particularly of 1 Corinthians 1-4.[26] By way of comparison, this is a distancing he does not attempt in his earliest letter, when he describes his ministry in Thessalonica as having been accomplished "in power and in the Holy Spirit and with full conviction" (1 Thess 1:5). In that passage Paul seems to have no compunction at all about his threefold description of the results of his ministry as an apostle: power, the Holy Spirit, and people being fully persuaded in the truth of the gospel, the message about Jesus Christ. Proper Christian apostolic ministry produced full conviction—full persuasion. Who among the Attic or Roman orators (or orators from any culture and any period of history) would not want their persuasive speeches to produce full conviction?

Some scholars clearly do not like the idea that Paul used rhetoric because of the often unfavorable reputation that rhetoric had in antiquity, thanks to Plato and others. It may also be that there are those in classics departments on college and university campuses who do not think that theologians should make any unauthorized border crossings. After all, they might say, good fences make good neighbors! Yet if we biblical scholars are going to do rhetorical criticism of the Bible based on ancient rhetoric, it certainly is necessary that we know enough about ancient rhetoric to be able to form a reasonable opinion about it. This is both the delight and the danger of attempting to think outside our respective envelopes. When we attempt to do rhetorical criticism as mere dilettantes, we will inevitably bring ourselves and our scholarship on the Bible into question by classical scholars and rhetoricians, not to mention other biblical scholars. This has happened in some cases.

A LARGER HORIZON

We can all be thankful that Kennedy has provided such a solid base for New Testament scholars, other classicists, other scholars of rhetoric, and other historians of literature and culture to be able to learn the complex and rich tradition of Greek and Roman rhetoric. His "History of Rhetoric," going back to the 1960s and 1970s, provides an excellent starting point from which to learn about the rhetoric of the Greeks and Romans. His *Classical Rhetoric*, from 1980, is an excellent and masterful survey of ancient and medieval rhetoric and its relation to the larger culture of the West. His *New Testament Interpretation through Rhetorical Criticism*, from 1984, both documents and facilitates some extremely interesting and invigorating points of contact and dialogue between the study of ancient rhetoric and the study of the New Testament. No doubt this dialogue clearly did provoke and should continue to provoke a *retour aux sources,* the *sources* being the texts that tell us the history of Greek and Roman rhetoric, both in theory and in practice. His translation and commentary on Aristotle's *Rhetoric,* from 1991, is a remarkably helpful tool in many ways to students and scholars alike. There is every reason why New Testament scholars, theologically oriented or otherwise, should get interested in ancient rhetoric as well as other matters pertaining to the world of late antiquity. There is no excuse for New Testament scholars to be ignorant of the history of rhetoric, one of the most important parts of the cultures of the Hellenistic world. With Kennedy's work, and the works of other scholars of rhetoric, there is no need to be ignorant. I remain convinced that we can use all the fresh air we can get.

Notes

[1] See especially the most helpful volume by Duane F. Watson and Alan J. Hauser, *Rhetorical Criticism of the Bible: A Comprehensive Bibliography with Notes on History and Method* (BIS 4; Leiden: Brill, 1994), especially the article by Duane F. Watson on pp. 101–25. See also Duane F. Watson, *The Rhetoric of the New Testament: A Bibliographic Survey* (Tools for Biblical Study 8; Blandford Forum: Deo Publishing, 2006).

[2] George L. Kennedy, *New Testament Interpretation through Rhetorical Criticism* (Chapel Hill: University of North Carolina Press, 1984).

[3] Kennedy, *New Testament Interpretation,* 3–38.

[4] Kennedy, *New Testament Interpretation,* 144–52; Hans Dieter Betz, *Galatians: A Commentary on Paul's Letter to the Churches in Galatia* (Hermeneia; Philadelphia: Fortress, 1979), 14–29.

[5] Kennedy, *New Testament Interpretation,* 33–38; Watson and Hauser, *Rhetorical Criticism of the Bible,* 110–11.

[6] Watson in Watson and Hauser, *Rhetorical Criticism of the Bible,* 110–11.

[7] Wilhelm Wuellner, "Paul's Rhetoric of Argumentation in Romans: An Alternative to the Donfried-Karris Debate over Romans," *CBQ* 38 (1976): 330–51. Repr. in *The Romans Debate* (ed. Karl P. Donfried; rev. and expanded ed.; Peabody, Mass.: Hendrickson, 1991), 128–46; F. Forrester Church, "Rhetorical Structure and Design in Paul's Letter to Philemon," *HTR* 71 (1978): 17–33; Wilhelm Wuellner, "Greek Rhetoric and Pauline Argumentation," in *Early Christian Literature and the Classical Intellectual Tradition* (ed. William R. Schoedel and Robert L. Wilken; ThH 54; Paris: Beauchesne, 1979), 177–88.

[8] Gerd Luedemann, *Paul, Apostle to the Gentiles: Studies in Chronology* (Philadelphia: Fortress, 1984), 46–59, referred to Betz's 1975 article in his chronological analysis of Galatians, although he did not refer to what Betz was doing as rhetorical criticism. George Strecker, *History of New Testament Literature* (trans. Calvin Katter with

Hans-Joachim Mollenhauer; Harrisburg, Pa.: Trinity Press International, 1997), 61–68. See also the dissertation by Johannes School-Janßen that Prof. Strecker both directed and published in his series: *Umstrittene "Apologien" in den Paulusbriefen. Studien zur rhetorischen Situation des 1. Thessalonicherbriefes, des Galaterbriefes, und des Philipperbriefes* (GTA 45: Göttingen: Vandenhoeck & Ruprecht, 1991).

[9] Carl Joachim Classen, "Paulus und die antike Rhetorik," *ZNW* 82 (1991): 1–32.

[10] Bruce C. Johanson, *To All the Brethren: A Text-Linguistic and Rhetorical Approach to 1 Thessalonians* (ConBNT 16; Stockholm: Almqvist & Wiksell, 1987).

[11] Wilhelm Wuellner, "Reading Romans in Context," in *Celebrating Romans: Template for Pauline Theology: Essays in Honor of Robert Jewett* (ed. Sheila E. McGinn; Grand Rapids & Cambridge: Eerdmans, 2004), 106–39; idem, "The Argumentative Structure of 1 Thessalonians as Paradoxical Encomium," in *The Thessalonian Correspondence* (ed. Raymond F. Collins; BETL 87; Leuven: Leuven University Press/ Peeters, 1990), 117–35.

[12] Paul Schubert, *The Form and Function of the Pauline Thanksgivings* (BZNW 20; Berlin: Töpelmann, 1939).

[13] Schubert, *Form and Function*, 180.

[14] Duane F. Watson, *Invention, Arrangement, and Style: Rhetorical Criticism of Jude and 2 Peter* (SBLDS 104; Atlanta: Scholars Press, 1988).

[15] Robert Jewett, *The Thessalonian Correspondence: Pauline Rhetoric and Millenarian Piety* (FFNT; Philadelphia: Fortress, 1986).

[16] David E. Mesner, "The Rhetoric of Citations: Paul's Use of Scripture in Romans 9" (Ph.D. diss., Northwestern University/Garrett-Evangelical Theological Seminary, 1991); K. K. Yeo, *Rhetorical Interaction in I Corinthians 8 and 10: A Formal Analysis with Preliminary Suggestions for a Chinese, Cross-Cultural Hermeneutic* (BIS 9; Leiden: Brill, 1995); Jeffrey A. Crafton, *The Agency of the Apostle: A Dramatistic Analysis of Paul's Responses to Conflict in 2 Corinthians* (JSNTSup 51; Sheffield: JSOT Press, 1991); Frank W. Hughes, *Early Christian Rhetoric and 2 Thessalonians* (JSNTSup 30; Sheffield: JSOT Press, 1989);

[17] Glenn S. Holland, *The Traditions That You Received from Us: 2 Thessalonians in the Pauline Tradition* (HUT 24; Tübingen: Mohr Siebeck, 1986); Margaret Mitchell, *Paul and the Rhetoric of Reconciliation: An Exegetical Investigation of the Language and Composition of 1 Corinthians* (HUT 28; Tübingen: Mohr Siebeck, 1991).

[18] Richard N. Longenecker, *Galatians* (WBC 41; Dallas: Word, 1990); G. Walter Hansen, *Abraham in Galatians: Epistolary and Rhetorical Contexts* (JSNTSup 29; Sheffield: JSOT Press, 1989); L. Gregory Bloomquist, *The Function of Suffering in Philippians* (JSNTSup 78; Sheffield: JSOT Press, 1993).

[19] Heinrich Lausberg, *Handbuch der literarischen Rhetorik* (2 vols.; Munich: Hueber, 1960).

[20] Karl Donfried and I. Howard Marshall, *The Theology of the Shorter Pauline Letters* (New Testament Theology; Cambridge: Cambridge University Press, 1993), 3–7; 83–84.

[21] Donfried in *The Thessalonians Debate: Methodological Discord or Methodological Synthesis?* (ed. Karl P. Donfried and Johannes Beutler; Grand Rapids and Cambridge: Eerdmans, 2000), vii–xii, 3–60. For other rhetorical analyses of 1 Thessalonians, see Frank W. Hughes, "The Rhetoric of 1 Thessalonians," in *The Thessalonian Correspondence* (ed.

Raymond F. Collins; BETL 87; Leuven: Leuven University Press and Peeters, 1990), 94–116; and Duane F. Watson, "Paul's Appropriation of Apocalyptic Discourse: The Rhetorical Strategy of 1 Thessalonians," in *Vision and Persuasion: Rhetorical Dimensions of Apocalyptic Discourse* (ed. Greg Carey and L. Gregory Bloomquist; St. Louis: Chalice, 1999), 61–81.

[22] J. Paul Sampley, "The First Letter to the Corinthians: Introduction, Commentary, and Reflections," in *The New Interpreter's Bible* (ed. Leander E. Keck et al.; 12 vols.; Nashville: Abingdon, 2002), 10:771–1003; idem, "The Second Letter to the Corinthians: Introduction, Commentary, and Reflections," in *The New Interpreter's Bible* (ed. Leander E. Keck et al.; 12 vols.; Nashville: Abingdon, 2000), 11:1–180.

[23] Robert Jewett, *Romans: A Commentary* (Hermeneia; Minneapolis: Fortress, 2006).

[24] Organized initially with the help of the late Wilhelm Wuellner, whose friendship with rhetorical critics of all ages will never be forgotten, and whose contacts with rhetorical and New Testament scholars around the world were indispensible.

[25] Ferdinand Christian Baur, *Paul, the Apostle of Jesus Christ* (2nd ed.; 2 vols.; London: Williams and Norgate, 1875–1876). First edition was *Paulus, der Apostel Jesu Christi* (Stuttgart: Becher & Miller, 1845). See also idem, "Die beiden Briefe an die Thessalonicher: Ihre Echtheit und Bedeutung für die Lehre von der Parusie Christi," *Theologische Jahrbücher* 14 (1855): 141–68.

[26] See the especially clear discussion of 2:1-5 in Raymond F. Collins, *First Corinthians* (SP 7; Collegeville, Minn.: Liturgical, 1999), 115–21.

CHAPTER 9

KENNEDY AND THE READING OF PAUL
THE ENERGY OF COMMUNICATION

James D. Hester

> *The previous chapter by Frank Hughes assesses the impact of George Kennedy's rhetorical approach upon Pauline studies in general. While the reader will be reminded of that survey in James Hester's contribution, the latter moves the conversation several steps further. In this chapter Hester concentrates our attention on a particular letter of Paul that for decades has been a storm center in rhetorical research: the Epistle to the Galatians. Moreover, by tracing the development in Kennedy's own thoughts across those decades, Hester shows us how the unfolding of Kennedy's theory offers Paul's interpreters fresh and specific insights into the exegesis of Galatians. In that process we are privileged to observe how a skillful Pauline commentator constructs an argument that is, in its own right, at once scholarly and rhetorical.*

THE EARLY KENNEDY: METHOD IN RHETORICAL CRITICISM

I categorize Professor George Kennedy as primarily a social and intellectual historian. At least in his earlier writing, it is that perspective that tends to inform his conversation with the New Testament's rhetorical critics. In the first chapter of *New Testament Interpretation through Rhetorical Criticism*, he observes that, while scholars had picked up on the need for rhetorical analysis of New Testament texts, they had not developed a widely accepted methodology. From his perspective, much of what had been written up to that time bore closer resemblance to adaptations of either biblical form criticism or literary criticism than to rhetorical criticism as such.[1] He wanted to correct that tendency by reminding us what rhetorical training was in the ancient world, how it functioned, how widely it was practiced in the educational system of the Hellenistic and Roman worlds, and, within that context, how its artifacts ought to be analyzed.

Kennedy's reminder of the extent and importance of rhetorical training is elaborated in the introduction to his translations of the *progymnasmata*. There he points out that, although the first full-fledged textbooks did not appear until the late first century C.E., earlier references to forms appearing in exercises are found in Aristotle. Cicero alludes to them in *De inventione rhetorica*; they appear also in *Ad Herenium*.[2] The textbooks themselves structure and formalize training in composition and rhetoric, and the educational system concentrated on those textbooks for several centuries.[3] Because the system of rhetorical education was so widespread in the Hellenistic and Roman world, and because everyday life exposed so many to the rhetorical artifacts produced by that education, Kennedy argues that not only would one expect New Testament authors to have had some exposure to such things as narration, elaboration of *chreiai*, paraphrase, encomia, description, and personification, but also that their readers and hearers would have been acquainted with such techniques.[4] It follows that rhetorical analysis of New Testament texts should include identification of argumentative tools and strategies common in first-century Greco-Roman society, as well as a description of their function.

The methodological, or analytical, program suggested to New Testament rhetorical critics by Kennedy is made up of the following elements:

1. Determining the rhetorical unit;
2. Defining the rhetorical situation;
3. Identifying the rhetorical problem, or stasis, and the species of rhetoric employed;
4. Analyzing the text's invention, style, and arrangement;
5. Evaluating the effectiveness of the rhetorical unit in meeting its exigence.[5]

While this program includes concepts defined in modern rhetorical theory—specifically the "rhetorical unit," the "rhetorical situation," and the "exigence," about which more will be said below—its goal seems to be the description and evaluation of the rhetorical abilities of a New Testament author as judged by the use of classical rhetorical models found in first-century imperial Rome. Rhetorical analysis is, therefore, largely an exercise in historical, style, and form criticism. Its underlying theory is found in the teaching of ancient rhetors.

Among the many important points Kennedy makes about aspects of rhetorical method, there are three I want to highlight: (1) the identification of a rhetorical unit, (2) the concept of the rhetorical situation, and (3) the exigence.[6]

1. A rhetorical unit is that segment of a rhetorical artifact that has an identifiable opening, middle, and closing, with the middle composed of some action or argument. In the New Testament these units can be as brief as five or six verses and as long as a couple of chapters. There can be units within units, and each unit may have its peculiar rhetorical situation.[7] A unit may be analogous with a form or formula, but the reverse is not true. Forms and formulae may be part of the pattern of persuasion in a rhetorical unit, but they themselves do not define a rhetorical unit.

2. Since its definition and description by Lloyd Bitzer in the late 1960s, the concept of the rhetorical situation has become a commonplace in New Testament rhetorical studies. Typically, the rhetorical situation is an event containing an exigence that a rhetor believes can be resolved through discourse.

3. It is important to distinguish the rhetorical situation from the larger historical situation, of which it may be only one part, and the argumentative situation, which is derived from the rhetorical situation and shifts as the attempted persuasion unfolds.[8] It is occasionally true that the rhetorical situation is represented as though it is the historical situation. That is, the historical situation may produce an exigence. Once it has produced that exigence, however, it ceases to be relevant. The *rhetorical* situation is the focus of the rhetor's interest. The argumentative situation encountered in the rhetorical situation depends on that situation and the intensity of adherence to relevant convictions held by the audience addressed.[9] The interaction of those elements may influence the arrangement of arguments as the speaker attempts self-adaptation to the audience.[10]

Bitzer describes three components for the rhetorical situation: the exigence, the audience, and the constraints, which may be invented by the speaker or present in the situation itself.[11] The exigence is an occurrence in the life of the community, the presence of which has caused some disruption, that a speaker, or for that matter a writer, believes can be resolved by discourse.[12] Bitzer describes exigence as "an imperfection marked by an urgency; it is a defect, an obstacle, something waiting to be done."[13] It becomes rhetorical when "it is capable of positive modification and when positive modification requires discourse or can be assisted by discourse." He goes on to point out that it is the exigence that "specifies the audience to be addressed and the change to be effected."[14]

Interestingly enough, Kennedy points out the need for the critic to identify both the immediate and universal audiences for the writing; yet he does not elaborate on the functional difference between the two audiences, nor does he refer to Chaim Perelman's work on the concept of the universal audience.[15] In any case the immediate audience is that group of individuals the rhetor identifies as capable of being influenced by her argument. In that sense, the audience is a construct. While there may be cases where all persons involved in the historical situation are also part of the rhetorical situation, it may also be true that the rhetor formulates an argumentative strategy for a subset of that group. Think, for example of Paul's strategy with Philemon. Philemon is the first in a list of recipients (vv. 1-2), but clearly he is the one whom Paul hopes to persuade. The others may be understood as the "universal audience" in the sense that Paul implies that they will sit in judgment on Philemon's response to Paul's argument. One might compare those circumstances with the more generalized audience of 1 Thessalonians, made even larger by Paul's instruction in 5:27 to have the letter read to "all the brothers."

I highlight these points because, as we see below, Kennedy develops a theory of rhetoric that modifies and elaborates these already conventional concepts and in doing so gives rise to the need to reexamine how they should be defined in Pauline rhetorical criticism.

Concerning rhetorical criticism, in *New Testament Interpretation* Kennedy writes: "Rhetorical criticism takes the text as we have it, whether the work of a single author or the product of editing, and looks at it from the point of view of the author's or editor's intent, the unified results, and how it would be perceived by an audience of near contemporaries."[16] In some ways it is the last part of that sentence that is the most important, because it obligates the rhetorical critic to be a kind of social-intellectual historian, a point that has been made in different ways by Ronald Hock and Vernon Robbins.[17] Kennedy wants the rhetorical critic to sift the text through the mesh of the ancient world's educational and cultural artifacts and to adopt preconceptions, in our own critical theories and models, about what constitutes appropriate discourse as informed by these artifacts. He further wants us to "read the Bible as speech,"[18] recognizing the distinctiveness of religious rhetoric and its use of sacred language that depends on authoritative declaration rather than rational argument. That point is stressed in virtually all his comments on the distinction between classical and Christian rhetoric. In other words, the rhetorical critic may be faced with recovering what I have called Christian *paideia*,[19] in which the kerygma is proclaimed by means of what Kennedy calls "radical Christian rhetoric."[20]

What, then, is the goal of rhetorical criticism? For Kennedy, it is "the discovery of the author's intent and of how that is transmitted through a text to an audience."[21] That intent is uncovered by discovering from the text such things as the rhetorical situation, exigence, and inventional strategies used by the speaker to influence the audience he had in mind. In doing this, the critic moves beyond the mining of the text for forms and formulae to questions of genre, the identification of the rhetorical unit and exigence, and such features as arrangement and style. Presumably, analysis of these elements, considered within the historical context of the artifact itself, will allow the critic to render some judgment as to the effectiveness of the argument on the immediate audience.

By the end of the first chapter of *New Testament Interpretation*, we may not have a full blown theory of rhetoric—that comes later in Kennedy's work—but we do have both a clearly outlined method and a clear definition of rhetorical criticism. My task now is to demonstrate how that method and definition are elaborated in Kennedy's later writings in ways that may assist us in a better understanding of the Pauline Letters than was possible through use of his earlier analytical model.

THE LATER KENNEDY: LEARNING THROUGH READING

One way to learn from Kennedy's reading of Paul is to analyze how he follows his own method and what he achieves by doing that. Thus we can seek to emulate him by focusing more closely on smaller rhetorical units or by otherwise applying his method to Pauline argumentation. In the more than twenty years since *New Testament Interpretation* appeared, a variety of rhetorical critics have done that, and we have learned much. I want, however, to approach the question of what Kennedy may teach us from another angle: I want to pick up on aspects of his rhetorical theory and then suggest what directions he intimates for future rhetorical-critical studies of Paul.

I begin with Kennedy's definition of rhetoric. In *New Testament Interpretation* he writes, "Rhetoric is that quality in discourse by which a speaker or writer seeks to accomplish his purposes."[22] It "originates in speech and its primary product is a speech act." On the other hand, the rhetoric of most historical periods can be studied only through texts.[23]

It is imperative, however, that we not limit ourselves to that definition of rhetoric as representative of Kennedy's thought. In order to understand the theoretical basis of his concept of a radical Christian rhetoric or how authorial intent would be transferred to an audience, we must look at later definitions he formulates. In the introduction to his translation of Aristotle's *On Rhetoric*, Kennedy writes: "Rhetoric, in the most general sense, is the energy inherent in emotion and thought, transmitted through a system of signs, including language, to others to influence their decisions and actions."[24] About a year after that translation appeared, his article "A Hoot in the Dark: The Evolution of General Rhetoric" was published in the journal *Philosophy and Rhetoric*. There he suggests, "Rhetoric in the most general sense may perhaps be identified with the energy inherent in communication: the emotional energy that impels the speaker to speak, the physical energy expended in the utterance, the energy level coded in the message, and the energy experienced by the recipient in decoding the message."[25] In that article's epilogue he writes, "[R]hetoric is a form of energy driven by a basic instinct to survive."[26] Still later, in *Comparative Rhetoric*, he pushes the definition even further:

> [R]hetoric, in essence, is a form of mental and emotional energy. This is most clearly seen when an individual, animal or human, is faced with some serious threat or opportunity that may be affected by utterance. . . . An emotional reaction takes place in the mind. . . . The probable source of such basic emotions, and thus of rhetoric, is the instinct for self-preservation.[27]

Because rhetoric takes less energy to affect change than the application of physical force, it is a "conservative faculty."

In Kennedy's earlier definition, rhetorical artifacts are speeches, which in the ancient world are preserved in texts. As he points out in *Comparative Rhetoric*, writing "makes a more efficient use of language than does speech"; it makes possible regularity, system, and analysis of complex thought. In writing, structure is more easily observed by the critic. Writing also provides a code to be used by both an author and readers, reducing the potential for misunderstanding.[28] In later definitions, however, Kennedy takes the meaning of rhetoric back to sound, or, as he puts it, to life-forms that can utter signals.[29] That sound must be sufficient to convey a message's energy. This observation reinforces the need for New Testament rhetorical critics to consider utterance in dealing with texts, as such scholars as Whitney Shiner are doing.[30] By now we are all familiar with the fact that Paul's contemporaries vocalized texts, including letters they received.[31] Kennedy argues that a weak speaker is an ineffective one because he or she cannot produce enough energy to convey the message. We can speculate that Paul occasionally had that problem, at least with the Corinthians.[32] Someone was better at conveying the energy of his letters than Paul himself was at preaching while visiting them (2 Cor 10:10). In any case, it is the act of vocalizing texts that optimizes the energy of a message.[33]

I want to elaborate on the concept of coding,[34] transferring the energy of vocalization to texts, by referring to something Kennedy once wrote about source criticism of the gospels. In his essay "Classical and Christian Source Criticism," he points out that it was common in the period in which the gospels appeared for secretaries and others so trained to take notes on speeches. He suggests that writers of the gospels might have had access to notes taken by disciples of the apostles and others who heard apostolic teaching.[35] If that were so, then the energy of the apostles' preaching was preserved in whatever coding system the disciples used, then transferred by the gospel writers to another generation. The plurality of the gospels suggests that this energy was channeled in a variety of ways.[36] Be that as it may, let us consider the role that notes and the process of note-taking may have played in the production of Paul's letters.[37]

It is commonplace to observe that most of Paul's extant letters are considerably longer than the typical letters of his era, to say nothing of those of the philosophers. For instance, the letters of Cicero range from 22 to 2,530 words in length, averaging about 295 words; those of

Seneca, 150 to 4,130, on average 955 words. Compare those figures to the seven undisputed letters of Paul, which range from Philemon's 335 words to Romans' 7,111 words. If one includes Philemon, Paul's letters average 3,442 words in length; excluding Philemon, the average length of a Pauline Letter is 3,959 words![38] It does not seem likely to me that Paul typically either (1) sat down and wrote out such long letters or (2) dictated them nonstop to a secretary. I can envision a more likely scenario in which Paul sketched out what he wanted to say, then had a secretary, using notes from both that conversation and other occasions on which Paul spoke, formulate a draft.[39] That draft could be reworked until a final product emerged.[40]

If my general scenario for a process of epistolary production is plausible, then I think we need to consider that yet another step in the production of a given letter's argument(s). Drawing from Perelman, I think Kennedy's refined definition of rhetoric allows us to reconsider the dynamics of the argumentative situation. Ancient teachers of rhetoric recognized that the speaker had to reckon with the effect of a speech on the audience. A speaker had to be flexible enough to respond to that effect.[41] Shiner has written of the occasionally raucous response an audience might be expected to give to a speech.[42] In Kennedy's terms, the audience expended energy in decoding the message while they were receiving it. If Kennedy is right, then it seems likely that such energy would have an effect on the speaker. In other words, the original argumentative situation shifts, and the speaker must decide what to do about it.

Now consider that, in every instance that Paul writes, his knowledge of the exigence is secondhand. So he creates or reshapes it, usually in his letter's thanksgiving but also in other sections as the argumentative situation evolves. Paul determines the issues he will argue and the audience for which he will make the argument. It is not a completely historical audience but a rhetorical one: an imaginative construct. As the energy of his argument is expended, Paul anticipates its effect on the audience, calculating how the argumentative situation shifts so that he can engage in further elaboration of issues or the introduction of new ones. This also allows for new energy to be encoded into the message. Later in this chapter I illustrate this phenomenon in Paul's letter to the Galatians.

The process proposed leads me to make three claims for Pauline rhetorical critics to consider. First, Kennedy's functionalist theory deconstructs structure, or at least structure as defined by the classical canons of Greco-Roman rhetoric. In Kennedy's reconstruction of rhetoric, structure grows out of (a) the coding system, (b) the rhetorical situation and exigence, and (c) the appropriateness of the response (or, as Bitzer puts it, the response's fittingness for the situation).[43]

Second, the conventional canons of classical rhetoric must now be viewed as the *handmaidens* of rhetoric, not (as most critics seem to assume) as its *substance*. Rhetorical topics, figures, and styles do not merely follow the models found in handbooks but are also influenced by codes, contexts, functions, and situations. That, I think, is what Kennedy means when he says that (a) rhetoric is prior to speech, (b) the rhetorical code evolves by selective variation, and (c) rhetorical invention, arrangement, style, memory, and delivery are "phenomena of nature," prior to speech.[44]

Third, the rhetorical situation of early Christianity demanded the creation of Christian *paideia*, one of whose aspects may well have been what Kennedy calls a radical rhetoric that is characterized by appeals to authority as a type of proof.[45] While the use of logos, ethos, and pathos can be found in all of Paul's letters, there are also times when he simply resorts to authority instead of reason to bolster his argument.[46] As Jack Levison points out in his essay for Kennedy's *Festschrift*,[47] there is prior literary warrant for this rhetorical move in Philo, Josephus, and the wisdom tradition. It cannot be argued that Paul is purely dependent on Spirit-generated rhetoric; rather, to quote Levison, Paul "reveals a *studied* and prepared display of rhetorical ability," including the use of irony.[48] On the other hand, and with apologies to Levison, I do not think Kennedy wants to characterize "radical Christian rhetoric" as the absence of traditional rhetorical devices. In fact, in *Comparative Rhetoric*, Kennedy argues that rhetoric is a "natural phenomenon" underlying all communication.[49] That phenomenon is present in the communication of nonhuman animals and can be found in some form in every culture. While the most developed system for describing the art of rhetoric is found in Greco-Roman rhetoric, rhetorical terms exist in almost every society, and deliberation as a species of rhetoric is nearly universal. As pointed out above, it is reasonable to assume that Paul would know common rhetorical devices. For Kennedy, therefore, radical rhetoric stands on the shoulders of history and tradition.

What does this mean for the Pauline rhetorical critic? For me it includes the following, and I ask forgiveness for some leaps in argument required by constraints of space. If inventional choices are driven by the need for survival, then Paul's preaching effects the creation of a new Christian rhetorical vision,[50] the energy of which creates communal reality. Paul's letters elaborate and sustain this vision. Because Paul's vision was radically new to most of his hearers, because place was always a factor in determining a code used to transmit energy, and because house-churches probably did not allow for public discourse in the traditional sense, Paul could and did tweak the coding system and the rhetoric it expressed: the patterns of persuasion he needed to articulate that vision.

Furthermore, in "Thesis II" of "A Hoot in the Dark," Kennedy claims, "the receiver's interpretation of a communication is prior to the speaker's intent in determining the meaning."[51] By this Kennedy means that the recipient's possession of a code preconditions what he or she does with the message sent. If the recipient does nothing, then "the message has no meaning." The code may not possess all the capabilities necessary to screen out noise and organize data into information, thus enabling the transfer of energy and action to be taken. This means that Paul's rhetorical system had to nurture his hearers along the trajectory of the argumentative situation so that in the end they would get his meaning and do something.[52] His manipulation of the code could not outstrip his hearers' ability to process the energy it conveyed. If it got too radical, then the power of the message and the inadequacy of the receivers' decoding system combined to confuse rather than to clarify.[53] The rhetorical critic has to be alert, therefore, to instances of what can be called "information overload."

Rhetorical analysis must be executed with the realization that Paul's rhetoric is functional, interactive, contextual, situational, and Christian, designed more to sustain his rhetorical vision than to comply with handbook models. Our analysis must also note the educational process unfolding in the arguments made, as Paul tries to unpack an often complex and difficult message for an audience that appears to have trouble decoding his rhetoric. Rhetorical criticism must describe the power of persuasion that operates as the energy of communication is transferred from speaker to hearer, in the speaker's attempt to get the audience to take action based on his or her argument.

GALATIANS AS A TEST CASE

The epistle to the Galatians illustrates the dynamic I have described.[54] Setting aside any attempt to identify precisely who was involved,[55] the letter's rhetorical situation seems clear. Opponents had emerged who challenged Paul's apostolic persona[56] and message. Identifying the details of an exigence is harder; I comment more on this problem later. The address is to the Galatian[57] "churches," and there is no internal evidence to decide whether the plural refers to house-churches in a single locale or churches located in various cities or towns in the province of Galatia.[58] The absence of any reference to another individual in the salutation or closing greetings—be it a companion of Paul or some associate of these churches—suggests that the letter was to be copied and carried by a number of emissaries, perhaps the "brothers" mentioned in 1:2, who would then read it to the various groups. If that was the case, then the task of conveying the message was made more difficult by the use of a variety of "speakers" and by the presence of multiple audiences who would likely have experienced slightly different exigences conditioned by their group reality. One would expect to find shifts in the trajectory of the argumentative situations, as both the intended audience and the universal audience changed in character as required by the multiple exigences addressed.

You can see some of that when circumscribing the larger rhetorical units.[59] The rhetorical situation is set out in 1:1-5. Only here and in the salutation of 2 Corinthians (1:1-2) does Paul make use of an unqualified statement to refer to his persona. In both letters it is important that the recipients hear a direct reference to his apostleship with no circumlocution. Even more importantly, that office is of divine origin. The significance of that is elaborated in the next unit of Galatians and revisited in the letter's final rhetorical unit (6:11-17).

The use of θαυμάζω ("I am amazed") in 1:6 introduces a direct expression of the controlling or "master" exigence for the letter: some churches' abandonment of the Pauline gospel in favor of other expressions of the gospel. That abandonment also implies rejection of Paul's apostolic office. However else the particulars of that exigence had been experienced in the churches—enthusiastic acceptance of circumcision, segregation of congregants, emergence of libertine behavior—falling away from Paul's gospel is the core issue.

The narrative response to that exigence is introduced by the body of the letter's opening formula—γνωρίζω δὲ ὑμῖν ("I want you to know")—in 1:11.[60] What follows is a narration of the claim that Paul's gospel is of divine origin (1:12-17) and has withstood challenges from the other apostles (2:1-10). The links in that narrative are signaled by the use of the temporal adverb ἔπειτα ("then") in 1:18 and 2:1.

The narrative link is broken at 2:11 with the use of a different temporal phrase ὅτε δέ ("but when"); the use of this phrase implies that there is no necessary linear continuity to the events preceding it. The episode reported in 2:11-14 could have happened within the fourteen-year period referred to by Paul in 2:1. The story of Paul's contact with the disciples and "pillars" in Jerusalem has served its argumentative purpose: Paul is a divinely commissioned apostle, equal to those in Jerusalem, and his message has been sanctioned by the "pillars" of the Jerusalem church. The energy of the argument has to be redirected to create and address a new argumentative situation, the so-called "incident at Antioch."[61]

Therefore, at 2:11 there is a reformulation of the rhetorical situation and exigence.[62] The situation is table-fellowship, and the exigence the rupture of that fellowship by Cephas.[63] To elaborate: The new situation is Peter's behavior in the presence of men sent from James; the new exigence is the fear of the "circumcision party" (2:12) these men aroused in Peter. Argumentatively the exigence is expressed by means of a *chreia*—"I said to Cephas, 'If you, though a Jew, live like a Gentile and not a Jew, how can you compel the Gentiles to live like Jews?'" (2:14)—and is elaborated in 2:15-21.[64] By the end of the chapter the futility of Peter's conduct is clear—"for if justification were through the law, then Christ died to no purpose" (2:21)—and that claim ends the first major rhetorical unit of the body of the letter.

Paul's rebuke—"O foolish Galatians"—in 3:1 signals a clear transition to a new argumentative situation and opens the next major rhetorical unit (3:1-5:12). It redirects the argument's energy from Paul's defense of his apostolic persona and message to his reminder to the Galatians of their experience in the Spirit, in preparation for elaborating some elements of what Paul had already taught them. The rebuke also serves to signal a transition in the character of the argument: Paul shifts the blame away from himself and the charge that he has not taught the gospel to the Galatians who are abandoning the true gospel.[65]

The rhetorical questions in Galatians 3:1-5 serve as reminders of the original effects of their hearing of Paul's gospel; 3:6-14, 15-18, 19-22, 3:23-4:7, 4:8-11 are rhetorical units that elaborate and illustrate the central tenets of that gospel. Believers are heirs of Abraham, who himself was justified by faith; the inheritance promised in Abraham's covenant belongs to those who, like Abraham, have faith; the law has pragmatic but not salvific function; the appearance of Christ has fulfilled the promise and made those in Christ "sons" and heirs; and such status frees those in Christ from old and inadequate beliefs and rituals.

The energy of the argument is again redirected at 4:12, and another rhetorical unit opens. Following a statement of despair at 4:11, the argumentative situation returns to Paul and his personal relationship with the Galatians, which he describes as at first caring and supportive, but which has become hostile. Paul suggests that he would rather not use ironic rebuke in his dealings with them (4:20) but must, because he cannot deal with them face to face. That device sets the stage for a new unit (4:21-5:1) in which a diatribe style of argumentation is used, with the presumed interlocutors being both those who have been persuaded by the other gospel ("those who want to live under law") and those who Paul believes are still sympathetic ("brothers").[66]

That situation is brought to an abrupt end by the intervention of another emotionally charged exigence, the opponents' insistence on the need for circumcision, at 5:2. With the use of the imperative "Look!" reinforced by the phrase "I, Paul, tell you," it appears that Paul inserts himself into the pattern of the argument to construct a proof from pathos on the subject of circumcision.[67] This argument ends just as abruptly with the expressed wish that those who are troubling the churches—or at least one of them—would undergo self-castration (5:12). I see this unit as an interpolation, but one done by Paul himself in editing what the secretary had given him.

At 5:13 the argumentative situation turns again, and another major rhetorical unit begins. Clearly at this point Paul has assessed the effect of his argument and has decided that he can move from persuasion to *paraenesis*,[68] or, as Betz would have it, to a group of exhortations.[69] The experience of the Spirit has practical application in the law of love. The indicative of life in the Spirit must be expressed pragmatically in the way the children of God behave toward one another and carry on their daily lives. The heirs of Abraham—those who have been baptized into Christ, those who have experienced the Spirit in their lives—now "work for the good of all" (6:10). Curiously, the moral exhortations in this unit are not drawn directly from the issue of circumcision but from the larger issue of the "law" of love (5:14). The exigence has shifted from the current practice of the Galatians to the values expected from members of the body of Christ. The practice of circumcision implies adherence to now discredited values (4:9), which in turn implies the potential for the collapse of values found in the Christian *paideia* (5:16-21). Acceptance of circumcision is the slippery slope leading to eschatological judgment (5:7-8). The resolution of that exigence is to "love your neighbor as yourself" (5:14) and "walk by the Spirit" (5:16, 25).

Finally, in 6:11, which many analysts identify as the beginning of the epistolary postscript, Paul again uses the imperative "Look!" to insert himself into the situation in order to change the argument's energy and trajectory. As in 4:19-20, there is a hint of the functionality of the "apostolic parousia"[70] in the instruction to observe Paul's own writing, and ethos is joined with pathos to challenge the proponents of "another gospel." But even more astonishingly, Paul in this new unit creates a new rhetorical situation by associating himself with the crucifixion and moving the argument into the realm of the new creation (6:15). In this new realm he, and presumably his gospel, is beyond the reach of his opponents (6:17). In rhetorician Perelman's terms, this is the apex of his appeal to the universal audience to sanction his argument. The exigence of the "other" gospel is resolved by the cross and new creation that Paul, the apostle, proclaims.

Reading the letter in this way helps us better to understand the character of Paul's letters. I have already noted that by the standards of his day Paul's letters are considerably longer than others, and Kennedy has supported the idea that they share characteristic features with species of speeches in the Greco-Roman world. How, then, does one explain the integration of the two genres? By paying greater attention to the dynamic, interactive nature of rhetorical and argumentative situations along the trajectory of common patterns of persuasion. While the epistolary genre is an *inventional* choice, persuasive speech and its formulae are *situational* choices. Paul must imagine his audiences, both particular and universal, and anticipate the progress of persuasion. When he believes that the audience has been persuaded of one thing, he can then shift the trajectory of his argument and bring to it new energy.[71] Thus he is creating new rhetorical or argumentative situations, or both, which need to be addressed. That, in turn, requires longer letters. In other words, there is a *rhetorical* reason for the length of Paul's letters.

CONCLUSION

The method and criticism found in Kennedy's early works can be described as "rhetorics"—that is, as analysis based on the special theories of rhetoric found in the classical handbooks of rhetoric. Special theories are useful in explaining how to conduct communication within the constraints of a certain time and place.[72] They deal with communication events in which models for communication are mutually agreed upon but could be ignored by some participants; they are "artistic formulations that specify the nature of conventional forms and provide practical advice on how to take part in the relevant communication episodes."[73] Handbook models of rhetoric reflect this practice.

On the other hand, the later Kennedy is proposing a general theory of rhetoric. A general theory of rhetoric is able to account for "broad classes of events" and "tendencies in human communications events that cannot be ignored or rescinded by the participants. . . . [They] are trans-cultural in that they explain events that take place in various cultural contexts. . . . [They] may include a description of the dynamic forces that can provide a necessary and sufficient set of causes to explain [a] discovered pattern" of longitudinal patterns of communication that "show an evolution from earlier forms to later forms."[74] Kennedy's understanding of rhetoric as the transference of energy in an attempt to motivate an audience to act satisfies the criteria of a general theory of rhetoric.

Kennedy's later thinking about and his elaboration of concepts of a general theory of rhetoric suggest new approaches to New Testament rhetorical criticism. In addition to those mentioned above, consider this: Kennedy admits that his contention that meaning resides in the hearer's response to the message gives comfort to pragmatists.[75] He does not go on to claim, however, that rhetoric is epistemic, a position that would follow directly from that. On the other hand, I believe that such a position can be inferred from his later writings. Accordingly, if he and others who believe rhetoric to be epistemic are correct, then one task of the Pauline rhetorical critic is to describe how Paul uses rhetoric to create knowledge. Regarding the letters as epistemic suggests that we might become less interested in how closely Paul's thought and teaching parallel that of the rabbis or philosophers, or even the Qumran community, and become more intentionally concerned with how in Paul's hands history and tradition function rhetorically—functionally, situationally, interactionally—to create and elaborate Christian *paideia*. That, for me, is the power of Robbins' metaphor of the tapestry: Some new reality is woven out of the threads of human culture and experience.

I would never make the argument that we have exhausted historical and literary-critical analyses of early Christian texts based on the Western rhetorical tradition. Analysis of "rhetorics" may well be the first step in rhetorical criticism. However, I urge us all to follow Kennedy's lead by paying more attention to *theories* of rhetoric, classical and modern, if we are to move from rhetorical *analysis* to rhetorical *criticism*, from descriptions of what the argument looks like to explanations of why it retains its persuasive power.[76]

Notes

[1] George A. Kennedy, *New Testament Interpretation through Rhetorical Criticism* (Chapel Hill: University of North Carolina Press, 1984), 3–5.

[2] George A. Kennedy, *Progymnasmata: Greek Textbooks of Prose Composition and Rhetoric, Translated into English, with Introductions and Notes* (WGRW 10; Atlanta and Leiden: Society of Biblical Literature/Brill, 2003), x–xi; and *New Testament Interpretation*, 12–13.

[3] Although Kennedy does not dwell on it explicitly, another point should be emphasized: Such handbooks were not studies of rhetorical theory, as such, but textbooks. Their intended use was for instruction, not analysis.

[4] Kennedy, *New Testament Interpretation*, 8–10.

[5] Kennedy, *New Testament Interpretation*, 33–38.

[6] In the paragraphs that follow, I will occasionally elaborate on elements of Kennedy's method, not simply describing what he lays out in *New Testament Interpretation*.

[7] Kennedy, *New Testament Interpretation*, 33–34.

[8] I borrow the concept of the "argumentative situation" from Chaim Perelman and Lucie Olbrechts-Tyteca, *The New Rhetoric: A Treatise on Argumentation* (trans. John Wilkinson and Purcell Weaver; Notre Dame: University of Notre Dame Press, 1969), 96, 460, 490–91.

[9] Perelman and Olbrechts-Tyteca, *The New Rhetoric*, 96.

[10] Perelman and Olbrechts-Tyteca, *The New Rhetoric*, 460–61.

[11] Kennedy simply appropriates Bitzer's definition of the rhetorical situation and exigence, as have many other rhetorical critics. Thus Bitzer: "Rhetorical situation may be defined as a complex of persons, events, objects, and relations presenting

an actual or potential exigence which can be completely or partially removed if discourse, introduced into the situation, can so constrain human decision or action as to bring about the significant modification of the exigence" ("The Rhetorical Situation," *PR* 1 [1968]: 6).

[12] As we shall see, Kennedy expands or perhaps simplifies the notion of discourse to that of utterance.

[13] Bitzer, "The Rhetorical Situation," 6.

[14] Bitzer, "The Rhetorical Situation," 7.

[15] For a definition of the universal audience, see Perelman and Olbrechts-Tyteca, *The New Rhetoric*, 31–35, and throughout. For its utility in rhetorical criticism of Paul, see James D. Hester, "Speaker, Audience and Situations: A Modified Interactional Model," *Neot* 32 (1998): 80–83.

[16] Kennedy, *New Testament Interpretation*, 4.

[17] While a number of works from these scholars would illustrate my point, I direct the reader's attention especially to Ronald F. Hock, *The Social Context of Paul's Ministry: Tentmaking and Apostleship* (Philadelphia: Fortress, 1980); idem, "The Chreia in Primary and Secondary Education," in *Alexander's Revenge* (ed. J. M. Asgeirsson and N. van Deusen; Reykjavik: University of Iceland Press, 2002), 11–35; Ronald F. Hock and Edward N. O'Neil, eds., *The Chreia in Ancient Rhetoric: The Progymnasmata* (Atlanta: Scholars Press, 1986); idem, *The Chreia and Ancient Rhetoric: Classroom Exercises* (Atlanta: Society of Biblical Literature, 2002); V. K. Robbins, ed., *Ancient Quotes and Anecdotes: From Crib to Crypt* (Sonoma, Calif.: Polebridge, 1989); idem, *The Tapestry of Early Christian Discourse: Rhetoric, Society, and Ideology* (London: Routledge, 1996); Burton L. Mack and V. K. Robbins, *Patterns of Persuasion in the Gospels* (Foundations and Facets: Literary Facets; Sonoma, Calif.: Polebridge, 1989).

[18] Kennedy, *New Testament Interpretation*, 6.

[19] See James D. Hester, "A Fantasy Theme Analysis of 1 Thessalonians," in *Rhetorical Criticism and the Bible* (ed. Stanley E. Porter and Dennis Stamps; JSNTSup 195; Sheffield: Sheffield Academic, 2002), 504; n. 2.

[20] Kennedy, *New Testament Interpretation*, 7, with emphasis in the original. Although, as far as I know, Kennedy does not use the phrase explicitly, I think it likely he would agree that "radical" Christian rhetoric is also "charismatic" rhetoric to some degree. That is, it is understood as derived from and responding to the Holy Spirit.

[21] Kennedy, *New Testament Interpretation*, 12.

[22] Kennedy, *New Testament Interpretation*, 3

[23] Kennedy, *New Testament Interpretation*, 5.

[24] George A. Kennedy, trans., *Aristotle, On Rhetoric, A Theory of Civic Discourse: Newly Translated, with Introduction, Notes, and Appendices* (New York: Oxford University Press, 1991), 7.

[25] George A. Kennedy, "A Hoot in the Dark: The Evolution of General Rhetoric," *PR* 25 (1992): 2.

[26] Kennedy, "A Hoot in the Dark," 20.

[27] George A. Kennedy, *Comparative Rhetoric: An Historical and Cross-Cultural Introduction* (New York: Oxford University Press, 1997 [1998]), 3–4.

[28] Kennedy, *Comparative Rhetoric*, 116, 117.

²⁹ Interestingly, scientists have recently reported that they were able to teach the common European starling to respond to certain vocalizations (see http://www.news.uchicago.edu.releases/06/060426.starling.shtml). Such a discovery tends to support Kennedy's claims in "A Hoot in the Dark."

³⁰ See Whitney T. Shiner, *Proclaiming the Gospel: First-Century Performance of Mark* (Harrisburg, Pa.: Trinity Press International, 2003).

³¹ See Paul J. Achtemeier, "*Omne verbum sonat*: The New Testament and the Oral Environment of Late Western Antiquity," *JBL* 109 (1990): 3–27, who describes the predominance of the orality of texts in the ancient world, followed by the emergence of silent reading more generally some time in the fourth century CE. Cf. Frank D. Gilliard, "More on Silent Reading in Antiquity: *Non Omne Verbum Sonabat*," *JBL* 112 (1993): 689–94.

³² Perhaps also with the Galatians; see 4:13-16; 5:8-11.

³³ Scholars of Islam have long known that about the Qur'an; see J. Coorigan, F. M. Denny, C. M. N. Eire, and M. S. Jaffe, *Jews, Christians, Muslims: A Comparative Introduction to Monotheistic Religions* (Upper Saddle River, N.J.: Prentice Hall, 1998), 415–16. New Testament rhetorical critics need to recognize it too.

³⁴ I borrow the concept of "code" from information theory, but I am also modifying it for use in the context of rhetoric. At the most basic level, "code" is a device to organize data. In order for information to get from the sender to the receiver, a code and a channel of communication have to be selected. Vocabulary and syntax can be thought of as "code." Meaning may depend in some measure not only on what is coded but also on how that code is sent and what measures are used to prevent "noise" from muddling the message. Three of the classical canons of rhetoric—invention, arrangement, and style—may be thought of as related to coding; another—delivery—to channels of communication. Obviously, such things as the social location of the sender and recipient, social and cultural norms, and literacy rates also enter the picture, because they can introduce "noise" and require some sort of feedback loop to ensure that effective communication takes place. In Paul's situation the most effective channel of communication open to him seems to have been the letter, carried by a trusted associate who could both read and interpret it for the recipient. Evidently, from what we see in his letters, feedback came either from that associate, returning with a description of how the message was received, or from emissaries sent from the recipients charged with getting more information from Paul. He would then have to assess the new rhetorical situation, elaborating his rhetorical vision to address the realities he and they faced.

³⁵ George A. Kennedy, "Classical and Christian Source Criticism," in *The Relationship among the Gospels: An Interdisciplinary Dialogue* (ed. William O. Walker; Trinity University Monograph Series in Religion 5; San Antonio: Trinity University Press, 1978), 126, 129, 131, 140, 141; 148–9, 151.

³⁶ Consider the prologue of Luke (1:1-4). The author acknowledges two earlier generations of "writers." He also implies that the information they provided needed modification or elaboration.

³⁷ There is a very useful discussion of notes and the role played by secretaries in the production of letters in E. Randolph Richards, *Paul and First-Century Letter Writing: Secretaries, Composition and Collection* (Downers Grove, Ill.: InterVarsity, 2004): 55–57, 59–80. Cf. P. J. J. Botha, "Letter Writing and Oral Communication in Antiquity: Sug-

gested Implications for the Interpretation of Paul's Letter to the Galatians," *Scriptura* 42 (1992): 19–23.

[38] See M. R. P. McGuire, "Letters and Letter Carriers in Christian Antiquity," *CW* 53 (1960): 148–53, 184–86, 199–200. McGuire's assessment of the Pauline corpus includes the thirteen letters traditionally ascribed to the apostle, which he says average 2,500 words. Jerome Murphy-O'Connor, *Paul the Letter-Writer* (Collegeville, Minn.: Liturgical 1995), 121, also provides a word count of each of the letters traditionally attributed to Paul, including even Hebrews (which makes no claim of having been written by Paul). According to Murphy-O'Connor's count, the average length of the seven undisputed letters is 3,442. On the basis of my own computerized computation, I corroborated his figures for the undisputed letters. David E. Aune, *The New Testament in Its Literary Environment* (Philadelphia: Westminster, 1987), 205, provides still other word counts for each of the letters; by his calculation the average length of the undisputed letters is 3,427 words. These differences could be explained by the use of different editions of the Greek text. In any case the variations are hardly significant.

[39] In Pliny the Younger's letter to Fuscus, he describes what I would call the inventional process used in composing letters. Pliny would seclude himself in a room for some time, call in his secretary when ready to dictate text, dismiss the secretary to reflect further on what he wanted to say, and then repeat the process of dictation. Although it is not clear from the letter to Fuscus, it seems logical that at some point Pliny would have had opportunity to read and possibly correct what his scribe had written. See Letter CVIII in Marcus Tullius Cicero, *Letters of Marcus Tullius Cicero, with His Treatises on Friendship and Old Age* (trans. E. S. Shuckburgh), and *Letters of Gaius Plinius Caecilius Secundus* (trans. W. Melmoth; rev. by F. C. T. Bosanquet; The Harvard Classics, vol. 9; New York: Collier, 1909).

[40] Richards, *Paul and First-Century Letter Writing*, 93, describes the process somewhat differently, but our variations are minor. The use of notes might help explain interpolations in the letters: Later editors had material they regarded appropriate to the topic and made use of it. One does not always need other letters to account for source material. If you accept the idea that notes might have been available to the editor, you do not have to explain why an editor would excise epistolary formulae to make things fit. Richards (109–21) takes a different view: He seems to regard all so-called interpolations as the product of a compositional process in which Paul and his "coauthors" engaged.

[41] See, e.g., Quintilian, *Inst.*, 7.10.5–17. One might compare "The Seventh, or Euboean, Discourse" from *Dio Chrysostom* (vol. 1; trans. J. W. Cohoon; LCL; Cambridge: Harvard University Press, 1932). In it Dio narrates a story told to him by a landless peasant who is tricked into appearing in the forum to defend himself against a series of increasingly outrageous charges. When the peasant begins his rejoinder by generously agreeing to share the elements of his meager existence, his ethos turns the sentiment of the crowd around, and by the end they try to reward him for his generosity. This episode illustrates almost perfectly the interaction of rhetorical and argumentative situations, the energy generated by the speeches and their effects on the crowd, and adaptations made by the speaker to the situations he faced.

[42] See Whitney T. Shiner, "Applause and Applause Lines," in *Rhetorics and Hermeneutics* (ed. James D. Hester and J. David Hester; New York: T&T Clark, 2004), 129–44.

[43] Bitzer, "Rhetorical Situation," 10.

[44] Kennedy, "A Hoot in the Dark," 10, 13, 14.

[45] See his description of Christian rhetoric in *Classical Rhetoric and Its Christian and Secular Tradition from Ancient to Modern Times* (Chapel Hill: University of North Carolina Press, 1980), 125–32; also Kennedy, *New Testament Interpretation*, 6–10, 104–5.

[46] See my essay, "The Rhetoric of Persona in Romans: Re-reading Romans 1:1-12," in *Celebrating Romans: Template for Pauline Theology* (ed. Sheila E. McGinn; Grand Rapids, Mich.: Eerdmans, 2004), 83–105, for a description of the use of a rhetorical device to establish the authority of Paul's arguments before he even made them to the Romans!

[47] John R. Levison, "Did the Spirit Inspire Rhetoric? An Exploration of George Kennedy's Definition of Early Christian Rhetoric," in *Persuasive Artistry: Studies in New Testament Rhetoric in Honor of George A. Kennedy* (ed. Duane F. Watson; JSNTSup 50; Sheffield: JSOT, 1991), 25–40.

[48] Levison, "Did the Spirit Inspire Rhetoric," 37–38. Building on Nils Dahl's work, Mark Nanos makes the case for Paul's extensive use of irony in Galatians in *The Irony of Galatians: Paul's Letter in First-Century Context* (Minneapolis: Fortress, 2002).

[49] Kennedy, *Comparative Rhetoric*, 4.

[50] As far as I know, Ernest Bormann is the first theoretician to give a formal definition to the concept of the "rhetorical vision." He describes it as a unifying or unified construction of code words, cues, dramatizing narratives, and other "scripts" that provide groups with a "broader view of things," which helps them to cope with their social realities. Those who participate in such visions often form rhetorical communities. See Bormann, *The Force of Fantasy: Restoring the American Dream* (Carbondale: Southern Illinois University Press, 1985), 6–8.

[51] Kennedy, "A Hoot in the Dark," 5.

[52] Rhetorically, that may explain the position of the majority of Paul's paraenetic material at the end of his letters.

[53] It would appear that later generations of readers had exactly that problem! See 2 Peter 3:15b-16.

[54] Mark Nanos has brought together an invaluable collection of the major articles on the rhetoric of Galatians in *The Galatians Debate* (Peabody, Mass.: Hendrickson, 2002). Limitations of space preclude my surveying all the issues raised and discussed by those authors and more recent commentators. I assume the reader's familiarity with most of them.

[55] In *The Irony of Galatians*, 127–31, Nanos argues that it is misleading to characterize the outsiders who are raising questions about Paul's gospel as "Judaizers," "agitators," or "troublemakers." He sees these designations as reflecting Paul's rhetorical strategy in characterizing those who have come in and questioned his teaching. Nanos prefers to understand them as those who are trying to influence the restoration of what they see as essential social order to the congregations (249–56). Nanos's preference for "influencers" seems a bit clumsy to me, however much the term is based on his socio-rhetorical reconstruction of the situation in the Galatian churches. Whatever else may be said about the outsiders, they were in opposition to the new social realities—"there is neither Jew nor Greek, nor slave nor freeman, not even male or female"—created

by the new Christian *paideia*. Thus I will use the designation "opponent," even while acknowledging the issues such use ignores.

⁵⁶ For a discussion of apostolic persona, see Hester, "The Rhetoric of Persona in Romans."

⁵⁷ Although I am not sure just what to make of it, it is interesting that Galatians is the only letter Paul addressed to a region rather than to an individual church. It certainly requires us to be open to a greater range of alternatives when trying to understand just what "immediate" audience he had in mind when writing it.

⁵⁸ In *Galatians* (New York: Routledge, 1998, 32–34), Philip Esler argues that the letter was addressed to churches in the northern sector, or what he terms "tribal Galatia," rather than "provincial Galatia." In "Choose Your Mother, Chose Your Master: Galatians 4:21–5:1 in the Shadow of the Anatolian Mother of the Gods" (*JBL* 118 [1999]: 661–83), Susan Elliott remarks, "Whether the venue was 'North Galatia' or 'South Galatia,' Paul wrote his letter to residents of central Anatolia" (671). See also Clinton E. Arnold, "'I am astonished that you are so quickly turning away': Paul and Anatolian Folk Belief," *NTS* 51 (2005): 429–49. The identification of place is important to these and other scholars because of their arguments concerning Paul's need to deal with social and cultural forces faced by the Galatian Christians and the issues of group and individual identity relevant to their experience. Although an interesting question, I am not convinced that the answer is ultimately relevant to a rhetorical critical reading of the letter. The larger question must always be: What group or individual identity, or both, did Paul want them to appropriate? What was he trying to persuade them to be and do?

⁵⁹ Kennedy, *New Testament Interpretation*, 148–51, outlines Galatians' rhetorical units as follows: proem, 1:6-10; proofs, 1:11–5:1; "specific commandments," 5:2–6:10; epilogue, 6:11-18. He breaks the proofs down into the following units: narrative, 1:13–2:14; "epicheireme," 2:15-21; argument from the experience of the Galatians, 3:1–4:11; personal appeal, 4:12-20; and allegory, 4:21–31. Although Kennedy does not say so, 5:1 presumably serves as a kind of summary of the proofs or transitional statement to the paranetic section.

⁶⁰ In "Apostasy to Paganism: The Rhetorical Stasis of the Galatian Controversy" (*JBL* 114 [1995]: 437–61), Troy Martin refers to epistolary features such as the body opening and body closing but seems to ignore the formulae associated with them, such as the disclosure formula in 1:11, which is typically associated with the body opening. He points to six transitional questions (1:10, 3:1, 4:9, 4:21, 5:7, 5:11) to identify rhetorical units within the body middle, but he does not distinguish between rhetorical questions and ones reflecting dismay. He regards 6:11-17 as the body closing. This analysis identifies the same units as I do—with the exception of incorporating 4:8 into the question posed in 4:9—until the fifth and sixth questions, though it does not do justice to the paranetic section (5:13–6:10).

⁶¹ For an analysis of the pattern of argumentation in Galatians 1–2, see my essay, "Epideictic Rhetoric and Persona in Galatians One and Two," in *The Galatians Debate* (ed. Nanos), 181–96.

⁶² Using the rhetorics of the handbooks, Hans Dieter Betz argues that 2:11-14 is part of the *narratio*, and 2:15–21, the *propositio* (*Galatians: A Commentary on Paul's Letter to the Churches in Galatia* [Hermeneia; Philadelphia: Fortress, 1979], 105–12, 113–27).

Betz's identification has been challenged, most recently by Ian W. Scott, "Common Ground? The Role of Galatians 2.16 in Paul's Argument," *NTS* 53 (2007): 425–35. Scott identifies 2:15-21 as a thesis structured in the style of a diatribe. I now hold that the larger rhetorical unit runs from 1:11–2:21, in which Paul's claim that his gospel is not dependent on human resources but divinely revealed is segmented as two "narrative" units: 1:11–2:10 and 2:11-21. The first unit corresponds loosely to a "statement of facts," or *narratio*; the second, to an episode elaborated by a *chreia*.

[63] It is interesting to note Paul's encoding of names for Peter in the arguments in 1:18-24, 2:1-10, and 2:11-14. The shift in the names for Peter seems to represent two different personae. On the one hand, "Cephas" is used for his persona in Jerusalem or with associates from Jerusalem. On the other, "Peter" is used for his persona as apostle to the circumcised (see 2:7). By doing this, Paul can imply in 2:11 that "Cephas" is among the opponents of the gospel and that "Peter" is not (compare 2:11 with 2:7, while noting that the reference to "Cephas" in 2:9 carries a negative overtone). In "Peter and Cephas: One and the Same," *JBL* 111 (1992): 489–95, Dale Allison contests Bart Ehrman's position ("Cephas and Peter," *JBL* 109 [1990]: 463–74) that Peter and Cephas were two different people, using historical and exegetical evidence to argue for those names as referring to the same person. Allison's evidence can make the case for Peter's having been identified by two names, but it seems to me that only rhetorical analysis can explain why Paul uses them in Galatians. No commentary I have consulted comments on this rhetorical strategy.

[64] See my essay "Placing the Blame: The Presence of Epideictic in Galatians 1 and 2," in *Persuasive Artistry* (ed. Watson), 299–306, for a full description of the elaboration process.

[65] Hester, "Placing the Blame," 307.

[66] Here it is important to note that, while the subjects of these two rhetorical units differ—Paul's personal relationship with the Galatians and the allegory of Sarah and Hagar—the argumentative situation is the same: the importance to the churches of Paul's persona as pastor and apostolic teacher.

[67] Betz, *Galatians*, 253–59, argues that the *probatio* ends at 4:31, with 5:1-12 serving as an *exhortatio*. Most analyses I have seen of this section of the letter tend to construe 5:1-12 as a unit. On the other hand, I prefer the view of Nanos, *Irony of Galatians*, 70–72, who understands 5:2 as beginning a "situational discourse." By that he means rhetoric "directly addressed to the Galatian recipients in their own local situations" (10).

[68] Nanos, *Irony of Galatians*, 72, identifies 5:2-18 and 5:24–6:10 as units of situational discourse, with 5:19-23 being a unit of a narrative catalog of virtues and vices.

[69] Betz, *Galatians*, 22–23, 271–311.

[70] For the classic definition of the function of this epistolary formula, see Robert Funk, "Apostolic Parousia: Form and Significance," in *Christian History and Interpretation: Studies Presented to John Knox* (ed. W. R. Farmer, C. F. D. Moule, and R. R. Niebuhr; Cambridge: Cambridge University Press, 1967), 249–69.

[71] Limitations of space forbid an exploration of the utility of information theory and chaos theory in analyzing Paul's coding of messages, but New Testament rhetorical theorists need to explore them in greater depth. See, e.g., N. Katherine Hay-

les, *Chaos Bound: Orderly Disorder in Contemporary Literature and Science* (Ithaca: Cornell University Press, 1985).

[72] Ernest Bormann, *Small Group Communication: Theory and Practice* (3rd ed.; New York: Harper & Row, 1990), 3–5.

[73] Ernest Bormann, John Cragan, and Donald Shields, "In Defense of Symbolic Convergence Theory: A Look at the Theory and Its Criticisms after Two Decades," *Communications Theory* 4 (1994): 265.

[74] Bormann, et al., "In Defense of Symbolic Convergenece Theory," 266.

[75] Kennedy, "A Hoot in the Dark," 7.

[76] I want to thank Professor Charles Wanamaker of the University of Cape Town, South Africa, for his careful reading and helpful comments on an earlier draft of this paper. It is a better piece for his insights, but I take full responsibility for the whole.

Chapter 10

MOVING AN AUDIENCE
One Aspect of Pathos in the Book of Revelation

Greg Carey

> *If not the most mystifying member of the New Testament, the Revelation to John is a strong contender for that position. Any level-headed study that helps us better to understand the Johannine Apocalypse is to be embraced. The reader should rejoice to receive Greg Carey's lucid inquiry into the persuasive role of pathos in Revelation. Here is a model of scholarship, proceeding with care and circumspection, which builds on previous research while opening onto the exegetical landscape a new vista. That perspective fosters deeper appreciation of one of the classical modes of persuasion, its adaptation for genres other than public speeches, and its potential for both illuminating and altering the social world of early Christians and the ambient world with which they experienced painful tension. By paying patient attention to the multiple "voices" that issue from Revelation, Carey's own voice continues to command our attention.*

How does one track the varieties of New Testament rhetorical criticism that have flourished since the publication of George A. Kennedy's *New Testament Interpretation through Rhetorical Criticism*?[1] In a recent dictionary article David E. Aune attempts this venture, helpfully diagnosing two major distinctions within the field: (1) some practitioners emphasize classical Greco-Roman categories, while others draw upon more "modern" rhetorics; (2) some stress rhetorical structures and classifications, while others focus on "style and development of argumentation."[2] Methodologically speaking, one might say that those who incline toward Greco-Roman categories and rhetorical structures demonstrate a methodological affinity for form criticism, while those who employ modern and postmodern rhetorics with an appreciation for argumentative flow gravitate toward narrative criticism.[3]

Coincidentally or not, Kennedy's introduction of Greco-Roman rhetoric arrived at about the same time that biblical scholars were encountering postmodern (or linguistic) sensibilities. We do not have the space here to pursue this complex development in a systematic way, yet it remains the case that some New Testament scholars began reading modern and postmodern literary theorists who appealed to the rhetorical traditions of antiquity. These theorists may not have used the specific conventions of Aristotle, Quintilian, or Cicero, but they did emphasize the ancients' awareness that language *performs*. In other words, one reads texts not simply as depositories of ideas or as static examples of aesthetic skill; rather, one reads texts as interventions in public or communal life. Unfortunately, scholars reading antique rhetoric rarely conversed with those sampling literary theory. The recent history of scholarship confirms this dichotomy.

Students of Revelation will recognize these distinctions in the scholarly literature. Some interpreters have appropriated Greco-Roman rhetorical categories, often citing or depending upon Kennedy's work,[4] though to my knowledge no monograph-scale work has adopted those categories as a primary rubric for Revelation's interpretation. On the other hand, perhaps Revelation's most influential rhetorical analyst, Elisabeth Schüssler Fiorenza, most often dons contemporary literary and ideological lenses for her work, rarely citing ancient rhetorical theorists.[5] In this respect some of the most widely appreciated rhetorical studies of Revelation follow her lead.[6] The full-time rhetorician Stephen D. O'Leary, also influential among Revelation's interpreters, occasionally employs Greco-Roman categories, though his rhetorical approach draws much more profoundly from the rhetoric of Kenneth Burke.[7] In my view, Greco-Roman categories have exercised far less influence on Revelation's interpretation than have more contemporary or "literary" rhetorics.

The problem with Revelation, of course, lies in its generic complexity. Revelation is neither a deliberative, judicial, nor epideictic speech; it is an apocalypse, one of many similar works from Jewish and Christian antiquity. Revelation calls itself an apocalypse (1:1), yet it also claims status as prophecy (1:3; 19:10; 22:7, 10, 18-19). Like all apocalypses, Revelation takes a narrative form; however, by presenting itself as directly addressed to seven Christian communities in Asia Minor, Revelation also draws upon epistolary conventions. How does one adapt the known canons of Greco-Roman rhetoric to the interpretation of such a book as Revelation, with its interwoven apocalyptic, prophetic, and epistolary textures?

Kennedy's work defies such simple taxonomy, holding greater promise than we may have assumed. New Testament scholars usually cite Kennedy when applying classical categories to the identification of argumentative parts of a given block of text or discerning its rhetorical species (i.e., deliberative, judicial, or epideictic). However, at least two trajectories in Kennedy's own work suggest the limitations of such an approach. First, Kennedy notes rhetoric's universal character. Aristotle set out not simply to describe Greek rhetoric but to provide an analysis of the art of persuasion in any context. Indeed, Kennedy argues, Aristotelian categories can apply in just about any cultural context.[8] Second, Kennedy himself has taken on such a project by articulating a comparative rhetoric with specific attention to diverse global cultures.[9] Taking a cue from Kennedy, my keen interest resides in how the classical and the contemporary, the micro and macro, can nourish one another.

Though I have not seen it discussed among biblical scholars, Kennedy does offer some thoughts on millennialism, which he defines as the doctrine that a "peaceful and prosperous time" lies in the future. Most often this future age represents a return to the conditions of an idealized past.[10] Locating it in "societies under stress," Kennedy contrasts millennialism with a more rational utopianism, the hope for a better world through social and political reform. Both millennialism and utopianism represent a "poetic" rhetoric.[11] My own work has explored the poetic dimensions of apocalyptic discourse, though with greater attention to its *creativity* than to its literary form.[12] Kennedy further identifies the critical role of authority in millennial rhetoric, something also pointed out by O'Leary.[13] Unfortunately, Kennedy does not demonstrate how one might investigate millennial rhetoric—or apocalyptic discourse, for that matter—by means of either Greco-Roman or comparative rhetorics.

PATHOS IN THE APOCALYPSE

Kennedy's tentative exploration in millennial rhetoric invites creative research. How might contemporary scholars, informed by Greco-Roman rhetorical categories, devise a rhetoric that can illuminate the book of Revelation? In previous work I have built upon ancient conventions regarding ethos, the persuasive potential of a speaker's character, to investigate how apocalyptic narrators construct their personae, what I have called an "apocalyptic ethos."[14] This work required, among other things, a comparative approach to apocalyptic literature, an inductive sifting of formal apocalypses in terms of how apocalyptic narrators represent themselves. It also demanded a look at ethos-building conventions in Greco-Roman rhetoric.

In this chapter I investigate one dimension of how the book of Revelation seeks to persuade through pathos, the appeal to its audience's emotion. No one doubts that the Apocalypse deals in pathos, what Loren L. Johns calls "pathetical persuasion."[15] Here I consider Revelation's pathetic appeal through its address to its literary audience. Revelation addresses its audience by means of direct address, dramatic pointing and showing, and a rhetoric of identification that links the audience to characters within the apocalyptic drama.[16] The present study will also rely upon ancient rhetorical sensibilities regarding pathos as a context against which to read Revelation's appeal, but my approach leans more toward the rhetoric of fiction. I propose that Revelation addresses its audience through a system of intricately related literary devices and that those devices were likely designed to foster particular responses within Revelation's audience.

One might hope for more. A creative and more thorough investigation of apocalyptic pathos would both rely upon and inform a study of pathos in Revelation. A study of pathos in the broader realm of apocalyptic discourse could prove especially valuable. Likewise, a broader look into pathos within Revelation itself would likely revise this study's conclusions, even as it would incorporate them. The aims of this essay are restricted to Revelation's address to its intended audience, especially with respect to Revelation's potential to foster emotional response.

GRECO-ROMAN PATHOS

In Greco-Roman rhetoric, pathos serves as one of three primary proofs, or means of crafting an argument. Ethos relates to the speaker's character, actual or perceived; logos to the content of his argument; and pathos to the appeal to an audience's emotions or psychology. Aristotle created the most systematic treatment of pathos by developing a psychology of human motivation. (Indeed, pathos often receives little or no attention in many of our ancient sources, though its significance is universally acknowledged.) Emotions affect people's judgments because they relate to both pleasure and pain. The most powerful emotions in this respect are anger and mildness, love and hate, fear and confidence, shame and honor, benevolence (χάρις) and unkindness, mercy and indignation, and envy and emulation (*Rhet.* 2.1.5–2.11.7).[17] Each of these pairs manifests itself in three respects: dispositions of mind, people who arouse these emotions, and the occasions on which we are prone to the emotions. Aristotle's classifications prove valuable, not because every ancient Mediterranean speaker knew them, but because they broadly represent the sensibilities of ancient speakers and audiences.

Brian Vickers has shown that the Latin oratorical tradition, represented most articulately by Cicero, elevated pathos even beyond the level it attains in Aristotle. Cicero's *De oratore* features a character that claims the orator's virtue consists primarily "in rousing men's hearts to anger, hatred, or indignation, or in recalling them from these same passions to mildness and mercy."[18] Thus the accomplished orator must master psychology. Cicero offers his own partial list of emotions: hatred or love, ill will or well wishing, fear or hope, desire or aversion, joy or sorrow, and compassion or the wish to punish (*De or.* 2.44.185, cf. 2.50.206).[19] Cicero frankly acknowledges that people make more decisions based upon emotion than upon empirical realities, authorities, or laws (2.42.178). Along this line Quintilian distinguishes rhetoric from scholarly discourse, as rhetoric requires moving the audience: If one wants to win people over to the just and the true, one must "allure them by gratification, attract them by force, and occasionally excite their feelings" (*Inst. or.* 5.14.29).[20]

John of Patmos probably did not consult the rhetorical handbooks of his day for guidance in composing the Apocalypse. While we ought not employ Aristotle or Cicero to create a binding interpretive grid for pathos in Revelation's address to its audience, their sensibilities do hold significant promise.[21] Specifically, my own study of how Revelation "speaks to" its audience reveals the importance of fear and emulation. Revelation draws on fear in the obvious sense that it warns its audience of potential judgment, but it also employs fear of John's enemies to build solidarity with John's program. As for emulation, Revelation encourages its audience to identify with the status and accomplishments of some characters in its story, accompanied by aversion to the values and deeds of others. We may describe this process in terms of identification and counter-identification.

HOW REVELATION "SPEAKS TO" ITS AUDIENCE

The Apocalypse is remarkable for the various voices that address its audience directly.[22] John, Revelation's primary narrating voice, obviously speaks not only at the book's introduction and conclusion but also, occasionally, within the vision itself. The audience also hears directly from Jesus and from other heavenly voices. Revelation demonstrates yet other ways of "speaking to" its audience, and these multiple devices carry fascinating potential for affecting its historical audience.

Direct Address

At the most general level, Revelation addresses its audience as a letter, naming its recipients—seven churches in seven cities—specifically (1:11). This is most apparent at the book's beginning and ending. In that sense the entire book addresses the audience directly. Yet most of Revelation conveys a third-person visionary report, as John tells the audience what he sees and hears (1:2). Within this framework John occasionally speaks directly to the churches. So does the risen Christ, particularly, though not exclusively, in the letters to the churches (2:1–3:22). So also do heavenly beings speak on a number of occasions (5:2, 11; 9:14; 16:5; 17:1, 7; 18:1-2; 22:8-9).

John himself speaks directly to the audience by framing the Apocalypse in terms of blessing and curse. Revelation 1:1-9 compactly informs the audience of the nature of the book (a revealed vision), its import (one finds blessing in reading, hearing, and doing what it says), the book's relationship to the seven churches (it addresses them as an epistle), and John's relationship to them (he shares their status). Very near the book's conclusion (22:17-19), John invites the audience to join the call for Christ's return, warning them that deviation from the book's contents invites dire consequences. The last phrase of the Apocalypse, "The grace of the Lord Jesus [be] with everyone" (22:21), reminds the audience of Revelation's epistolary nature. The whole of Revelation addresses them directly.

That is the *logical* content of these framing addresses. In terms of pathos, their potential *effects* are multiple. As I have argued in other places, Revelation's address demands that the audience adopt a conflicted posture with respect to John and his message. The message offers status (royalty, priesthood, dominion) and blessing, elevating the audience to share John's status and recognizing their common distress (θλῖψις), but it also requires their submission. Perhaps compensating for John's assertion of authority, Revelation also invites the audience to own its message. The readers, like John, receive the extraordinary privilege of esoteric knowledge through the vision's specific address to them. If, like John, they share in the struggles of faithful witness (1:9), they are invited to own an alternative status as kings, priests, and witnesses. The call for submission accompanies an invitation to exalted status.

Direct address to the audience in the book's body takes a different tone. It still invites the audience's participation, but it also calls forth their discernment. Having introduced the dragon and the beast, John echoes the speech of Jesus in chapters 2–3: "If someone has an ear, let him hear" (13:9). Then John announces that those who capture and kill others face reciprocal fates; the saints' endurance and faith in the face of beastly violence apparently rests upon this confidence (13:10). In a similar case of direct discourse, the saints' endurance grounds itself in the knowledge that God will exact vengeance upon those who yield allegiance to the beast (14:11-12). Revelation 18:20 calls for the apostles and prophets to rejoice because of God's vengeance on their behalf. This also may pose a case of direct address, as Revelation loosely identifies its audience with the prophets' fate (16:6; 18:24). Likewise, Revelation 20:6 pronounces blessing upon the martyrs, those who participate in the first resurrection (20:4-5). This blessing implicitly invites the audience to envision themselves as potential martyrs (12:11, 17; 17:6; 19:10).

John also calls forth the audience's "wisdom" or discerning capacity with two symbolic riddles (13:18; 17:9). To modern eyes the second instance seems fairly straightforward: Recognizing that "seven hills" alludes to Rome, the city on seven hills, requires a modest level of "wisdom." But decoding "the number of the beast" poses a far greater challenge. The most popular interpretation of 666 among scholars—*Neron Caesar*—would have required terribly creative accounting from any ordinary hearer of Revelation. These riddles reach out to the audience, rewarding them for their code-breaking abilities. I am at a loss to estimate their larger effect on the audience, though I can offer a suggestion. Perhaps the presentation of an easy riddle *after* a nearly impossible one resembles the precarious balance of identification and submission that Revelation has already called forth. In other words, the riddles invite the audience to enter the world of the Apocalypse: The easier one rewards them with a sense of ownership, while the more difficult chastens excessive levels of comfort with its message.

Informed by Aristotle and Cicero, we might say that John's direct address to the audience nurtures a tense combination of fear and hope, aversion and emulation. On the obverse of blessing lies threat. While John offers himself as one with whom to identify, he insists upon the audience's submission.

The risen Jesus also speaks directly to the audience, most conspicuously in the letters to the churches but also in some other contexts. The letters to the churches pose a notorious problem.[23] At a literal level they generally, albeit inconsistently, address not the churches but the *angels* of the churches. Careful attention to the modes of address in these letters, however, shows that they assess the conditions and performance of those churches. Perhaps these angels are the heavenly caretakers of their churches, held accountable for the churches themselves; perhaps they serve as a literary device through which to address the churches. In any event, I read the letters to the churches as direct address to the audience, specifically in the case of members of particular churches and generally through the common point of view they pose for all of the churches. For example, the letter to the church in Ephesus (2:1-7) directs its address entirely to the angel of that church in the singular, just as Revelation 2:8 speaks directly to the angel of the church in Smyrna in the singular. On the other hand, 2:10 warns the church of its coming distress in the plural. Revelation 2:14-15 bears special attention:

> But I hold a few things against you [sing.], that you [sing.] have there those [implied] holding the teaching of Balaam. . . . Also you [emphatic sing.] have those [implied] holding the teaching of the Nicolaitans in a similar manner. (author's trans.)

One might object that 2:14-15 does not represent direct address but, instead, allows the audience to overhear information concerning themselves. In this narrow context such an objection would be accurate. But 2:23-25—the most intense invective in these letters—speak to the audience in the second-person plural. Thus I conclude that these letters address John's audience directly.

And what of these letters? Essentially they reinforce Revelation's combination of blessing and cursing. This pattern at once exhorts the audience toward faithfulness, even as it admonishes them against laxness and offers comfort in their distress.[24] The letters are the only part of Revelation that address the specific conduct, circumstances, debates, and challenges within the seven churches. By speaking directly to the churches through the voice of Jesus, rather than simply in John's own voice, they amplify what is at stake in how the audience responds. "Those with ears, let them hear what the Spirit says to the churches" (2:7, 11, 17, 29; 3:6, 13, 22).

Other instances of direct address by Jesus serve largely to keep the audience perched on the edge of fear and hope. Revelation 16:15 warns of Christ's stealthy coming and blesses those who are prepared. In my view, Revelation 22:7a, 12-13, 16, 20 all feature direct discourse from Jesus. These brief speeches attest to the imminence of Jesus' return, Jesus' preeminence, and the book's reliability.[25]

Other heavenly voices address Revelation's audience directly. After the announcement of Babylon's fall, a heavenly voice in 18:4-5 basically summarizes the message of the whole book: "Come out from her, my people. . . ." The voice continues in the second-person plural, calling the audience to "give her [Babylon] a torment and mourning to a similar degree" (18:7; the unit extends from 18:4-8). In chapter 19 a voice from the throne calls God's slaves to praise God (19:5); Revelation's audience attends to that voice alongside a great heavenly multitude. Through this revelatory moment, the audience observes its own worship.

In conclusion, various voices address Revelation's audience directly, and for diverse ends. Fear and hope combine with emulation to draw the audience into the book's vision and its call for resistance. Those ends include emphasizing the stakes involved in their response to the vision, inviting them to identify their own role as potential participants in the vision, soliciting their discernment, and reinforcing the book's larger message of pure resistance and faithful witness.

Pointing and Showing

John routinely reminds the audience of what he has heard (ἤκουσα) and seen (εἶδον).[26] However, a subcategory of direct discourse occurs when multiple voices invite the audience to "behold" (ἰδού) aspects of the vision. As a dramatic narrative Revelation routinely places its imagery "before the eyes" of the audience; ἰδού lays particular emphasis on key points. When paying attention to who calls for the audience's attention, we see that ἰδού connotes different things depending upon who voices it.

When ἰδού issues from John, it nearly always focuses the audience's attention upon a turning point or some especially significant point in the visionary narrative. The first instance proclaims Jesus' imminent return (1:7), while the second and third open John's heavenly tour (4:1, 2). Subsequent cases introduce three of the four horses and their riders (6:2, 5, 8), the countless multitude (7:9), the dragon (12:3), the Lamb (14:1), and the Son of Man (14:14). Other examples mark transitions from one woe to another (9:12; 11:14).

On the lips of Jesus, ἰδού focuses attention upon urgent values admonished or exhorted. The term occurs six times in the letters to the churches. Jesus warns the church in Smyrna of impending persecution (2:10), admonishes the church in Thyatira not to share "Jezebel's" fate (2:22), and encourages the lukewarm church in Laodicea that he still awaits their response (3:20). In a cluster of three instances in three Greek sentences, Jesus assures an open door to the Philadelphians, promising the submission of their (apparently) Jewish enemies (3:8-9). Beyond the letters to the churches, ἰδού reinforces the urgency of Jesus' imminent return, again mixing warning with encouragement (16:15; 22:7, 12).

Other heavenly voices rarely pronounce ἰδού. In Revelation 5:5 one of the elders comforts John by announcing that the Lion of Judah is able to open the scroll. In chapter 21 a "great voice" from the throne, probably the voice of God, announces God's dwelling among mortals (v. 3), making all things new (v. 5). Throne imagery in Revelation is notoriously difficult to parse. One naturally expects the throne to be God's seat, as 1:4-5 implies (cf. 5:13; 7:10). Jesus, however, claims God's throne as his own (3:21; cf. 22:1, 3) and stands in the throne's midst (5:6), though he receives the scroll from "the one seated upon the throne" (5:7).

In John's voice ἰδού directs the audience's attention to transitional moments and significant characters within the story. From Jesus, ἰδού emphasizes the weight attached to their response to his message.

IDENTIFICATION AND COUNTER-IDENTIFICATION

Revelation relies upon a complex web of identification and counter-identification, encouraging the audience to align itself for and against specific characters within the story and the values that transcend it.[27] In Greco-Roman terms, this dimension of Revelation involves emulation (Aristotle) and aversion (Cicero). If Jesus is the truly "faithful witness" (1:5; 3:14), Antipas' martyrdom emulates that of his Lord (2:13). So does John the visionary, who faithfully testifies to "all that he saw" (1:2, 9; 22:6). John invites the audience as well to imagine itself as a potential witness (6:9; 12:11, 17; 17:6; 19:10; 20:4). (The case of the two witnesses in chapter 11 is more difficult, though they too may function as potential models for the audience.) If John is God's slave (1:1), as are the prophets and the angelic interpreter (10:7; 22:9), so also may the audience stand as God's servant (1:1; 2:20; 7:3; 11:18; 19:2, 5; 22:3, 6).

Fundamentally, Revelation's rhetoric of *identification* invites the audience to participate in the book's story and its program. Consider the praise of the "few" in Sardis who have kept their garments clean (3:4), as well as that voiced by the 144,000 and the numberless multitude (7:4-9; cf. 15:2-8; 18:20). These groups encourage the audience's emulation. The audience may aspire to participate in the prayers of the saints, which elicit a spectacular, divine response (8:3-5). The audience might also desire elevation to angelic status (19:10; 22:8). Revelation even encourages identification with the martyrs, the "blessed and holy" who share the first resurrection (20:6; cf. 6:9-11). Short of that exalted status, it offers inclusion among the saints who worship the Lamb in the new Jerusalem (22:3-5).

Identification mingles with fear at several points in the Apocalypse. Those who oppose the Lamb attack God's people, often with deadly effect. The way of death leads to their conquest (12:11). The faithful face attack from the horrific dragon (12:17), as well as conquest and slaughter by the beast (13:7, 15) and the whore (17:6; 18:24). Even after the millennium, the saints endure a final assault (20:9). Beyond the well-founded fear of what may happen if the Lamb rejects them, Revelation seeks to harden the audience's resolve against its enemies by portraying such threats in dire terms.[28]

Counter-identification, as I use the term here, occurs when Revelation associates people or conduct, often though not always in symbolic guise, with values the audience would likely detest or avoid. For example, John's Christian opponents include "Balaam," the "Nicolaitans," and "Jezebel." Jesus promises harsh judgment on them and on those who adopt their teachings (2:16, 22-23). We have seen how Revelation 3:4 praises the "few" in Sardis who have not "soiled their garments"; these stand over against the (presumably) many who have. The audience knows that those lacking God's seal will endure horrific plagues (9:4), while the violent (11:18; 13:10), those who worship the beast (13:8: 20:4-5), and those whose names are missing from the Book of Life (20:15)—not to mention the balance of the earth's sinners (21:8)—will face judgment.

Perhaps Revelation's most prominent, and most telling, case of counter-identification involves "the inhabitants of the earth" (3:10; 6:10; 8:13; 11:10; 13:8, 12, 14; 17:2, 8). Held guilty for the blood of the martyrs (6:10; 11:10), they worship the beast (13:8, 12, 14) and cavort with the whore (17:2, 8). They await judgment soon and presumably at the end as well. It is hardly overreading to suggest that Revelation's rhetoric concerning these "inhabitants" reflects the book's dramatically sectarian outlook. The Book of Revelation fosters aversion of the larger society, considering all outsiders as enemies.

Burke has argued that identification and counter-identification lie at the heart of rhetoric. Skillful persuaders invite their audiences into shared interests, identities, and dispositions, and they discourage competing interests, identities, and dispositions.[29] Revelation invites emulation of the martyrs, heavenly beings, and the community of the saints, but it stirs revulsion against the earth's general population. It encourages participation in the saints' prayer and witness, calling for withdrawal from the larger society and its evils. Revelation urges its audience to fear powers beyond the Christian community, solidifying identity and resolve among the churches.

CONCLUSION

One can only imagine how Revelation's first audiences responded when they heard it read or performed aloud. We cannot know for sure how friendly they were to John or to his program before receiving the Apocalypse, nor can we assess how they were moved by it. Everything we say about pathos and the Apocalypse is unavoidably speculative.

I do think it highly probable, however, that Revelation addressed primarily a group of churches in Asia Minor and that its author intended to intervene in their communal lives by changing their dispositions and behaviors. In other words, it makes sense to read Revelation rhetorically. Without knowing the intentions of John or the attitudes of his first audiences, we may at least look for signs of rhetorical design in the book's formal features. In this case, I have chosen a fairly limited dimension of Revelation: How does its literary design reflect the potential to move its audience through its mode of address?

This study calls attention to how Revelation speaks directly to its audience through the voices of John the narrator, Jesus, and other heavenly figures; how Revelation invites the audience to appreciate or participate in its story world by directing the listeners' attention at key moments, and how Revelation builds networks of identification and counter-identification between its audience and the values or characters within its story world. These devices all enhance Revelation's larger aims: to foster communal resistance to and withdrawal from the imperial and polytheistic environment of its audience. Among other things, Revelation promotes a combination of fear and hope, aversion and emulation. Revelation appeals to fear by reminding the audience of divine judgment and warning it to be wary of imperial authorities and their neighbors. This fear of authorities and neighbors seems designed to create an aversion to the larger society. On the other hand, Revelation fosters hope by promising blessing and inclusion. This hope is closely tied to emulation, as the Apocalypse encourages the audience to identify with John, with Jesus, with the martyrs, and with all the saints—all of whom are destined for honor and blessing.

Of all the dimensions of biblical rhetoric, I suspect that pathos may prove most elusive for analysis. For one thing, it demands attention to the values and sensibilities of ancient persons. Despite intense, current investigation of ancient social conventions, such cross-cultural interpretation implies a challenging level of speculation. It also puts interpreters on the precarious spot of building links between texts and their actual or potential effects. Those of us who received our training during the apex of literary theory are especially leery of advancing claims concerning textual intentions and effects. Nevertheless, authors do design texts to affect their audiences, and pathos represents an essential dimension of that process. In this case, an assessment of how Revelation engages its audience complements our appreciation of its larger social and religious aims.

Notes

[1] George A. Kennedy, *New Testament Interpretation through Rhetorical Criticism* (Chapel Hill: University of North Carolina Press, 1984).

[2] David E. Aune, "Rhetorical Criticism," in *The Westminster Dictionary of New Testament and Early Christian Literature and Rhetoric* (Louisville, Ky.: Westminster John Knox, 2003), 416–17; cf. C. Clifton Black, *The Rhetoric of the Gospel: Theological Artistry in the Gospels and Acts* (St. Louis: Chalice, 2001), 4–12. For a similar discussion with a focus on Revelation, see Edith M. Humphrey, "In Search of a Voice: Rhetoric through Sight and Sound in Revelation 11:15–12:17," in *Vision and Persuasion: Rhetorical Dimensions of Apocalyptic Discourse* (ed. Greg Carey and L. Gregory Bloomquist; St. Louis: Chalice, 1999), 141–60.

[3] A developing alternative, socio-rhetorical criticism, seeks to integrate the culture-specific conventions of Greco-Roman rhetoric with attention to literary patterns of repetition and progression. See the seminal work of Vernon K. Robbins, *The Tapestry of Early Christian Discourse: Rhetoric, Society, and Ideology* (London: Routledge, 1996), idem, *Exploring the Texture of Texts: A Guide to Socio-Rhetorical Interpretation* (Valley Forge, Pa.: Trinity Press International, 1996). For application of such an approach to the book of Revelation and apocalyptic discourse in general, see David A. deSilva, "Toward a Socio-Rhetorical Taxonomy of Divine Intervention: Miracle Discourse in the Revelation to John," in *Fabrics of Discourse: Essays in Honor of Vernon K. Robbins* (ed. David B. Gowler, L. Gregory Bloomquist, and Duane F. Watson; Harrisburg, Pa.: Trinity Press International, 2003), 303–16; Duane F. Watson, ed., *The Intertexture of Apocalyptic Discourse in the New Testament* (SBLSymS 14; Atlanta: Society of Biblical Literature, 2002); and Carey and Bloomquist, eds., *Vision and Persuasion*.

[4] Among them, chronologically: John T. Kirby, "The Rhetorical Situations of Revelation 1–3," *NTS* 34 (1988): 197–207; Robert M. Royalty Jr., "The Rhetoric of Revelation," *SBLSP* 36 (1997): 596–617; Loren L. Johns, "The Lamb in the Rhetorical Program on the Apocalypse of John," *SBLSP* 37 (1998): 762–84; Ben Witherington III, *Revelation* (New Cambridge Bible Commentary; New York: Cambridge University Press, 2003); Antonius King Wai Siew, *The War Between the Two Beasts and the Two Witnesses: A Chiastic Reading of Revelation 11.1–14.5* (JSNTSup 283; New York: T&T Clark, 2005).

[5] Elisabeth Schüssler Fiorenza, "The Followers of the Lamb: Visionary Rhetoric and Socio-Political Situation," *Semeia* 36 (1986): 147–74. See also her critique of efforts to conform Revelation to ancient rhetorical categories in *Revelation: Vision of a Just World* (Proclamation Commentaries; Minneapolis: Fortress, 1991), 20–37, cited in Johns, "The Lamb in the Rhetorical Program on the Apocalypse of John," 763.

[6] See Paul Duff, *Who Rides the Beast? Prophetic Rivalry and the Rhetoric of Crisis in the Churches of the Apocalypse* (Oxford: Oxford University Press, 2001); Robert M. Royalty Jr., *The Streets of Heaven: The Ideology of Wealth in the Apocalypse of John* (Macon, Ga.: Mercer University Press, 1998). My own work largely fits this model; see especially *Elusive Apocalypse: Reading Authority in the Revelation to John* (StABH 15; Macon, Ga.: Mercer University Press, 1999). See also David A. deSilva, "The Construction and Social Function of a Counter-Cosmos in the Revelation of John," *Forum* 9.1-2 (1993): 47–61.

⁷ Stephen D. O'Leary, *Arguing the Apocalypse: A Theory of Millennial Rhetoric* (New York: Oxford University Press, 1994).

⁸ Kennedy, *New Testament Interpretation*, 10–11. Aune observes this as well ("Rhetorical Criticism," 417).

⁹ George A. Kennedy, *Comparative Rhetoric: An Historical and Cross-Cultural Introduction* (New York: Oxford University Press, 1997 [1998]).

¹⁰ Kennedy, *Comparative Rhetoric*, 90.

¹¹ Kennedy, *Comparative Rhetoric*, 71.

¹² Greg Carey, *Ultimate Things: An Introduction to Jewish and Christian Apocalyptic Literature* (St. Louis: Chalice, 2005).

¹³ O'Leary, *Arguing the Apocalypse*.

¹⁴ By "narrators" I mean to set aside the problem of authorship in apocalyptic works, almost all of which are pseudonymous. See Greg Carey, "Apocalyptic Ethos," *SBLSP* 37 (1998): 731–61.

¹⁵ Loren L. Johns, *The Lamb Christology of the Apocalypse of John: An Investigation into Its Origins and Rhetorical Force* (WUNT 167; Tübingen: Mohr [Siebeck], 2003), 157.

¹⁶ See Stephen Pattemore, *The People of God in the Apocalypse* (SNTSMS 128; New York: Cambridge University Press, 2004), esp. 64–67. Pattemore, however, does not emphasize Revelation's rhetorical dimensions, even less its potential for pathos.

¹⁷ See the brief discussion in Brian Vickers, *In Defence of Rhetoric* (Oxford: Clarendon, 1988), 24. Thomas H. Olbricht identifies six, not seven, pairs of opposites in Aristotle, positing shame and benevolence as opposites and eliminating honor and unkindness from the list ("Pathos as Proof in Greco-Roman Rhetoric," in *Paul and Pathos* [ed. Thomas H. Olbricht and Jerry L. Sumney; SBLSymS 16; Atlanta: Society of Biblical Literature, 2001], 15).

¹⁸ Cicero, *De oratore* 1.12.53 (trans. E. W. Sutton and H. Rackham; LCL; Cambridge and London: Harvard University Press/Heinemann, 1942); cf. 2.44.186.

¹⁹ This list came to my attention through Olbricht, "Pathos as Proof," 17.

²⁰ Trans. John Shelby Watson (http://honeyl.public.iastate.edu/quintilian/index.html). The present discussion relies heavily upon Vickers, *In Defence of Rhetoric*, 74–80, though I have corrected Vickers's reference to *Inst. or.* 5.14.29. Cf. Jakob Wisse, *Ethos and Pathos from Aristotle to Cicero* (Amsterdam: Hakkert, 1989).

²¹ For a persuasive argument to this effect regarding Paul, consult Steven J. Kraftchick, "Πάθη in Paul: The Emotional Logic in 'Original Argument,'" in *Paul and Pathos* (ed. Olbricht and Sumney), 39–68.

²² Dal Lee provides, to date, the most systematic study of Revelation's narrative asides: *The Narrative Asides in the Book of Revelation* (Lanham, Md.: University Press of America, 2002). Lee cites many more examples than does this study, including clarifications and explanations that I do not regard as calls to the audience, such as "And the name of the star is called Apsinthos" (8:11a). However, these common features of Revelation do hold potential for drawing the audience's participation into the vision, thus fostering their goodwill. Choosing to study the role of Revelation's narrator, Lee does not investigate other voices that speak to Revelation's audience. For direct address, Lee cites only 13:9-10; for indirect address, only 22:18-19. For further assessment, see my review of his study in *CBQ* 65 (2003): 643–44.

[23] See the excursus, "The 'Angels' of the Seven Churches," in *Revelation* (ed. David E. Aune; WBC 52A; Waco, Tex.: Word, 1997), 108–12.

[24] Duff, *Who Rides the Beast?*, includes an excellent study of the diverse modes of address among the letters to the churches.

[25] Revelation 22:7a ("Behold, I am coming soon") sounds like it must convey Jesus' voice, though the literary context of 22:6-7 implies that the speaking voice is that of the interpreting angel from 21:9. As Gregory Beale points out, Revelation 22:6-21 lacks an "explicit flow of thought" but instead voices "a series of repeated exhortations based on prior portions of the Apocalypse" (*The Book of Revelation: A Commentary on the Greek Text* [NIGTC; Grand Rapids, Mich.: Eerdmans, 1999], 1123). I agree, and on this basis judge 22:6 as the angel's voice, 22:7a as Jesus', and 22:7b as John's.

[26] Carey, *Ultimate Things*, 109.

[27] Carey, *Ultimate Things*, 118–28.

[28] On the role of fear in contemporary public discourse in the United States, see George Lakoff, *Don't Think of an Elephant: Know Your Values and Frame the Debate* (White River Junction, Vt.: Chelsea Green, 2004), 6–8, 52–68.

[29] Kenneth Burke, *A Rhetoric of Motives* (repr., Berkeley: University of California Press, 1969), 35, 46, 55, 67.

CHAPTER 11

AFTERWORD

George A. Kennedy

The invitation from the editors, Clifton Black and Duane Watson, to contribute an afterword to this volume offers me a welcome opportunity to thank them and the authors of the chapters for their thoughtful contributions to the rhetorical criticism of the New Testament—a minor school of biblical interpretation that I seem inadvertently to have fathered in classrooms in Chapel Hill. Without underestimating the fine scholarship of others, the development of rhetorical interpretation owes more to the patient dedication of Duane Watson than to any other laborer in this vineyard, and it thus is a special pleasure to acknowledge once again his fine work and to express my pleasure in his friendship.

Professor Thomas Olbricht has encapsulated some features of my education and professional activities that provided a background to my studies of biblical rhetoric.[1] In the preface to *Greek Rhetoric under Christian Emperors*,[2] as he notes, I looked back nostalgically over sources of my interest in rhetoric, something not common among students of classics in the mid-twentieth century. Among other things I mentioned being taken to church as a boy, "where I became an early, if sometimes impatient, critic of the eloquence of the pulpit." That was in the Methodist church (at the time, Methodist Episcopal), or sometimes the Congregational church (that is, the First Church of Christ) in Simsbury, Connecticut, a pleasant country town near Hartford where I grew up. My experience of preaching was greatly enlarged as an undergraduate at Princeton, where I regularly attended the chapel services, which retained little trace of their austere Presbyterian ancestry.[3] The pulpit was often occupied by leading American religious leaders from many denominations invited to come and speak at the university, but I confess that I was attracted more by the superb music directed by the noted organist, Carl Weinrich, and have little memory of what these worthy divines said. The only exception is one aged Congregational minister who was, or had been, I believe, president of some small New England college and whose theme was that "man has a right to live in a habitable portion of the globe"; whether this included New Jersey I do not recall. I had not realized it was a Christian doctrine, and I thought the universal application of the thesis questionable. I also occasionally attended services of some of the local churches, brought there by friends of different faiths who had some illusory hope of converting me to Episcopalianism, Lutheranism, or (least likely) Christian Science. In addition to going to church, at Princeton I took a course in Christian ethics with Paul Ramsey—my only exposure to the thought of Kierkegaard—began reading New Testament Greek with Paul R. Coleman-Norton, and as a senior enjoyed a fine course on Ancient Near Eastern History, taught by Cuyler Young.

Despite my lack of memory of details, I think it would be fair to say that the sermons I heard in Simsbury and Princeton in the 1930s and 1940s, though orthodox in principle, were almost never concerned with theology and avoided tasteless evangelical enthusiasms. The preachers drew on the Bible, and sometimes on secular literature, current events, or personal experiences, to teach Christian ethics and how to deal with the challenges of life. In Simsbury and in most Princeton churches, the Apostles' Creed was regularly recited. I had mental reservations about this, and I sometimes wondered what other members of the congregation made of it, but I hesitated to ask. Our prayers were regularly addressed to God the Father, and though they sometimes ended "in Jesus' name, Amen," I do not think we ever prayed directly to Jesus, whom my father referred to as "a remarkable young man." Later in life I found some people praying to Jesus, and it seemed shocking to me. My impression in Simsbury had been that the only part of Christian doctrine that much interested folks was the immortality of the soul. It became clear over time that this was not regarded as being brought before a divine judge and joining a chorus in white gowns with harps and wings: among my early acquaintances, the afterlife was idealized as a kind of ongoing family reunion where husband and wife, mother and child, would be happily reunited. After a generation or two, their shades probably slowly faded away so the gathering would not become too crowded. These views, of course, were contrary to New Testament doctrine and more like those of some classical Greeks. As time passed I came to regard any concept of an immortal soul as implausible, something whose role in society has been ambiguous, at best, and often exploited in the self-interest of the powerful.

I continued my dilettantish, undemanding survey of religious services when in graduate school at Harvard. Before a nine o'clock class I often went to "daily prayers" in the choir of the University Chapel to sing a hymn (which I enjoyed), hear a reading from Scripture, and listen to a brief homily by some member of the faculty; and sometimes on Sundays I went to hear the Preacher to the University in the Harvard chapel—Harvard being Harvard less often invited outsiders to its pulpit than had Princeton. More often, I visited the handsome historic churches of Boston—Old North, New Old South, Arlington Street, Trinity Church, occasionally the Church of the Advent (taken there by my avid High Church roommate), and especially King's Chapel, which combined the liberal theology of the Unitarians with the eloquence of the eighteenth-century Anglican prayer book. Although the exterior of the building is a forbidding gray, inside one discovers, in elegant Georgian style, one of the most beautiful interior spaces in Boston. Until the Revolutionary War this was the church of the British governor (whose box pew survives) and the Anglican community of Boston, but after the war, in a burst of post-enlightenment rationalism, it became the first self-proclaimed Unitarian church in the United States and kept—and still keeps—the Prayer Book but with creeds and references to the Trinity deleted. In Cambridge I also sampled the First Parish (Unitarian), where Emerson had given his American Scholar address (1837); Christ Church (Episcopal), where George Washington had worshiped; and other local churches—once even Catholic mass with a friend who had recently converted. The Mass was still celebrated in Latin at this time. The church was crowded, the congregation seemed to pay little attention to the service, and the priests could hardly be heard. A few times I went with my High Church friends to compline at the Cowley Father's monastery on Charles River Drive, a soothing way to end the day.

When I was a young faculty member at Haverford College the undergraduates were expected to attend a specified number of Quaker "Fifth Day" (i.e., Thursday) meetings, and because they had to go I thought a faculty member ought to go, at least sometimes. I have a great respect for the Friends and developed a warm admiration for Henry Cadbury, one of the most distinguished religious scholars of his age, then living in retirement in Haverford, but Quaker meeting in the Philadelphia tradition was, shall we say, not distinguished homiletically—sometimes the hour was passed in silence, and I missed singing hymns. At North Carolina, where the original college chapel building survives but the university no longer sponsored any religious services, I felt no inclination to frequent the local churches except for weddings, funerals, and special services. Although I have never myself given a sermon, I probably could; I did once conduct a funeral, and on another occasion (at the request of my Anglo-Catholic sister-in-law) I substituted for the organist at the communion service at a small church in Chapel Hill, which was a refuge for those Episcopalians to whom women priests and the revised Prayer Book were anathema.

While in Chapel Hill my progress into more serious study of Christianity was accelerated by an invitation to participate in a seminar, lasting several days at Trinity University in San Antonio, on the relationship among the gospels as seen by scholars from disciplines other than religious studies. My topic was "Classical and Christian Source Criticism" treated comparatively, the preparation for which led me for the first time to read Eusebius and other early church historians. In the paper I stressed the importance of *hypomnēmata*, note-taking, and the redaction of notes into narrative or other discourse by Greek and Latin prose writers, which provided a partial model for the composition of the gospels. It was in this talk and the published paper[4] that I uttered what is perhaps the most often quoted of my *sententiae*: that "ancient writers sometimes meant what they said and occasionally knew what they were talking about." I intended this to apply to the church historians of antiquity and left open the question of whether it should apply to the evangelists. Today I would be inclined to say that the first clause can well be applied to them, the second more doubtfully. Subsequently, consistent with my belief that rhetoric was a universal phenomenon, not solely a Western tradition, I began research on what became *Comparative Rhetoric: An Historical and Cross-Cultural Introduction*,[5] my most original and potentially most important book. It includes chapters on animal communication; the rhetorical origins of human speech; oral rhetoric in traditional cultures in Australia, Africa, and the Americas; and written rhetoric in the ancient Near East (Sumeria, Egypt, and Palestine), China, India, and Greece. Necessarily I raised the issue of the rhetoric of religious traditions (except Islam, which fell outside the chronological scope of my study), and this in turn led me back to the Bible.

By this time I had retired from Chapel Hill and had in 1994 sought refuge from the Carolina climate at the foot of the Rocky Mountains in Fort Collins, where Colorado State University provided me an agreeable environment and library resources. After completing *Comparative Rhetoric*, much of my time went into preparation of revised editions of my two best-selling works, *Classical Rhetoric and Its Christian and Secular Tradition from Ancient to Modern Times*, and Aristotle's *On Rhetoric: A Theory of Civic Discourse*. I also published a book on a subject that amused me and had become something of a hobby: *Fictitious Authors and Imaginary Novels in French, English, and American Literature from the 18th to the Start of the 21st Century*.[6] This brought me to the study of nineteenth-century literature and thought in England and America. In the process I became fascinated with the religious crisis in the Church of England in the nineteenth century and the numerous references to it in English fiction. It was the time of the ritualist or Oxford movement, of the shocking conversion of John Henry Newman to Roman Catholicism (1845), of the Broad Church movement that sought (unsuccessfully) to provide a home in the national church for clergy and communicants who could no longer accept the Athanasian Creed and the inconsistencies between Scripture and the Thirty-Nine Articles, and of the abandonment of the Church by numerous distinguished individuals, among them Newman's brother Francis, who moved in the liberal direction.

Of the many novels in which soul-searching and conversions in one direction or another are depicted, the finest in my estimation is *Robert Elsmere* (1888) by Mrs. Humphrey Ward. Elsmere is depicted as a graduate of Oxford and an Anglican priest, but his studies of historical criticism in German, French, and English lead him to resign his cure, leave the church, and found the "New Brotherhood of Christ," a religious and educational settlement in London. Mrs. Ward, who later founded such a settlement house, was the granddaughter of Dr. Thomas Arnold of Rugby, an opponent of ritualism and one of the first in England to view the Scriptures "as fit a subject as any other book for free inquiry and the exercise of the individual judgment,"[7] something that opens up the possibility of rhetorical criticism. Matthew Arnold, the famous poet and essayist, was his son, thus Mrs. Ward's uncle, and the author of two closely argued attacks on traditional Christianity: *Literature and Dogma* (1873) and *God and the Bible* (1875), both highly controversial in mid-Victorian England. Matthew Arnold, Mrs. Ward, Benjamin Jowett at Oxford, and many other "modernists" were convinced that the victory of liberal religion over orthodoxy, the abandonment of creeds and much dogmatic theology, and the development of Christianity into an enlightened, humanistic social movement based on the moral teachings of Jesus were only a matter of time—a hope that proved unrealistic in the popular needs for religion during the horrors of war and depression that engulfed the people of Britain in the twentieth century, followed in times of peace and prosperity by a decline in interest in any form of religion on the part of much of the British public.

My interest in nineteenth-century religious movements—including Transcendentalism and other developments in America—led me to begin reading important works of historical criticism: David Strauss' first *Life of Jesus* (1835–1836),[8] Ludwig Feuerbach's *Essence of Christianity* (1841), both in the fine translations (1846 and 1854, respectively) of the novelist George Eliot, and Albert Schweitzer's *Quest of the Historical Jesus* (first German edition, 1906; revision, 1913), with its many expositions of biblical criticism from Reimarus in the eighteenth century to Schweitzer's own time.[9] The inconsistencies and improbabilities of much biblical narrative were the inspiration for new, more historically and rationally based interpretations. Strauss' *Life* is particularly important for rhetorical criticism in its introduction of "myth" as a Hegelian synthesis between the thesis of supernaturalism, the antithesis of rationalism, and a new synthesis of mythical interpretation.[10] The need to read the creation story and other portions of the Old Testament as myth was already gaining ground in the early nineteenth century; Strauss applied the technique to the New Testament, including the tales of Jesus' nativity and resurrection. Soon after, Bruno Bauer "built his *Criticism of the Gospel History of the Synoptists*" (1841–1842), to quote Schweitzer, "on the site which Strauss had leveled."[11] Bauer came to view the gospels—John first, then the Synoptics—as literary creations, something resembling, but shorter and less literary than, the historical novels that were appearing in his time. Feuerbach's *Essence of Christianity* is an early classic of the anthropology of religion: it argues that God or gods have no objective reality. They are projections of the human psyche, imaginative searches for inspiration, comfort, and help in confronting death and in times of trouble or rejoicing. One of the most startling parts of the work is an extended chapter attacking the whole Christian concept of "faith," which Feuerbach argues, with some cogency, has been the source of prejudice, bigotry, violence, and oppression on the part of religious zealots from the time of the apostles to his own day.

From an early time Christians showed an inability to be content with pure monotheism and began the creation of a panoply of additional gods and demi-gods to fill their needs, with some regarded as the patron of some human activity and thus replacements for the pagan gods with their special domains. Among Christians the process began, in my personal view, with the multiplication of one Jewish god into three persons—Father, Son, and Holy Ghost—each to be adored and capable of independent (but presumably coordinated) action and intervention in human affairs. The cult of the divine Virgin Mary was already flourishing in the second century, as seen in the Proto-Gospel of James, in which her immaculate conception, her earthly career, and her bodily assumption to heaven are described in detail.[12] The apostles and martyrs of the church became the first of a long series of saints who, in return for the adoration of the faithful, conferred favors upon them, performed miracles, and sometimes appeared to admonish or warn individuals. Christians often prayed to a patron saint who might intervene on their behalf with the divinities of higher rank, awesome beings whom a humble individual might hesitate to bother with personal concerns. The growth of this hierarchy was partially checked by the Reformation, but it is still sponsored by the Church of Rome: saints' relics perform healing, and the Virgin continues to appear from time to time in unexpected places.

Schweitzer did not share the optimism of nineteenth-century British reformers that a new rational Christianity would soon necessarily win out: the historical Jesus, whose central message Schweitzer believed was eschatological and predestinational, developed his message in the context of "primitive late-Jewish metaphysics," which is difficult to translate into modern terms. The historical Jesus, he says, "will no longer be a Jesus Christ to whom the religion of the present can ascribe its own thought and ideas.... Nor will he be a figure who by a popular historical treatment can be made as sympathetic and universally intelligible to the multitude. With the specific characteristics of his notions and his actions, the historical Jesus will be to our time a stranger and an enigma."[13] Schweitzer was not, however, willing to relinquish Jesus as an inspiration. "Our relationship to Jesus," he claims, "is ultimately of a mystical kind.... We can achieve a relation to such a personality only when we become united with him in the knowledge of a shared aspiration, when we feel that our will is clarified, enriched and enlivened by his will and when we discover ourselves through him."[14] Noble as this seems, I instinctively distrust it as too mystical. How can we know Jesus' "will" except from historical criticism of the New Testament? The eschatological teachings attributed to Jesus and preached by Saint Paul, together with the prophecies of Revelation, have proven a distraction for the church throughout the ages. They have consistently disappointed but continually reemerged in times of stress, and some today eagerly expect the coming of "the rapture."[15]

The invitation to write an afterword has thus provided me with an opportunity to say something about my recent studies of New Testament interpretation and to suggest the presence of rhetorical features that I have not previously marked out. It cannot be too often stressed that the original purpose of rhetorical criticism of the New Testament as I conceived it was to provide modern readers with a technique to hear the transmitted texts of the gospels and epistles as they might have been heard by a Greek-speaking audience when read aloud in the time of the Roman Empire. Some in those audiences would have had an education in written composition, as taught in schools of grammar or rhetoric throughout the Mediterranean world, or practice in public declamation, and even those lacking much formal education would have become accustomed to the rhetorical conventions of narrative and epistolary texts by hearing or reading them repeatedly. These latter, less lettered folk might not have been able to name a figure of speech or identify the stasis of a pericope, but they could have directly responded to its pathos, ethos, or logos. Rhetoric, as I argue in *Comparative Rhetoric*, is a form of mental energy, transmitted through a medium from "rhetor" to audience, and reception and reaction to a message does not require knowledge of theory. But given this assumption, I think we might now move another step in understanding the texts through rhetoric. Rhetorical criticism of smaller units has told us little about the historical truth of the content—for example, whether a pericope represents the actual teaching and actions of the historical Jesus of Nazareth. What I say below about large-scale rhetorical features of the gospels may also tell us little about the actual teachings of the historical Jesus, though it should contribute to peeling away later theological accretions to it.

As noted above, relying on the canonical books of the New Testament, Schweitzer believed that the teachings of the historical Jesus were fundamentally eschatological. There is, however, a possibility that this is not correct. During the last fifteen years the members of the Jesus Seminar have been engaged in a controversial reconsideration of the historical Jesus,[16] making much use of the *Gospel of Thomas*. This is a collection of "The Secret Sayings of Jesus" in Coptic, discovered in 1945 in Upper Egypt and unknown to Schweitzer when he made his last revisions of *The Quest* in 1913.[17] It could be comparable in date to the earliest material in Mark and contains no reference to the nativity, no eschatological teaching, and no mention of the resurrection. Some of the "Sayings" are derived from Jewish wisdom literature, and some show signs of an early form of Gnosticism, but without gnostic theology. Comparing *Thomas* with other early evidence, members of the Jesus Seminar have concluded that the eschatology of the canonical gospels should not be regarded as teaching of the historical Jesus but derives from John the Baptist, taken up by the evangelists a generation or more after Jesus' death. With later accretions removed, we are left with a historical Jesus as a Jewish reformer who taught, primarily by parables, an austere social ethic and a belief that the kingdom of heaven is already present if we will only sincerely embrace it.

The most conspicuous rhetorical features of the gospels considered over all include myth, narrative, *chreia*, topos,[18] *ethopoeia*, thesis, and other structures. These are compositional units called *progymnasmata*, elementary exercises in grammar and rhetorical schools that are useful in constructing a discourse and can be given elaboration in more sophisticated writing, including epic poetry, historiography, and the novel.[19] They are lacking in the *Gospel of Thomas* and probably were lacking also in Mark's sources, which appear to have been simple, unedited collections of material. Sophisticated rhetorical devices were apparently imposed on the stories of Jesus two generations or more after his death, probably in the belief that something like them was necessary—and thus must be valid—to establish his authority as a prophet in the culture of the time. The grand topoi of the mythical nativity and resurrection were developed in analogy with pagan mythology and reflect knowledge of Jewish Scriptures and traditions about prophets and wise men in the Near East and in the Greco-Roman world. They are the credentials of someone with supernatural powers; thus their rhetorical function was to provide authority to Christ as a prophet in a way that would be understood by those who knew of Jewish, Egyptian, and Greco-Roman precedents. The three great master topoi—without which Christianity might well not have spread and survived in competition with Mithraism and other eastern cults—are a supernatural birth, the account of Jesus as a miracle worker, and his return from the dead, the latter probably developed out of a real psychological experience of seeming to see a vision of the risen Jesus on the part of some of his original followers.

The story of Jesus' nativity is historically the most suspect of the three. It is lacking in Mark and John, and the versions in Matthew and Luke are very different.[20] Matthew's may well have originated in stories of baby Jesus told by Christian parents to their children in the middle of the first century C.E., modeled on folk tales, with Herod playing the role of bogeyman ("if you don't behave, see what may happen to you"). These are reminiscent of stories of the birth of gods and heroes in many cultures. Classical parallels include tales of the infancy of Hermes, Theseus, Romulus, Lycurgus, and others. The two evangelists imitated or chose their versions in accord with their audiences: Matthew's account features Herod, consistent with interest of his Jewish audience, while Luke introduces the Roman census, though his chronology is confused. The flight into Egypt and massacre of the innocents, perhaps the coming of the Magi, if they had any historical validity, would surely have been known to Josephus, a contemporary who was well informed about the actions of Herod (died 4 B.C.E.), but he never mentions them. The nativity stories, as myth, can be read in universal terms: to quote Harriet Beecher Stowe (herself an orthodox Christian), "The wise men of the east at the feet of an infant, offering gifts, gold, frankincense, and myrrh, is just a parable of what goes on in every house where there is a young child. All the hard and the harsh, and the common and the disagreeable, is for the parents—all the bright and beautiful for their child."[21] The enormous popularity of the Christmas story with artists, musicians, and parents for centuries has had much to do with establishing belief in the divinity of Jesus, and the Christmas story as commonly told, in competition with the myth of Santa Claus, is so important for Western culture that to many it may seem offensive to question its historicity at this late date. In both versions of the nativity, that in Matthew and much more in Luke, the narrative is elaborated and rendered vivid by *ethopoeia*, or speeches in character, attributed to angels, Mary, Zechariah, and Simeon. The author of the Fourth Gospel omitted an account of the nativity, if it was known to him, and, influenced by the Jewish philosopher Philo of

Alexandria (30 B.C.E.–45 C.E.), he substituted the proclamation of the logos, which he supports by testimony attributed to John the Baptist and the earliest disciples. So far as I know, no account of the nativity is found in early Christian narratives except in Matthew and Luke until late in the second century, when it appears in the Proto-Gospel of James, in which Jesus' conception and birth (though not in Bethlehem), Matthew's wise men, Herod, and the slaughter of the innocents reappear.[22] Accounts of Jesus as a miracle-maker or healer are also a feature of stories of other prophets, the most striking classical parallel being Apollonius of Tyana, a wonder worker of the first century who raised the dead, healed the sick, and ascended bodily into heaven.[23] The members of the Jesus Seminar retain some miracles in their *Gospel of Jesus*,[24] regarding them as examples of psychosomatic healing.

Turning to the resurrection accounts, Mark's account of the crucifixion in chapter 15 is an elegant narrative, terse and filled with pathos. Some believe that the original end of Mark's gospel has been lost. What follows in 16:1-8 is the discovery of the empty tomb by Mary Magdelene, Mary the mother of James, and Salome, and the explanation by "a young man dressed in white" that Jesus has risen. This seems to me to be very moving. The following verses (9-20) are lacking in most early manuscripts and usually are regarded as the work of a later editor who did not understand Mark's rhetoric and was dissatisfied with the abrupt climax of the original text. The resurrection story resembles stories of disappearance, rebirth, or return from the dead in classical mythology and legend. As found in other gospels and in noncanonical sources, it has been elaborated by the writers or their sources and as such its literal historicity is suspect, but I do not doubt that Jesus' friends felt his presence among them.

It will take a hundred years or more of peace, the eradication of poverty and disease, and universal scientific education—as unlikely as all this may seem—for any historically valid, humanistic Christianity to gain a victory over orthodox Christianity with its entrenched bureaucracy, supernatural mechanisms, and offer of immortality. As Feuerbach realized a century-and-a-half ago, religions, even though illusions, fulfill important social and psychological needs, and they have been sponsored by both kings and popular leaders in the interests of maintaining order and for their ceremonial value. All people encounter tragedies and disasters, natural or man-made; all face pain, suffering, and death; and all of us, at least at times, live lives of quiet desperation when we seek the aid of a father figure, a just God, a loving Jesus, and a better life beyond the grave. I wish it were feasible to discourage required recitation of theological creeds in those church services where it has a traditional place and replace them with an affirmation of Christian principles and values. Nothing even in the Apostles' Creed, the simplest of the traditional creeds (except reference to the crucifixion in the time of Pontius Pilate[25]) has historical or rational validity, and except for "the forgiveness of sins," the creed is strangely lacking in ethical values. Modern Christians in democratic societies should have freedom of conscience to form their own theological beliefs on the basis of the evidence and their personal experience, but they can reasonably be expected to subscribe to the teaching of their church in the way they lead their lives and serve their neighbor, society, and the environment. I hope statements of Christian principles will increasingly include a declaration of respect for the interdependent web of nature that we share with the plants and animals of the Earth. Concern for the environment has recently begun to emerge as an issue that scientists, humanists, and Christians, both conservative and liberal, share—and as something that can bring many of us together in a common effort to improve the future of the world.[26]

Notes

[1] Additional biographical and bibliographical information, updated regularly, can be found in the listing under my name in the latest edition of *Who's Who in America*. The article on me in *Encyclopedia of Rhetoric and Composition* (ed. Theresa Enos; New York: Garland Publishing 1996), 375–76, follows immediately after the article on Immanuel Kant and gives my date of birth as ten years later than what is found in other sources. The result of that chronology would be that I must have received my Ph.D. from Harvard at the age of fifteen!

[2] George A. Kennedy, *Greek Rhetoric under Christian Emperors* (Princeton: Princeton University Press, 1983), xv.

[3] In my time at Princeton (1946–1950), freshmen and sophomores were required to attend a certain number of weekly services either in the chapel or in a local place of worship.

[4] George A. Kennedy, "Classical and Christian Source Criticism," in *The Relationship among the Gospels: An Interdisciplinary Dialogue* (ed. William O. Walker; Trinity University Monograph Series in Religion 5; San Antonio: Trinity University Press, 1983), 125–55.

[5] George A. Kennedy, *Comparative Rhetoric: An Historical and Cross-Cultural Introduction* (New York: Oxford University Press, 1997 [1998]).

⁶ George A. Kennedy, *Classical Rhetoric and Its Christian and Secular Tradition from Ancient to Modern Times* (2nd ed., rev. and enl.; Chapel Hill: University of North Carolina Press, 1998); Aristotle, *On Rhetoric: A Theory of Civic Discourse* (trans. with intro., notes, and appendices by George A. Kennedy; 2nd rev. ed.; Oxford: Oxford University Press, 2006); George A. Kennedy, *Fictitious Authors and Imaginary Novels in French, English, and American Fiction from the 18th to the Start of the 21st Century* (Lewiston, N.Y.: Edwin Mellen, 2005).

⁷ See Lytton Strachey, *Eminent Victorians* (ed. John Sutherland; Oxford: Oxford University Press, 2003), 158.

⁸ A later version (1863) was intended to be a popular work addressed to "the German people" and is less satisfactory.

⁹ Albert Schweitzer, *The Quest of the Historical Jesus* (trans. J. R. Coates, Susan Cuprit, and John Bowden; ed. John Bowden; Minneapolis: Fortress, 2001).

¹⁰ More will be said about myth, below.

¹¹ Schweitzer, *The Quest of the Historical Jesus*, 126.

¹² See Bart Ehrman, *Lost Christianities: The Battles for Scripture and the Faiths We Never Knew* (New York: Oxford University Press, 2003), 207–9.

¹³ Schweitzer, *The Quest of the Historical Jesus*, 478.

¹⁴ Schweitzer, *The Quest of the Historical Jesus*, 486. The "shared aspiration" to which Schweitzer refers is how to achieve the kingdom of God on earth.

¹⁵ Millenianism is a feature of many societies under pressure. In *Comparative Rhetoric*, I noted examples among the native inhabitants of Indonesia (71), North America (90–91), and ancient China (155–56).

¹⁶ The Jesus Seminar, a project of the Weststar Institute in Santa Rosa, California, is a large group of scholars from a variety of Christian backgrounds who study the evidence for the sources of New Testament texts and vote, by a system of color-coding, about the probability that material can be attributed to the historical Jesus. They sponsor oral seminars throughout the country and have an ongoing publication program. Among their publications are *The Complete Gospel* (ed. Robert J. Miller; Santa Rosa, Calif.: Polebridge, 1994); *The Five Gospels: The Search for the Authentic Words of Jesus* (ed. Robert W. Funk, Roy W. Hoover, and the Jesus Seminar; San Francisco: Polebridge, 1993); and *The Acts of Jesus: The Search for the Authentic Deeds of Jesus* (ed. Robert W. Funk and the Jesus Seminar; Santa Rosa, Calif.: Polebridge, 1998).

¹⁷ See Schweitzer, *The Quest of the Historical Jesus*, xiii, xxxiv, and xxxv.

¹⁸ The term topos ("place") is used in two senses in rhetorical theory. There are "commonplaces"—logical topoi, such as argument from the more to the less—and "material" topics, which have a specific subject matter (see my *New Testament Interpretation through Rhetorical Criticism* [Chapel Hill: University of North Carolina Press, 1984], 20). It is the latter type I am discussing here.

¹⁹ See George A. Kennedy, *Progymnasmata: Greek Textbooks of Prose Composition and Rhetoric, Translated into English, with Introduction and Notes* (WGRW 10; Atlanta and Leiden: Society of Biblical Literature/Brill, 2003).

²⁰ The gospels are entitled *kata*, "according to" Matthew, Mark, Luke, and John, suggesting their sources in the teaching of a famous person, but they lack the identification of the author usually found in Greek historical texts. I shall refer to them here by the traditional names, but the actual authors are unknown.

[21] Harriet Beecher Stowe, *The Pearl of Orr's Island* (Sampson: Low, Son, 1862), 15.

[22] See Ehrman, *Lost Christianities*, 209. This gospel exists in over a hundred manuscripts and was very popular with readers in the East.

[23] See the biography by Philostratus (c. 200 C.E.), *The Life of Apollonius of Tyana* (ed. and trans. Christopher P. Jones: LCL; 2 vols.; Cambridge: Harvard University Press, 2003).

[24] *The Gospel of Jesus, According to the Jesus Seminar* (ed. Robert W. Funk and the Jesus Seminar; Santa Rosa, Calif.: Polebridge, 1999).

[25] For which we have, for instance, the evidence of the Roman historian Tacitus, *Annals* 15.44, writing soon after 100 C.E. Pontius Pilatus was procurator of Judaea from 27 to 37.

[26] A number of recent books by distinguished thinkers advocate this approach; see, e.g., Edward O. Wilson, *The Creation: An Appeal to Save Life on Earth* (New York: Norton, 2006).

CURRICULUM VITAE
George Alexander Kennedy

Although George Kennedy has been honored with two Festschriften, *to date a comprehensive list of his principal publications has not been published. The vita that follows rectifies that omission and is offered by the editors as an ancilla to research scholars in classics, biblical studies, speech communication, philology, and other fields. Prepared in consultation with Professor Kennedy, the following is complete up to October 2007; it omits only book reviews and lectures, some of which were subsequently published and appear herein.*

PERSONAL

Born: Hartford, Connecticut, 26 November 1928, son of George and Ethel Hall Kennedy; married Mary Lee Hunnicutt, 25 March 1955; one child: Claire Alexandra (Mrs. Jerrald) Morton; three grandchildren: Alexander, Amy, and Emily Morton.

EDUCATION

Public schools of Simsbury, Connecticut; Princeton University, 1946–50 (A.B. in Classics, magna cum laude); Harvard University, 1950–54 (A.M. in Classics, 1952; Ph.D. in Classical Philology, 1954).

ACADEMIC APPOINTMENTS
1. Full-Time

HARVARD UNIVERSITY: Instructor and Tutor in Classics and in History and Literature, 1955–58; Secretary of the Classics Faculty, 1955–58; Board of Freshman Advisors, 1956–58; Visiting Assistant Professor, Summer 1959.

HAVERFORD COLLEGE: Assistant Professor of Greek, 1958–59; Assistant Professor of Classics, 1959–63; Associate Professor of Classics, 1963–65.

UNIVERSITY OF PITTSBURGH: Professor of Classics and Chairman, Department of Classics, 1965–66.

UNIVERSITY OF NORTH CAROLINA AT CHAPEL HILL: Professor of Classics, 1966–72; Paddison Professor of Classics, 1972–95; Chairman, Department of Classics, 1966–76; Chairman, Department of Linguistics, 1975–76; Chair of the University Faculty, 1985–88; Chairman, Curriculum of Comparative Literature, 1989–93.

UNIVERSITY OF NORTH CAROLINA PRESS: Board of Governors, 1968–90; Chairman of the Board, 1973–88.

2. *Visiting Appointments*

UNIVERSITY OF PENNSYLVANIA: Visiting Professor, Summer 1963.

UNIVERSITY OF COLORADO: Visiting Professor, Summer 1982.

WASHINGTON UNIVERSITY IN ST. LOUIS: Lewin Distinguished Visiting Professor, Spring 1988.

COLORADO STATE UNIVERSITY: Faculty Affiliate in Speech Communication, 1994–2002.

RESEARCH FELLOWSHIPS

Harvard University: Traveling Fellow in Europe, 1954–55.

Fulbright Fellow to Italy and Guggenheim Fellow in Greece, 1964–65.

National Endowment for the Humanities Research Fellow and Fellow of the Dumbarton Oaks Center for Byzantine Studies, 1979–80.

National Endowment for the Humanities Fellowship for University Teachers, 1994–95.

HONORS

Phi Beta Kappa, 1950.

Golden Anniversary Award, Speech Communication Association, 1973, 1981.

James Allen Winans Award, Speech Communication Association, 1973.

Charles J. Goodwin Award of Merit, American Philological Association, 1975.

Johns Hopkins Centennial Scholar, 1976.

Elected Fellow of the American Academy of Arts and Sciences, 1978.

Thomas Jefferson Award, University of North Carolina at Chapel Hill, 1983.

Elected member of the American Philosophical Society, 1984.

Distinguished Scholar Award, Speech Communication Association, 1992.

Rhetoric Society of America Fellow (honorary), 2006.

In 2007 the University of North Carolina at Chapel Hill created the George A. Kennedy Professorship in the College of Arts and Sciences, using funds from the bequest of the late Paul A. Johnson. The Kennedy Chair's first holder is Dr. Stefan Litwin in the Department of Music.

FESTSCHRIFTEN

Persuasive Artistry: Studies in New Testament Rhetoric in Honor of George A. Kennedy. Edited by Duane F. Watson. Journal for the Study of the New Testament Supplement Series 50. Sheffield: JSOT Press/ Sheffield Academic, 1991.

The Orator in Action & Theory in Greece & Rome: Essays in Honor of George A. Kennedy. Edited by Cecil W. Wooten. Mnemosyne: bibliotheca classica Batava. Supplementum 225. Leiden and Boston: Brill, 2001.

SERVICE IN PROFESSIONAL ORGANIZATIONS

AMERICAN ACADEMY IN ROME: Advisory Council, School of Classical Studies, 1963–83; Fellowship Selection Committee, 1968–69; Trustee, 1978–80.

AMERICAN JOURNAL OF PHILOLOGY: Editor, 1989–94; Honorary Editor, 1994.

AMERICAN PHILOSOPHICAL ASSOCIATION: Board of Directors, 1969–73; Vice-President, 1977–78; President, 1978–79; Delegate to the American Council of Learned Societies, 1980–83.

AMERICAN SCHOOL OF CLASSICAL STUDIES IN ATHENS: Managing Committee, 1959–95; Executive Committee, 1976–80; Publications Committee, 1981–84.

CENTER FOR HELLENIC STUDIES: Senior Fellow, 1990–95.

FÉDÉRATION INTERNATIONAL DES ASSOCIATIONS DES ÉTUDES CLASSIQUES: Membre de bureau, 1985–94; Vice-président, 1989–94.

INTERNATIONAL SOCIETY FOR THE HISTORY OF RHETORIC: Council, 1977–87; Vice–President, 1979–83; President, 1983–85.

MELLON GRADUATE FELLOWSHIPS IN THE HUMANITIES: Chairman, Southeastern Region Selection Committee, 1984–87, 1988–89.

NATIONAL ENDOWMENT FOR THE HUMANITIES: Member, National Humanities Council, 1980–87 (appointed by President Carter and confirmed by the U.S. Senate); Chairman, Committee on Research, 1982–85; Vice-Chairman of the Council, 1983–85; Chairman of the Budget Committee, 1983–85; Chairman of the Jefferson Lecture Committee, 1984–85.

PHI BETA KAPPA: Christian Gauss Award Panel, 1991–93.

PUBLICATIONS

1. Books

The Art of Persuasion in Greece. Princeton: Princeton University Press, 1963. Pp. xi + 350.

Quintilian. Twayne's World Authors Series 66. New York: Twayne, 1969. Pp. 155.

The Art of Rhetoric in the Roman World: 300 B.C.–A.D. 300. Princeton: Princeton University Press, 1972. Pp. xvi + 658.

Classical Rhetoric and Its Christian and Secular Tradition from Ancient to Modern Times. Chapel Hill: University of North Carolina Press, 1980. Pp. xvii + 291. 2nd ed., revised, 1998. Slovenian translation: *Klasicna retorika ter njen krscanska in posvetna traadicija od antike do sodobnosti*. Edited by Nada Groselj. Zalozba ZRC, Ljubljana, 2001. Spanish translation: *La Retórica Clásica y su Tradución Cristiana y Secular, desde La Antiguëdad hasta Nuestros Días*. Edited by Luisa López Grigera. Logroño: Instituto de Estudios Riojanos, 2003.

Greek Rhetoric under Christian Emperors. Princeton: Princeton University Press, 1983. Pp. xvi + 333.

New Testament Interpretation through Rhetorical Criticism. Chapel Hill: University of North Carolina Press, 1984. Pp. x+171. Spanish translation by Federico de Carlos Otto: *Retórica y Nuevo Testamento.* Madrid: Ediciones Cristiana, 2003. Pp. 315. Italian translation by Donatella Zoroddy: *Nuovo Testamento e critica retorica.* Brescia: Paideia Editrice, 2006. Pp. 214.

A Woman's Version of the Faust Legend: George Sand's Seven Strings of the Lyre. Introduction, English Translation, and Notes. Chapel Hill: University of North Carolina Press, 1989. Pp.185.

General Editor, *The Cambridge History of Literary Criticism.* Volume I: *Classical Criticism.* Cambridge: Cambridge University Press, 1989. Pp. xv + 378. Also author of this volume's Preface (pp. ix–xv); Chapter 2: "Language and Meaning in Archaic and Classical Greece" (pp. 78–91); Chapter 5: "The Evolution of a Theory of Artistic Prose" (pp. 184–99); Chapter 6: "Hellenistic Literary and Philosophical Scholarship" (pp. 200–14), and Chapter 11: "Christianity and Criticism" (pp. 330–46).

Aristotle. *On Rhetoric: A Theory of Civic Discourse.* Translated with introduction, notes, and appendices by George A. Kennedy. Oxford: Oxford University Press, 1991. Pp. xiv + 335. 2nd rev. ed., 2006. Pp. viii + 337.

A New History of Classical Rhetoric. Princeton: Princeton University Press, 1994. Pp. xii + 301.

Two Greek Rhetorical Treatises from the Roman Empire. Introduction, Text, and Translation of the Arts of Rhetoric attributed to Anonymous Seguerianus and to Apsines of Gadara (in collaboration with Mervin R. Dilts). Mnemosyne: bibliotheca classica Batava. Supplementum 168. Leiden: Brill, 1997. Pp. xxvii + 249.

Comparative Rhetoric: An Historical and Cross-Cultural Introduction. New York: Oxford University Press, 1997 (1998). Pp. ix + 238.

The Latin Iliad: Introduction, Text, Translation, and Notes. Privately printed, Fort Collins, Colo., 1998. Pp. 78.

Progymnasmata: Greek Textbooks of Prose Composition and Rhetoric, Translated into English, with Introductions and Notes. WGRW 10. Atlanta and Leiden: Society of Biblical Literature/Brill, 2003. Pp. xviii + 231.

Fictitious Authors and Imaginary Novels in French, English, and American Fiction, from the 18th to the Start of the 21st Century. Lewiston, N.Y.: Edwin Mellen Press, 2005. Pp. vi + 304.

Invention and Method: Two Rhetorical Treatises from the Hermogenic Corpus. WGRW 15. Atlanta and Leiden: Society of Biblical Literature, 2005/Brill, 2006. Pp. xix + 267.

2. *Articles, Pamphlets, and Essays in Books*

"Theophrastus and Stylistic Distinctions." *Harvard Studies in Classical Philology* 62 (1957): 92–104.

"The Ancient Dispute over Rhetoric in Homer." *American Journal of Philology* 78 (1957): 23–35.

"The Oratory of Andocides." *American Journal of Philology* 79 (1958): 32–43.

"Isocrates' Encomium of Helen: A Panhellenic Document." *Transactions of the American Philological Association* 89 (1958): 77–83.

"Aristotle on the Period." *Harvard Studies in Classical Philology* 80 (1959): 169–78.

"Focusing of Arguments in Greek Deliberative Oratory." *Transactions of the American Philological Association* 90 (1959): 131–38.

"An Estimate of Quintilian." *American Journal of Philology* 83 (1962): 130–46.

"Non-Western Studies: A Challenge to the Classics." *Classical Journal* 58 (1963): 157–59.

"Two Problems in the Historical Study of Rhetoric." *Pennsylvania Speech Annual* 21 (1964): 17–22.

"Speech Education in Greece." *Western Speech* 31 (1967): 2–9.

"Crassus, Cicero, and Caplan." Addresses delivered at the meeting honoring Professor Harry Caplan. Speeches delivered in Washington, D.C., at a meeting of the Speech Communication Association; subsequently published in Ithaca, N.Y.: Cornell University Press, 1967.

"The Oratorical Career of Demosthenes." Pp. 28–47 in *Demosthenes' On the Crown*, edited by J. J. Murphy. New York: Random House, 1967. (Reprint of *The Art of Persuasion in Greece*, pp. 208–29.)

"Antony's Speech at Caesar's Funeral." *Quarterly Journal of Speech* 54 (1968): 99–106.

"The Rhetoric of Advocacy in Greece and Rome." *American Journal of Philology* 89 (1968): 419–36.

"The Shadow of Isocrates." *Colorado Journal of Educational Research* 2 (1972): 16–23.

"Apuleius," "Homer," "Iliad," and "Odyssey": articles in *The World Book Encyclopedia*. Chicago: Field Enterprises, 1972 (and subsequently).

"A Reading List on the Classical Humanities." *Humanities* (22.5). Washington: National Endowment for the Humanities, 1972.

"Gorgias." Pp. 30–47 in *The Older Sophists*, edited by Rosamond Sprague. Columbia: University of South Carolina Press, 1972; reprinted, Indianapolis: Hackett, 2001. Reprinted also as "Gorgias"/"Encomium of Helen," pp. 38–42 in *The Rhetorical Tradition: Readings from Classical Times to the Present*, edited by Patricia Bizzell and Bruce Herzberg. Boston: Bedford Books, 1990.

Careers for Classicists. Pamphlet, American Philological Association, 1972; rev. ed. with Laura Barnard, 1976.

"Introduction." Pp. 1–7 in *The Speeches in Thucydides*, edited by Philip A. Stadter. Chapel Hill: University of North Carolina Press, 1973.

"The Sophists as Declaimers." Pp. 17–22 in *Approaches to the Second Sophistic*, edited by G. W. Bowersock. American Philological Association, 1974.

"A Selective Bibliography of the Second Sophistic," with Mark Barnard. Pp. 30–42 in *Approaches to the Second Sophistic*, edited by G. W. Bowersock. American Philological Association, 1974.

"The Present State of the Study of Ancient Rhetoric." *Classical Philology* 70 (1975): 278–82.

"Classical Influences on The Federalist." Pp. 119–38 in *Classical Traditions in Early America*, edited by J. W. Eadie. Ann Arbor: Center for Coordination of Ancient and Modern Studies, 1976.

Chapter 9 (pp. 35–39) in *A Composite Translation of a Life of George Washington in Latin Prose*, by Francis Glass, edited by John F. Latimer. Washington, D.C.: George Washington University, 1976.

"Toward a Methodology for Study of Classics in America." Pp. 3–5 in *The Usefulness of Classical Learning in the Eighteenth Century*, edited by Susan F. Wiltshire. American Philological Association, 1977.

"A Southerner in the Peloponnesian War." Pp. 21–25 in *Southern Humanities Review*, special issue: "The Classical Tradition in the South," 1977.

"Encolpius and Agamemnon in Petronius." *American Journal of Philology* 9 (1978): 171–78.

"Later Greek Philosophy and Rhetoric." *Philosophy and Rhetoric* 13 (1980): 181–97.

"Gildersleeve, the Journal, and Philology in America." *American Journal of Philology* 101 (1980): 1–11; reprinted with some changes as pp. 42–49 in Basil Lanneau Gildersleeve, edited by W. Ward Briggs and Herbert W. Benario. Baltimore: Johns Hopkins University Press, 1986.

"Classical and Christian Source Criticism." Pp. 125–55 in *The Relationship among the Gospels: An Interdisciplinary Dialogue*, edited by William O. Walker. Trinity University Monograph Series in Religion 5. San Antonio: Trinity University Press, 1983.

"The Classical Tradition in Rhetoric." Pp. 20–34 in *Byzantium and the Classical Tradition*. Birmingham: Center for Byzantine Studies, 1981.

"Quintilian." Pp. 943–59 in *Ancient Writers, Greece and Rome*, edited by T. J. Luce. New York: Scribner's, 1982.

"Afterword: An Essay on Classics in America since the Yale Report." Pp. 325–51 in *Classica Americana*, edited by Meyer Reinhold. Detroit: Wayne State University Press, 1984.

"An Introduction to the Rhetoric of the Gospels." *Rhetorica* 1 (1983): 17–23.

"Forms and Functions of Latin Speech." Pp. 45–73 in *Medieval and Renaissance Studies*, edited by G. Mallory Masters. Institute for Medieval and Renaissance Studies at Duke University and the University of North Carolina 10. Chapel Hill: University of North Carolina Press, 1984.

"Sophists and Physicians of the Greek Enlightenment" (pp. 472–77) and "Oratory" (pp. 498–526) in *The Cambridge History of Greek Literature*, edited by P. Easterling and B. M. W. Knox. Cambridge: Cambridge University Press, 1985.

"Helen's Web Unraveled." *Arethusa* 19 (1986): 7–14.

"Helen's Husbands and Lovers: A Query." *Classical Journal* 82 (1987): 152–53.

"The Story of Helen: Myth and Rhetoric." Inaugural lecture as Lewin Visiting Distinguished Professor, subsequently published as a pamphlet by Washington University, St. Louis, 1987.

"Fin de siècle Classicism: Henry Adams and Thorstein Veblen; Lew Wallace and W. D. Howells." *Classical and Modern Literature* 8 (1987): 15–21.

"The Rhetorica of Guillaume Fichet (1471)." *Rhetorica* 5 (1987): 411–18.

"Some Reflections on Neomodernism." *Rhetoric Review* 6 (1988): 213–16.

"Process or Content? Language or Literature? The Future of the Latin Curriculum." *North Carolina Classical Association Newsletter*, special issue (1988): 1–4.

"Quintilian on Early Childhood Education." *Primus* 1.2 (1988): 4–9.

"Foreword." Pp. 7–8 in *Early Christian Rhetoric and 2nd Thessalonians*, by Frank Witt Hughes. Sheffield: Sheffield Academic, 1989.

"Truth and Rhetoric in the Pauline Epistles." Pp. 195–202 in *The Bible as Rhetoric*, edited by Martin Warner. Warwick Studies in Philosophy and Literature. London: Routledge, 1990.

"Classics and Canons." *South Atlantic Quarterly* 89 (1990): 217–25. Reprinted as pp. 223–31 in *The Politics of Liberal Education*, edited by Darryl Gless and Barbara H. Johnson. Durham: Duke University Press, 1992.

"The Rhetoric of the Early Christian Liturgy." Pp. 26–43 in *Language and the Worship of the Church*, edited by David and R. C. D. Jasper. London: Macmillan, 1990.

"The Roman Tradition in Rhetoric." Pp. 41–51 in *Retorikk*, edited by Øvind Andersen. Trondheim Universitetet, 1990.

"Rhetoric and Society: Some Comparative Evidence." *Carolinas Speech Communication Annual* 6 (1990): 7–13.

"Brief Mention" as Editor of *American Journal of Philology*, 1989–94.

"Running a Locomotive in 1856: The Log of H. S. Haines," *Railroad History* 146 (1991): 86–93.

"A Hoot in the Dark: The Evolution of General Rhetoric." *Philosophy and Rhetoric* 25 (1992): 1–21. Reprinted in *Rhetoric: Concepts, Definitions, Boundaries*, edited by William A. Covino and David A. Jolliffe. New York: Allyn & Bacon, 1995.

"Chapter IV: Rhetoric." Pp. 269–94 in *The Heritage of Rome*, edited by Richard Jenkyns. Oxford: Oxford University Press, 1992.

"Response by George A. Kennedy at the Rhetoric Society of America's Meeting on His Translation of Aristotle's Rhetoric." Pp. 244–46 in *Rhetoric in the Vortex of Cultural Studies: Proceedings of the Fifth Biennial Conference*, edited by Arthur Walzer. Minneapolis: Rhetoric Society of America, 1993.

"Visions of Beauty: The Western Rhetorical Tradition." Pp. 284–90 in *Proceedings of the XIIIth Congress of the International Comparative Literature Association*. Tokyo: University of Tokyo Press, 1995.

"Shifting Visions of Classical Paradigms: The 'Same' and the 'Other.'" *International Journal of the Classical Tradition* 1 (1994): 1–16.

"Reworking Aristotle's Rhetoric." Pp. 169–84 in *Theory, Text, Context*, edited by Christopher L. Johnstone. Albany: State University of New York Press, 1996.

"Reading Disraeli with Stendhal." Pp. 253–66 in *Narrative Ironies*, edited by Raymond A. Prier and Gerald Gillespie. Amsterdam: Rodopit, 1997.

"The Contributions of Rhetoric to Literary Criticism." Pp. 349–64 in *The Cambridge History of Literary Criticism*, Volume 4: *The Eighteenth Century*, edited by H. B. Nisbet and Claude Rawson. Cambridge: Cambridge University Press, 1997.

"Historical Survey of Rhetoric" (Chapter 1) and "The Genres of Rhetoric" (Chapter 2). Pp. 3–50 in *Handbook of Classical Rhetoric in the Hellenistic Period, 330 B.C.–A.D. 400*, edited by Stanley E. Porter. Leiden: Brill, 1997.

"Foreword." Pp. xix–xxi in the English translation of Heinrich Lausberg's *Handbook of Literary Rhetoric*, edited by David E. Orton and R. Dean Anderson. Leiden: Brill, 1998.

"Rhetoric and Culture/Rhetoric and Technology" (Selections from the Charles Kneupper Memorial Lecture for the Rhetorical Society of America, 1998). Pp. 55–61 in *Rhetoric, the Polis, and the Global Village*, edited by C. Jan Swearingen. Mahwah, N.J.: Lawrence Erlbaum Associates, 1999.

"Quintilian on Retirement." Pp. 151–58 in *Quintiliano: Historia y Actualidad de la Retórica*, vol. 1, edited by Tomás Albaladejo and Emilio del Río Sanz. Logroño: Instituto de Estudios Riojanos, 1998.

"The Origin of the Concept of a Canon and Its Application to the Greek and Latin Classics." Pp. 105–16 in *Canon vs. Culture: Reflections on the Current Debate*, edited by Jan Gorak. New York: Garland, 2000.

"Classical Rhetoric" (pp. 92–115), "Comparative Rhetoric" (pp. 137–43), and "Imitation" (pp. 381–84) in *Encyclopedia of Rhetoric*, edited by Thomas O. Sloane (Oxford: Oxford University Press, 2001.

"Rhetoric." Pp. 13, 317–13, 323 in *The International Encyclopedia of the Social & Behavioral Sciences*, edited by N. J. Smelse and Paul B. Baltes. Oxford: Elsevier Science, 2001.

"Cicero's Oratorical and Rhetorical Legacy." Pp. 481–501 in *Brill's Companion to Cicero: Oratory and Rhetoric*, edited by James M. May. Leiden: Brill, 2002.

"Brief Mention: Some Recent Controversies in the Study of Later Greek Rhetoric." *American Journal of Philology* 124 (2003): 295–301.

"Electrifying Rhetoric of 1906." *Newsletter of the Railroad and Locomotive Historical Society* 23.3 (2003): 3–8.

Short articles on the history of nine North Carolina railroads in the *Encyclopedia of North Carolina*, edited by William Powell. Chapel Hill: University of North Carolina Press, 2006.

Translation of chapter 6 of *Aspects de la logographie judiciaire antique* by M. Lavency (1964) as "The Written Plea of the Logographer," pp. 32–36 in *The Attic Orators*, edited by Edwin Carawan. Oxford: Oxford University Press, 2007.

"Roman Declamation in the Generation after Quintilian," a review article in *International Journal of the Classical Tradition* 13 (2007): 592–97.

Choricius of Gaza, *Declamation* 8, "A Spartan Citizen," and *Declamation* 23, "An Orator." Forthcoming in *Choricius of Gaza, Declamations in English Translations*, edited by Robert Panella (Cambridge: Cambridge University Press, 2008).

BIBLIOGRAPHY

Primary Literature

Aristotle. *On Rhetoric: A Theory of Civic Discourse*. Translated with introduction, notes, and appendices by George A. Kennedy. Oxford: Oxford University Press, 1991.

———. *Poetics*. Edited and translated by Stephen Halliwell. Cambridge and London: Harvard University Press, 1995.

———. *Rhetoric to Alexander*. Translated by H. Rackham. With Problems. 2 vols. Loeb Classical Library. Cambridge: Harvard University Press, 1936–37.

Augustine. *On Christian Doctrine*. Translated by D. W. Robertson Jr. The Library of the Liberal Arts 80. Indianapolis: Bobbs-Merrill, 1958.

Cicero, Marcus Tullius. *De oratore*. Translated by E. W. Sutton and H. Rackham. 2 vols. Loeb Classical Library. Cambridge and London: Harvard University Press/Heinemann, 1942 (addendum, 1988).

———. *Letters of Marcus Tullius Cicero, with his Treatises on Friendship and Old Age*. Translated by E. S. Shuckburgh. With *Letters of Gaius Plinius Caecilus Secundus*. Translated by W. Melmoth; revised by F. C. T. Bosanquet. Volume 9 in The Harvard Classics. New York: Collier, 1909.

Demetrius. *On Style*. Edited and translated by Doreen C. Innes. Based on W. Rhys Roberts. Loeb Classical Library. Cambridge and London: Harvard University Press, 1995.

Dio Chrysostom. Translated by J. W. Cohoon and H. L. Crosby. 5 vols. Loeb Classical Library. Cambridge: Harvard University Press, 1932–1964.

Longinus. *On the Sublime*. Translated by W. H. Fyfe and revised by Donald Russell. Cambridge and London: Harvard University Press, 1995.

Philostratus. *The Life of Apollonius of Tyana*. Edited and translated by Christopher P. Jones. Loeb Classical Library. 2 vols. Cambridge: Harvard University Press, 2003.

Plato. *Phaedrus*. Translated by Harold North Fowler. 12 vols. Rev. ed. Cambridge: Harvard University Press, 1990.

Quintilian. *The Institutio Oratoria of Quintilian*. Translated by H. E. Butler. Loeb Classical Library. Cambridge and London: Harvard University Press/Heinemann, 1920–1922 (addendum, 1980).

———. *Institutiones oratoriae*. Translated by John Shelby Watson. No pages. Online: http://honeyl.public.iastate.edu/quintilian/index.html.

Rhetores Latini Minores. Edited by C. Halm. Leipzig: Teubner, 1863.

Rhetorica ad Herennium. Translated by Harry Caplan. Loeb Classical Library. Cambridge and London: Harvard University Press/Heinemann, 1954 (addendum, 1981).

Tacitus, Cornelius. *The Annals*. Translated by John Jackson. 4 vols. Loeb Classical Library. London and New York: W. Heinemann/G. P. Putnam's, 1925–1937.

Secondary Literature

Achtemeier, Paul J. "*Omne verbum sonat*: The New Testament and the Oral Environment of Late Western Antiquity." *JBL* 109 (1990): 3–27.

Adams, John Quincy. *Lectures on Rhetoric and Oratory*. 2 vols. Cambridge: Hilliard and Metcalf, 1810. Reprint. New York: Russell & Russell, 1962.

Allison, Dale. "Peter and Cephas: One and the Same." *JBL* 111 (1992): 489–95.

Anderson, R. Dean Jr. *Ancient Rhetorical Theory and Paul*. Kampen: Kok Pharos, 1996. Rev. ed. CBET 18. Leuven: Peters, 1998.

Arnold, Carroll, and John F. Wilson. *Public Speaking as a Liberal Art*. Boston: Allyn & Bacon, 1964.

Arnold, Clinton E. "'I am astonished that you are so quickly turning away': Paul and Anatolian Folk Belief." *NTS* 51 (2005): 429–49.

Atkinson, Jane M. "'Wrapped Words': Poetry and Politics among the Wana of Central Sulawesi, Indonesia." Pages 34–68 in *Dangerous Words: Language and Politics in the Pacific*. Edited by Donald Brennis and Fred R. Meyers. Prospect Heights, Ill.: Waveland, 1984.

Attridge, Harold W. "Argumentation in John 5." Pages 188–99 in *Rhetorical Argumentation in Biblical Texts: Essays from the Lund 2000 Conference*. Edited by Anders Eriksson, Thomas H. Olbricht, and Walter Übelacker. Harrisburg, Pa.: Trinity Press International, 2002.

Aune, David E. *The New Testament in Its Literary Environment*. Philadelphia: Westminster, 1987.

———. *Revelation*. WBC 52A. Waco, Tex.: Word, 1997.

———. "Rhetorical Criticism." Pages 416–18 in *The Westminster Dictionary of New Testament and Early Christian Literature and Rhetoric*. Edited by David E. Aune. Louisville, Ky.: Westminster John Knox, 2003.

Ayres, Lewis. *Nicaea and Its Legacy: An Approach to Fourth-Century Trinitarian Theology*. Oxford: Oxford University Press, 2006.

Barclay, J. M. G. "Mirror-Reading a Polemical Letter: Galatians as a Test Case." *JSNT* 31 (1987): 73–93.

Barthes, Roland. "The Imagination of the Sign." Pages 205–11 in *Critical Essays*. Translated by Richard Howard. Evanston: Northwestern University Press, 1972.

———. "Literature and Signification." Pages 261–79 in *Critical Essays*. Translated by Richard Howard. Evanston: Northwestern University Press, 1972.

———. "The Old Rhetoric: An Aide-Memoire." In *The Semiotic Challenge*. Translated by Richard Howard. New York: Hill and Wang, 1988.

Bauer, Karl Ludwig. *Rhetoricae Paulinae*. 2 vols. Halae: Impensis Ophanotrophei, 1782.

Baur, Ferdinand Christian. "Die beiden Briefe an die Thessalonicher: Ihre Echtheit und Bedeutung für die Lehre von der Parusie Christi." *Theologische Jahrbücher* 14 (1855): 141–68.

———. *Paul, the Apostle of Jesus Christ*. 2nd ed. 2 vols. London: Williams and Norgate, 1875–1876. 1st ed. *Paulus, der Apostel Jesu Christi*. Stuttgart: Becher & Miller, 1845.

Beale, Gregory. *The Book of Revelation: A Commentary on the Greek Text*. NIGTC. Grand Rapids, Mich.: Eerdmans, 1999.

Betz, Hans Dieter. *Galatians: A Commentary on Paul's Letter to the Churches in Galatia*. Hermeneia. Philadelphia: Fortress, 1979.

———. "In Defense of the Spirit: Paul's Letter to the Galatians as a Document of Early Christian Apologetics." Pages 99–114 in *Aspects of Religious Propaganda in Judaism and Early Christianity*. Edited by Elizabeth Schüssler Fiorenza. Notre Dame and London:

University of Notre Dame, 1976. Reprinted pages 98–109 in *Paulinische Studien*. Edited by Hans Dieter Betz. Gessamelte Aufsätze 3. Tübingen: Mohr (Siebeck), 1994.

———. "The Literary Composition and Function of Paul's Letter to the Galatians." *NTS* 21 (1975): 353–79. Reprinted pages 63–97 in *Paulinische Studien*. Edited by Hans Dieter Betz. Gessamelte Aufsätze 3. Tübingen: Mohr (Siebeck), 1994. Reprinted pages 3–28 in *The Galatians Debate: Contemporary Issues in Rhetorical and Historical Interpretation*. Edited by Mark D. Nanos. Peabody, Mass.: Hendrickson, 2002.

———. *The Sermon on the Mount*. Hermeneia. Minneapolis: Augsburg Fortress Press, 1995.

Bingham, Caleb. *The Columbian Orator: Containing a Variety of Original and Selected Pieces; Together with Rules, Calculated to Improve Youth and Others in the Ornamental and Useful Art of Eloquence*. Boston: Caleb Bingham, 1794, 1815.

Bitzer, Lloyd. "Functional Communication: A Situational Perspective." Pages 21–38 in *Rhetoric in Transition: Studies in the Nature and Uses of Rhetoric*. Edited by E. E. White. University Park: Pennsylvania State University Press, 1980.

———. "The Rhetorical Situation." *PR* 1 (1968): 1–14.

Black, C. Clifton. *Mark: Images of an Apostolic Interpreter*. Columbia: University of South Carolina, 1994. Reprint, Minneapolis and Edinburgh: Fortress/T&T Clark, 2001.

———. "An Oration at Olivet: Some Rhetorical Dimensions of Mark 13." Pages 66–92 in *Persuasive Artistry: Studies in New Testament Rhetoric in Honor of George A. Kennedy*. Edited by Duane F. Watson. Journal for the Study of the New Testament: Supplement Series 50. Sheffield: JSOT Press, 1991, 66–92. Reprinted and expanded, pages 47–73 in *The Rhetoric of the Gospel: Theological Artistry in the Gospels and Acts*. St. Louis: Chalice, 2001.

———. "The Rhetorical Form of the Hellenistic Jewish and Early Christian Sermon: A Response to Lawrence Wills." *HTR* 81 (1988): 1–18.

———. *The Rhetoric of the Gospel: Theological Artistry in the Gospels and Acts*. St. Louis: Chalice, 2001.

Bloomquist, L. Gregory. *The Function of Suffering in Philippians*. Journal for the Study of the New Testament: Supplement Series 78. Sheffield: JSOT Press, 1993.

———. "Rhetorical Analysis and Sociological Analysis in Historical Jesus Research." *MTSR* 9.2 (1997): 139–54.

———. "The Rhetoric of the Historical Jesus." Pages 98–117 in *Whose Historical Jesus?* Edited by W. E. Arnal and M. Desjardins. Studies in Christianity and Judaism 7. Waterloo, Ont.: Wilfrid Laurier University Press, 1997.

Booth, Wayne. *The Rhetoric of Fiction*. Chicago: The University of Chicago Press, 1961.

Bormann, Ernest. *The Force of Fantasy: Restoring the American Dream*. Carbondale: Southern Illinois University Press, 1985.

———. *Small Group Communication: Theory and Practice*. 3rd ed. New York: Harper & Row, 1990.

Bormann, Ernest, John Cragan, and Donald Shields. "In Defense of Symbolic Convergence Theory: A Look at the Theory and Its Criticisms after Two Decades." *Communications Theory* 4 (1994): 259–94.

Botha, P. J. J. "Letter Writing and Oral Communication in Antiquity: Suggested Implications for the Interpretation of Paul's Letter to the Galatians." *Scriptura* 42 (1992): 19–23.

Brandt, W. J. *The Rhetoric of Argumentation*. New York: Bobbs-Merrill, 1970.

Brinton, Alan. "Situation in the Theory of Rhetoric." *PR* 14 (1981): 234–48.

Bromiley, G. W., ed. *International Standard Bible Encyclopedia*. 4 vols. Grand Rapids, Mich.: Eerdmans, 1979–1988.

Bruehler, Bart B. "Karma Yoga and Christian Ethics: Reading Bhagavad Gita 3 in Light of Ephesians 4–6." Pages 23–48 in *Song Divine: Christian Commentaries on the Bhagavad Gita*. Edited by Catherine Cornille. Leuven: Peeters Press, 2006.

Bullinger, E. W. *Figures of Speech Used in the Bible*. London: Eyre and Spottiswoode, 1898.

Bultmann, Rudolf. *Die Geschichte der synoptischen Tradition*. Göttingen: Vandenhoeck, 1921. Published in English as *The History of the Synoptic Tradition*. Translated by John Marsh. New York: Harper & Row, 1963.

———. *Der Stil der paulinischen Predigt und die kynisch-stoische Diatribe*. Göttingen: Vandenhoeck and Ruprecht, 1910.

Burke, Kenneth. *Counter-Statement*. 3rd rev. ed. Berkeley: University of California Press, 1968.

———. "A Dramatistic View of the Origins of Language." *QJS* 38.3 (1952): 251–64; 38.4 (1952): 446–60; 39.1 (1953): 79–91.

———. *A Rhetoric of Motives*. Englewood Cliffs, N.J.: Prentice-Hall, 1950. Reprint. Berkeley: University of California Press, 1969.

———. *The Rhetoric of Religion: Studies in Logography*. Berkeley and Los Angeles: University of California Press, 1970.

Burridge, Richard. "The Gospels and Acts." Pages 507–32 in *Handbook of Classical Rhetoric in the Hellenistic Period 330 B.C.–A.D. 400*. Edited by Stanley E. Porter. Leiden: Brill, 2001.

———. *What Are the Gospels? A Comparison with Graeco-Roman Biography*. Cambridge: Cambridge University Press, 1992. 2nd ed. Grand Rapids, Mich.: Eerdmans, 2004.

Buttrick, G. A., ed. *The Interpreter's Dictionary of the Bible*. 4 vols. Nashville: Abingdon, 1962.

Butts, James R. "The Chreia in the Synoptic Gospels." *BTB* 16 (1986): 132–38.

Cadbury, Henry Joel. *The Style and Literary Method of Luke*. Harvard Theological Studies 6. Edited by George F. Moore, James H. Ropes, and Kirsopp Lake. Cambridge and London: Harvard University Press/Oxford University Press, 1920.

Campbell, George. *The Philosophy of Rhetoric*. Edited by Lloyd Bitzer. Carbondale: Southern Illinois University Press, 1963.

Campbell, Karlyn Kohrs. "Conventional Wisdom—Traditional Form: A Rejoinder." *QJS* 58 (1972): 451–53.

Carey, Greg. "The Apocalypse and Its Ambiguous Ethos." Pages 163–80 in *Studies in the Book of Revelation*. Edited by Steven Moyise. Edinburgh: T&T Clark, 2001.

———. "Apocalyptic Ethos." Pages 731–61 in *SBLSP* 37. Atlanta: Scholars Press, 1998.

———. *Elusive Apocalypse: Reading Authority in the Revelation to John*. StABH 15. Macon, Ga.: Mercer University Press, 1999.

———. Review of Dal Lee, *The Narrative Asides in the Book of Revelation*. *CBQ* 65 (2003): 643–44.

———. *Ultimate Things: An Introduction to Jewish and Christian Apocalyptic Literature*. St. Louis: Chalice, 2005.

Carey, Greg, and L. Gregory Bloomquist, eds. *Vision and Persuasion: Rhetorical Dimensions of Apocalyptic Discourse*. St. Louis: Chalice, 1999.

Carmack, William R. "Studies in Classical Rhetoric." *QJS* 49 (1963): 325–28.

Chatman, Seymour. *Story and Discourse: Narrative Structure in Fiction and Film.* Ithaca: Cornell University Press, 1980.

Church, F. Forrester. "Rhetorical Structure and Design in Paul's Letter to Philemon." *HTR* 71 (1978): 17–33.

Classen, Carl Joachim. "Paulus und die antike Rhetorik." *ZNW* 82 (1991): 1–32.

———. *Rhetorical Criticism of the New Testament.* Tübingen: Mohr (Siebeck), 2000.

———. "St. Paul's Epistles and Ancient Greek and Roman Rhetoric." *Rhetorica* 10 (1992): 319–44.

Cmiel, Kenneth. *Democratic Eloquence: The Fight over Popular Speech in Nineteenth-Century America.* New York: William Morrow, 1990.

Cohen, Herman. *The History of Speech Communication: The Emergence of a Discipline, 1914–1945.* Annandale, Va.: The Speech Communication Association, 1994.

Collins, Adela Yarbro. *Crisis and Catharsis: The Power of the Apocalypse.* Philadelphia: Westminster, 1984.

Collins, Raymond F. *First Corinthians.* SP 7. Collegeville, Minn.: Liturgical, 1999.

Conley, Thomas. *Rhetoric in the European Tradition.* New York: Longman, 1990.

Connors, Robert, Lisa Ede, and Andrea Lunsford, eds. *Essays on Classical Rhetoric and Modern Discourse.* Carbondale: Southern Illinois University Press, 1984.

Consigny, Scott. "Rhetoric and Its Situation." *PR* 7 (1974): 175–85.

Coorigan, J., F. M. Denny, C. M. N. Eire, and M. S. Jaffe. *Jews, Christians, Muslims: A Comparative Introduction to Monotheistic Religions.* Upper Saddle River, N.J.: Prentice Hall, 1998.

Corbett, Edward P. J. *Classical Rhetoric for the Modern Student.* New York: Oxford University Press, 1965.

Corbett, Edward P. J., James L. Golden, and Goodwin F. Berquist, eds. *Essays on the Rhetoric of the Western World.* Dubuque: Kendall/Hunt, 1990.

Coulton, Thomas E. "Trends in Speech Education in American Colleges." Ph.D. dissertation, New York University, 1935.

Crafton, Jeffrey A. *The Agency of the Apostle: A Dramatistic Analysis of Paul's Responses to Conflict in 2 Corinthians.* Journal for the Study of the New Testament: Supplement Series 51. Sheffield: JSOT Press, 1991.

Crouch, Frank. "The Persuasive Moment: Rhetorical Resolutions in Paul's Defense before Agrippa." Pages 333–41 in *SBLSP* 35. Atlanta: Scholars Press, 1996.
Culpepper, R. Alan. *Anatomy of the Fourth Gospel: A Study in Literary Design*. Philadelphia: Fortress, 1983.
Czachesz, Istvan. "Socio-Rhetorical Exegesis of Acts 9.1-10." *CV* 37 (1995): 5–32.
Davies, W. D., and Dale C. Allison Jr. *A Critical and Exegetical Commentary on the Gospel According to Saint Matthew*. 3 vols. ICC. Edinburgh: T&T Clark, 1988.
Deissmann, Adolf. *Bible Studies*. Translated by A. Grieve. Edinburgh: T&T Clark, 1901.
———. *Light From the Ancient East*. Translated by L. R. M. Strachan. New York: Doran, 1927.
———. *Paul: A Study in Social and Religious History*. Translated by W. Wilson. 2nd ed. London: Hodder & Stoughton, 1926.
deSilva, David A. "The Construction and Social Function of a Counter-Cosmos in the Revelation of John." *Forum* 9.1-2 (1993): 47–61.
———. "Honor Discourse and the Rhetorical Strategy of the Apocalypse of John." *JSNT* 71 (1998): 79–110.
———. "Toward a Socio-Rhetorical Taxonomy of Divine Intervention: Miracle Discourse in the Revelation to John." Pages 303–16 in *Fabrics of Discourse: Essays in Honor of Vernon K. Robbins*. Edited by David B. Gowler, L. Gregory Bloomquist, and Duane F. Watson. Harrisburg, Pa.: Trinity Press International, 2003.
Dibelius, Martin. *Aufsätze zur Apostelgeschichte*. Göttingen: Vandenhoeck & Ruprecht. 1951. Published in English as *Studies in the Acts of the Apostles*. Translated by Heinrich Greeven. New York: Scribner's Sons, 1956.
———. *Die Formgeschichte des Evangeliums*. Tübingen: Mohr, 1919. Published in English as *From Tradition to Gospel*. 2nd ed. Translated by Bertram L. Woolf. New York: Charles Scribner's Sons, 1934.
Donfried, Karl P. "The Epistolary and Rhetorical Context of 1 Thessalonians 2.1-12." Pages vii–xii, 3–60 in *The Thessalonians Debate: Methodological Discord or Methodological Synthesis?* Edited by Karl P. Donfried and Johannes Beutler. Grand Rapids, Mich., and Cambridge: Eerdmans, 2000.

Donfried, Karl, and I. Howard Marshall. *The Theology of the Shorter Pauline Letters*. New Testament Theology. Cambridge: Cambridge University Press, 1993.

Douglass, Frederick. *Narrative of the Life of Frederick Douglass, An American Slave*, in *Frederick Douglass: Autobiographies*. Edited by Henry Louis Gates Jr. Los Angeles and New York: Literary Classics of the United States, 1994.

Duff, Paul. *Who Rides the Beast? Prophetic Rivalry and the Rhetoric of Crisis in the Churches of the Apocalypse*. Oxford: Oxford University Press, 2001.

Duhamel, P. Albert, and Richard E. Hughes. *Rhetoric: Principles and Usage*. Englewood Cliffs, N.J.: Prentice-Hall, 1962.

Dupont, Jacques. "La structure oratoire du discourse d'Étienne." *Bib* 66 (1985): 153–67.

Easton, John. "'Uniquely human' component of language found in gregarious birds." No pages. Online: http://www-news.uchicago.edu.releases/06/060426.starling.shtml.

Ehrman, Bart. "Cephas and Peter." *JBL* 109 (1990): 463–74.

———. *Lost Christianities: The Battles for Scripture and the Faiths We Never Knew*. New York: Oxford University Press, 2003.

Elliott, John H. "The Evil Eye and the Sermon on the Mount: Contours of a Pervasive Belief in Social Scientific Perspective." *BibInt* 2 (1994): 51–84.

Elliott, Susan. "Choose Your Mother, Choose Your Master: Galatians 4:21–5:1 in the Shadow of the Anatolian Mother of the Gods." *JBL* 118 (1999): 661–83.

Else, Gerald F. *Aristotle's Poetics: The Argument*. Cambridge: Harvard University Press, 1957.

Enos, Theresa, ed. *Encyclopedia of Rhetoric and Composition*. New York: Garland Publishing, 1996.

Eriksson, Anders, Thomas H. Olbricht, and Walter Übelacker., eds. *Rhetorical Argumentation in Biblical Texts: Essays from the Lund 2000 Conference*. Harrisburg, Pa.: Trinity Press International, 2002.

Ernesti, J. C. G. *Initia rhetorica*. Leipzig: Fritsch, 1784.

———. *Lexicon technologiae Graecorum rhetoricae*. Leipzig: Fritsch, 1795.

———. *Lexicon technologiae Latinorum rhetoricae*. Leipzig: Fritsch, 1797.

Esler, Philip. *Galatians*. New York: Routledge, 1998.

Fauconnier, Gilles, and Mark Turner. *The Way We Think: Conceptual Blending and the Mind's Hidden Complexities*. New York: Basic Books, 2002.

Fisher, Walter R. *Human Communication as Narration: Toward a Philosophy of Reason, Value, and Action*. Columbia: University of South Carolina Press, 1987.

Funk, Robert. "Apostolic Parousia: Form and Significance." Pages 249–69 in *Christian History and Interpretation: Studies Presented to John Knox*. Edited by W. R. Farmer, C. F. D. Moule, and R. R. Niebuhr. Cambridge: Cambridge University Press, 1967.

Funk, Robert, and the Jesus Seminar, eds. *The Acts of Jesus: The Search for the Authentic Deeds of Jesus*. Santa Rosa, Calif.: Polebridge, 1998.

———, eds. *The Gospel of Jesus, According to the Jesus Seminar*. Santa Rosa, Calif.: Polebridge, 1999.

Funk, Robert, Roy W. Hoover, and the Jesus Seminar, eds. *The Five Gospels: The Search for the Authentic Words of Jesus*. San Francisco: Polebridge, 1993.

Gempf, Conrad. "Public Speaking and Published Accounts." Pages 259–303 in *The Book of Acts in Its Ancient Literary Setting*. Edited by Bruce W. Winter and Andrew D. Clarke. Volume 1 of *The Book of Acts and Its First-Century Setting*. Edited by Bruce W. Winter. Grand Rapids, Mich.: Eerdmans, 1993.

Gilders, William K. *Blood Ritual in the Hebrew Bible: Meaning and Power*. Baltimore: The Johns Hopkins University Press, 2004.

Gilliard, Frank D. "More on Silent Reading in Antiquity: *Non Omne Verbum Sonabat*." *JBL* 112 (1993): 689–94.

Given, Mark D. *Paul's True Rhetoric: Ambiguity, Cunning, and Deception in Greece and Rome*. ESEC 7. Harrisburg, Pa.: Trinity Press International, 2001.

Goldstein, Jonathan A. *The Letters of Demosthenes*. New York and London: Columbia University Press, 1968.

Grams, Rollin. "The Temple Conflict Scene: A Rhetorical Analysis of Matthew 21–23." Pages 41–65 in *Persuasive Artistry: Studies in New Testament Rhetoric in Honor of George A. Kennedy*. Edited by Duane F. Watson. Journal for the Study of the New Testament: Supplement Series 50. Sheffield: Sheffield Academic, 1991.

Grant, F. C. "Rhetoric and Oratory." Pages 4:75–77 in *IDB*. Edited by George A. Buttrick. Nashville: Abingdon, 1962.

Grant, Robert M. *The Earliest Lives of Jesus*. New York: Harper & Brothers, 1961.

Green, Joel B., Scot McKnight, and I. Howard Marshall, eds. *Dictionary of Jesus and the Gospels*. Downers Grove, Ill.: InterVarsity, 1992.

Grube, G. M. A. *The Greek and Roman Critics*. Toronto: University of Toronto Press, 1965.

Gunn, David M., and Paula M. McNutt, eds. *'Imagining' Biblical Worlds: Studies in Spatial, Social and Historical Constructs in Honor of James W. Flanagan*. JSOTSup 359. Sheffield: Sheffield Academic, 2002.

Guthrie, W. K. C. *The Fifth-Century Enlightenment*. Volume 3 of *A History of Greek Philosophy*. 6 vols. Cambridge: Cambridge University Press, 1969.

Guthrie, Warren. "Rhetorical Theory in Colonial America." Pages 48–59 in *History of Speech Education in America: Background Studies*. Edited by Karl R. Wallace. New York: Appleton–Century–Crofts, 1954.

Haberman, Frederick W. "English Sources of American Elocution." Pages 105–26 in *History of Speech Education in America: Background Studies*. Edited by Karl R. Wallace. New York: Appleton–Century–Crofts, 1954.

Hansen, G. Walter. *Abraham in Galatians: Epistolary and Rhetorical Contexts*. Journal for the Study of the New Testament: Supplement Series 29. Sheffield: JSOT Press, 1989.

Harshbarger, H. Clay. *Some Highlights of the Department of Speech and Dramatic Art*. Iowa City: University of Iowa, 1976.

Hary, Benjamin H. "Adaptations of Hebrew Script." Pages 727–34, 741–42 in *The World's Writing Systems*. Edited by P. T. Daniels and W. Bright. New York: Oxford University Press, 1996.

———. "Judeo-Arabic in Its Socio-Linguistic Setting." *IOS* 15 (1995): 73–99.

———. *Multiglossia in Judeo-Arabic*. Leiden: Brill, 1992.

Hauser, Gerard A. "Henry W. Johnstone, Jr.: Reviving the Dialogue of Philosophy and Rhetoric." *RC* 1 (2000): 1–25.

Hayles, N. Katherine. *Chaos Bound: Orderly Disorder in Contemporary Literature and Science*. Ithaca: Cornell University Press, 1985.

Heever, Gerhard van den. "Finding Data in Unexpected Places (Or: From Text Linguistics to Socio-Rhetoric): A Socio-Rhetorical Reading of John's Gospel." Pages 629–76 in volume 2 of *SBLSP* 37. 2 vols. Atlanta: Scholars Press, 1998.

Hester, James D. "Epideictic Rhetoric and Persona in Galatians One and Two." Pages 181–96 in *The Galatians Debate*. Edited by Mark Nanos. Peabody, Mass.: Hendrickson, 2002.

———. "A Fantasy Theme Analysis of 1 Thessalonians." Pages 504–25 in *Rhetorical Criticism and the Bible*. Edited by Stanley E. Porter and Dennis Stamps. Journal for the Study of the New Testament: Supplement Series 195. Sheffield: Sheffield Academic, 2002.

———. "Placing the Blame: The Presence of Epideictic in Galatians 1 and 2." Pages 281–307 in *Persuasive Artistry: Studies in New Testament Rhetoric in Honor of George A. Kennedy*. Edited by D. F. Watson. Journal for the Study of the New Testament: Supplement Series 50. Sheffield: Sheffield Academic, 1991.

———. "The Rhetoric of Persona in Romans: Re-reading Romans 1:1-12." Pages 83–105 in *Celebrating Romans: Template for Pauline Theology*. Edited by Sheila E. McGinn. Grand Rapids, Mich.: Eerdmans, 2004.

———. "The Rhetorical Structure of Galatians 1:11–2:14." *JBL* 103 (1984): 223–33.

———. "Speaker, Audience and Situations: A Modified Interactional Model," *Neot* 32 (1998): 80–83.

———. "The Use and Influence of Rhetoric in Galatians 2:1-14." *TZ* 42 (1986): 386–408.

Hester, James D., and J. David Hester (Amador), eds. *Rhetorics and Hermeneutics: Wilhelm Wuellner and His Influence*. New York: T&T Clark International, 2004.

Hill, Forbes. "Conventional Wisdom—Traditional Form: The President's Message of November 3, 1969." *QJS* 58 (1972): 373–86.

———. "Reply to Professor Campbell." *QJS* 58 (1972): 454–60.

Hock, Ronald F. "The Chreia in Primary and Secondary Education." Pages 11–35 in *Alexander's Revenge*. Edited by J. M. Asgeirsson and N. van Deusen. Reykjavik: University of Iceland Press, 2002.

———. "Paul and Greco-Roman Education." Pages 198–227 in *Paul in the Greco-Roman World: A Handbook*. Edited by J. Paul Sampley. Harrisburg, Pa.: Trinity Press International, 2003.

———. *The Social Context of Paul's Ministry: Tentmaking and Apostleship*. Philadelphia: Fortress, 1980.

Hock, Ronald F., and Edward N. O'Neil, eds. *The Chreia and Ancient Rhetoric: Classroom Exercises*. Writings from the Greco-Roman World 3. Atlanta: Society of Biblical Literature, 2002.

———. *The Chreia in Ancient Rhetoric: The Progymnasmata*. Greco-Roman Religions Series 9. Atlanta: Scholars Press, 1986.

Hogan, Derek. "Paul's Defense: A Comparison of the Forensic Speeches in Acts, Callirhoe, and Leucippe and Clitophon." *PRS* 29 (2002): 73–87.

Holland, Glenn S. *The Traditions That You Received from Us: 2 Thessalonians in the Pauline Tradition.* HUT 24. Tübingen: Mohr Siebeck, 1986.

Hoshor, John P. "American Contributions to Rhetorical Theory and Homiletics." Pages 129–52 in *History of Speech Education in America: Background Studies.* Edited by Karl R. Wallace. New York: Appleton–Century–Crofts, 1954.

Hudson, Hoyt H. "Alexander M. Drummond." Pages 3–10 in *Studies in Speech and Drama in Honor of A. M. Drummond.* Ithaca: Cornell University Press, 1944.

Hughes, Frank W. *Early Christian Rhetoric and 2 Thessalonians.* Journal for the Study of the New Testament: Supplement Series 30. Sheffield: JSOT Press, 1989.

———. "The Parable of the Rich Man and Lazarus (Luke 16:19-31) and Graeco-Roman Rhetoric." Pages 29–41 in *Rhetoric and the New Testament: Essays from the 1992 Heidelberg Conference.* Edited by Stanley E. Porter and Thomas H. Olbricht. Journal for the Study of the New Testament: Supplement Series 90. Sheffield: Sheffield, 1993.

———. "The Rhetoric of 1 Thessalonians." Pages 94–116 in *The Thessalonian Correspondence.* Edited by Raymond F. Collins. BETL 87. Leuven: Leuven University Press and Peeters, 1990.

Humphrey, Edith M. "In Search of a Voice: Rhetoric through Sight and Sound in Revelation 11:15–12:17." Pages 141–60 in *Vision and Persuasion: Rhetorical Dimensions of Apocalyptic Discourse.* Edited by Greg Carey and L. Gregory Bloomquist. St. Louis: Chalice, 1999.

Hunsaker, David M., and Craig R. Smith. "The Nature of Issues: A Constructive Approach to Situational Rhetoric." *Western Speech Communication* 40 (1976): 144–56.

Jeal, Roy R. "Blending Two Arts: Rhetorical Words, Rhetorical Pictures and Social Formation in the Letter to Philemon." No pages. Online: http://rhetjournal.net/Jeal.pdf.

———. "Clothes Make the (Wo)man." No pages. Online: www.arsrhetorica.net/Queen/VolumeSpecialIssue5/Articles/Jeal.pdf.

———. "Writing Socio-Rhetorical Commentary: Colossians 1:15-20." Paper presented at the annual meeting of the SBL, RRA Seminar. Washington, D.C., November 17, 2006.

Jebb, Richard Claverhouse. *The Attic Orators from Antiphon to Isaeos*. 2 vols. New York: Russell & Russell, 1962.
Jewett, Robert. *Romans: A Commentary*. Hermeneia. Minneapolis: Fortress, 2006.
———. *The Thessalonian Correspondence: Pauline Rhetoric and Millenarian Piety*. FFNT. Philadelphia: Fortress, 1986.
Johanson, Bruce C. *To All the Brethren: A Text-Linguistic and Rhetorical Approach to 1 Thessalonians*. ConBNT 16. Stockholm: Almqvist & Wiksell, 1987.
Johns, Loren L. *The Lamb Christology of the Apocalypse of John: An Investigation into Its Origins and Rhetorical Force*. WUNT 167. Tübingen: Mohr (Siebeck), 2003.
———. "The Lamb in the Rhetorical Program on the Apocalypse of John." Pages 762–84 in *SBLSP* 37. Atlanta: Scholars Press, 1998.
Johnson, Luke Timothy. *The Creed: What Christians Believe and Why It Matters*. New York: Doubleday, 2003.
Johnson, Robert Underwood. *Remembered Yesterdays*. Boston: Little, Brown, 1923. Reprint. Whitefish, Mont.: Kessinger Publishing, 2004.
Jolivet, Ira J. "The Lukan Account of Paul's Conversion and Hermagorean Stasis Theory." Pages 210–20 in *The Rhetorical Interpretation of Scripture: Essays from the 1996 Malibu Conference*. Edited by Stanley E. Porter and Dennis L. Stamps. Journal for the Study of the New Testament: Supplement Series 180. Sheffield: Sheffield Academic, 1999.
Jordan, Harold M. "Rhetorical Education in American Colleges and University, 1850–1915." Ph.D. dissertation, Northwestern University, 1952.
Kelly, J. N. D. *Early Christian Creeds*. London, New York, and Toronto: Longmans, Green, 1952.
Kim, Johann D. *God, Israel, and the Gentiles: Rhetoric and Situation in Romans 9–11*. SBLDS 176. Atlanta: Society of Biblical Literature, 2000.
Kirby, John T. "The Rhetorical Situations of Revelation 1–3." *NTS* 34 (1988): 197–207.
König, Eduard. *Stilistik, Rhetorik, und Poetik in Bezug auf die biblische Literatur*. Leipzig: Weicher, 1900.
Kraftchick, Steven J. "Πάθη in Paul: The Emotional Logic in 'Original Argument.'" Pages 39–68 in *Paul and Pathos*. Edited by Thomas H. Olbricht and Jerry L. Sumney. SBLSymS 16. Atlanta: Society of Biblical Literature, 2001.

Kurz, William. "Hellenistic Rhetoric in the Christological Proof of Luke-Acts." *CBQ* 42 (1980): 171–95.

———. "Narrative Models for Imitation in Luke-Acts." Pages 171–98 in *Greeks, Romans, and Christians: Essays in Honor of Abraham J. Malherbe*. Edited by David L. Balch, Everettt Ferguson, and Wayne A. Meeks. Minneapolis: Fortress, 1990.

Lakoff, George. *Don't Think of an Elephant: Know Your Values and Frame the Debate*. White River Junction, Vt.: Chelsea Green, 2004.

———. *Women, Fire, and Dangerous Things: What Categories Reveal about the Mind*. Chicago and London: University of Chicago Press, 1987.

Lausberg, Heinrich. *Handbook of Literary Rhetoric: A Foundation for Literary Study*. Edited by David E. Orton and R. Dean Anderson. Translated by Matthew T. Bliss, Annemiek Jansen, and David E. Orton, with foreword by George A. Kennedy. Leiden: Brill, 1998. Translation from *Handbuch der literarischen Rhetorik: Eine Grundlegung der Literaturwissenschaft*. 2 vols. Munich: Hueber, 1960.

Lee, Dal. *The Narrative Asides in the Book of Revelation*. Lanham, Md.: University Press of America, 2002.

Leon, Judah Messer. *The Book of the Honeycomb's Flow (Sepher Nopheth Suphim)*. Translated by Isaac Rabinowitz. Ithaca: Cornell University Press, 1982.

Levison, John R. "Did the Spirit Inspire Rhetoric? An Exploration of George Kennedy's Definition of Early Christian Rhetoric." Pages 25–40 in *Persuasive Artistry: Studies in New Testament Rhetoric in Honor of George A. Kennedy*. Edited by Duane F. Watson. Journal for the Study of the New Testament: Supplement Series 50. Sheffield: JSOT, 1991.

Lincoln, Andrew T. *Truth on Trial: The Lawsuit Motif in the Fourth Gospel*. Peabody, Mass.: Hendrickson, 2000.

Longenecker, Bruce W. "Linked Like a Chain: Rev 22.6-9 in Light of Ancient Translation Technique." *NTS* 47 (2001): 105–17.

———. "Lukan Aversion to Humps and Hollows: The Case of Acts 11.27–12.25." *NTS* 50 (2004): 185–204.

———. *Rhetoric at the Boundaries: The Art and Theology of New Testament Chain-Link Transitions*. Waco, Tex.: Baylor University Press, 2005.

Longenecker, Richard N. *Galatians*. WBC 41. Dallas: Word, 1990.

Lösch, Stephen. "Die Dankesrede des Tertullus, APG 24.1-4." *ThQ* 112 (1931): 295–319.

Lowth, Robert. *De Sacra Poesi Hebraeorum. Praelectiones Academicae Oxonii Habitae a Roberto Lowth.* Oxford: Clarendon, 1753.

Luedemann, Gerd. *Paul, Apostle to the Gentiles: Studies in Chronology.* Philadelphia: Fortress, 1984.

Lyons, George. *Pauline Autobiography: Toward a New Understanding.* SBLDS 73. Atlanta: Scholars Press, 1985.

Lyons, Joseph A. *The American Elocutionist and Dramatic Reader for the Use of Colleges, Academies, and Schools.* 2nd rev. ed. Philadelphia: Butler, 1872.

Mack, Burton L. *Anecdotes and Arguments: The Chreia in Antiquity and Early Christianity.* Occasional Papers 10. Claremont, Calif.: The Institute for Antiquity and Christianity, 1987.

———. *Rhetoric and the New Testament.* GBSNTS. Minneapolis: Fortress, 1990.

Mack, Burton, and Vernon K. Robbins. *Patterns of Persuasion in the Gospels.* Foundations and Facets: Literary Facets. Sonoma, Calif.: Polebridge, 1989.

Malherbe, Abraham J. *Ancient Epistolary Theorists.* SBLSBS 19. Atlanta: Scholars Press, 1988.

———. "'Seneca' on Paul as Letter Writer." Pages 414–21 in *The Future of Early Christianity: Essays in Honor of Helmut Koester.* Edited by Birger A. Pearson. Minneapolis: Fortress, 1991.

Mannheim, Karl. "Erwin Panofsky and Karl Mannheim: A Dialogue on Interpretation." *Critical Inquiry* 19 (1993): 534–66.

Martin, Troy. "Apostasy to Paganism: The Rhetorical Stasis of the Galatian Controversy." *JBL* 114 (1995): 437–61.

Martyn, J. Louis. *History and Theology in the Fourth Gospel.* 3rd ed. NTL. Louisville, Ky.: Westminster John Knox, 2003.

Marxsen, Willi. *Der Evangelist Markus: Studien zur Redaktionsgeschichte des Evangeliums.* Göttingen: Vandenhoeck & Ruprecht, 1956. Translated into English as *Mark the Evangelist.* Translated by James Boyce, et. al. Nashville: Abingdon, 1968.

Maryono, Petrus. "Luke's Use of Biblical History and Promise in Acts 13.16-41." Ph.D. dissertation, Dallas Theological Seminary, 2001.

McCauley, Robert N., and E. Thomas Lawson. *Bringing Ritual to Mind: Psychological Foundations of Cultural Forms.* Cambridge: Cambridge University Press, 2002.

———. *Rethinking Religion: Connecting Cognition and Culture.* Cambridge: Cambridge University Press, 1990.

McDonald, J. Ian H. "Rhetorical Issue and Rhetorical Strategy in Luke 10:25-37." Pages 59–73 in *Rhetoric and the New Testament: Essays from the 1992 Heidelberg Conference*. Edited by Stanley E. Porter and Thomas H. Olbricht. Journal for the Study of the New Testament: Supplement Series 90. Sheffield: Sheffield Academic, 1993.

McGuire, M. R. P. "Letters and Letter Carriers in Christian Antiquity." *CW* 53 (1960): 148–53, 184–86, 199–200.

McKerrow, Raymie. "Critical Rhetoric: Theory and Praxis." *CM* 56 (1989): 91–111.

Meeks, Wayne A. "*Hypomnēmata* from an Untamed Sceptic: A Response to George Kennedy." Pages 157–72 in *The Relationship Among the Gospels: An Interdisciplinary Dialogue*. Edited by William O. Walker Jr. San Antonio: Trinity University Press, 1978.

Melanchthon, Philip. *Commentarii in epistolam ad Romanos hoc anno M.D.XL. recogniti et locupletati*. Argentorati: Apud C. Mylium, 1540.

Mesner, David E. "The Rhetoric of Citations: Paul's Use of Scripture in Romans 9." Ph.D. dissertation, Northwestern University/Garrett-Evangelical Theological Seminary, 1991.

Meynet, Roland. "Histoire de 'L'analyse rhetorique' en exégèse biblique." *Rhetorica* 8 (1990): 291–320.

Miles, Jack. *God: A Biography*. New York: Vintage Books, 1996.

Miller, Arthur B. "Rhetorical Exigence." *PR* 5 (1972): 111–18.

Miller, Melvin. Review of George A. Kennedy, *The Art of Persuasion in Greece*. *LJ* 48 (1964): 57–58.

Miller, Robert J. *The Complete Gospel*. Santa Rosa, Calif.: Polebridge, 1994.

Mitchell, Margaret. *Paul and the Rhetoric of Reconciliation: An Exegetical Investigation of the Language and Composition of 1 Corinthians*. HUT 28. Tübingen: Mohr Siebeck, 1991.

Mitchell, W. J. T. *Picture Theory: Essays on Verbal and Visual Representation*. Chicago and London: University of Chicago Press, 1994.

Moreland, Milton. "The Jerusalem Commentary in Acts: Mythmaking and the Socio-Rhetorical Functions of a Lukan Setting." Pages 285–310 in *Contextualizing Acts: Lukan Narrative and Greco-Roman Discourse*. Edited by Todd Penner and Caroline Vander Stichele. SBLSymS 20. Atlanta: Society of Biblical Literature, 2003.

Muilenburg, James. "Form Criticism and Beyond." *JBL* 88 (1969): 1–18.

Murphy-O'Connor, Jerome. *Paul the Letter-Writer*. Collegeville, Minn.: Liturgical, 1995.

Nanos, Mark, ed. *The Galatians Debate*. Peabody, Mass.: Hendrickson, 2002.

———. *The Irony of Galatians: Paul's Letter in First-Century Context*. Minneapolis: Fortress, 2002.

Neyrey, Jerome H. "The Social Location of Paul: Education as the Key." Pages 126–64 in *Fabrics of Discourse: Essays in Honor of Vernon K. Robbins*. Edited by David B. Gowler, L. Gregory Bloomquist, and Duane F. Watson. Harrisburg, Pa.: Trinity Press International, 2003.

Nikolakopoulos, Constantin. "Rhetorische Auslegungsaspekte der Theologie in der Johannesoffenbarung." Pages 166–80 in *"... Was ihr auf dem Weg verhandelt haben": Beiträge zur Exegese und Theologie des Neuen Testaments: Festschrift für Ferdinand Hahn zum 75. Geburtstag*. Edited by C. Gerber, T. Knoppler, and P. Muller. Neukirchen-Vluyn: Neukirchener Verlag, 2001.

Norden, Eduard. *Agnostos Theos: Untersuchungen zur Formengeschichte religiöser Rede*. Leipzig and Berlin: Teubner, 1913.

———. *Die antike Kunstprosa vom VI. Jahrhundert vor Christus in die Zeit der Renaissance*. 2 vols. Leipzig: Teubner, 1898.

Okoronkwo, Michael Enyinwa. *The Jerusalem Compromise as a Conflict-Resolution Model: A Rhetoric-Communicative Analysis of Acts 15 in the Light of Modern Linguistics*. AI 1. Bonn: Borengässer, 2001.

O'Leary, Stephen D. *Arguing the Apocalypse: A Theory of Millennial Rhetoric*. New York: Oxford University Press, 1994.

———. "A Dramatistic Theory of Apocalyptic Rhetoric. *QJS* 79 (1993): 385–426.

Olbricht, Thomas H. "An Aristotelian Rhetorical Analysis of 1 Thessalonians." Pages 216–36 in *Greeks, Romans, and Christians, Essays in Honor of Abraham J. Malherbe*. Edited by David L. Balch, Everett Ferguson, and Wayne A. Meeks. Minneapolis: Fortress, 1990.

———. "The Flowering of Rhetorical Criticism in America." Pages 79–102 in *The Rhetorical Analysis of Scripture: Essays from the 1995 London Conference*. Edited by Stanley E. Porter and Thomas H. Olbricht. JSNTSup 146. Sheffield: Sheffield Academic, 1997.

———. "Pathos as Proof in Greco-Roman Rhetoric." Pages 7–22 in *Paul and Pathos*. Edited by Thomas H. Olbricht and Jerry L. Sumney. SBLSymS 16. Atlanta: Society of Biblical Literature, 2001.

———. "A Rhetorical Analysis of Representative Homilies of Basil the Great." Ph.D. dissertation, University of Iowa, 1959.

Oliver, Robert T. *Communication and Culture in Ancient India and China.* Syracuse, N.Y.: Syracuse University Press, 1971.

———. *Culture and Communication: The Problem of Penetrating National and Cultural Boundaries.* Springfield, Ill.: Thomas, 1962.

Panofsky, Erwin. *Studies in Iconology: Humanistic Themes in the Art of the Renaissance.* New York: Oxford University Press, 1939.

Parker, William Riley. "Where Do English Departments Come From?" *College English* 28 (1967): 339–51. Reprinted pages 1–15 in *Essays on the Rhetoric of the Western World.* Edited by Edward P. J. Corbett, James L. Golden, and Goodwin F. Berquist. Dubuque: Kendall/Hunt, 1990.

Parrish, Wayland M. "Elocution—A Definition and a Challenge." *QJS* 43 (1957): 1–11.

Parsons, Mikeal. "Luke and the Progymnasmata: A Preliminary Investigation into the Preliminary Exercises." Pages 43–63 in *Contextualizing Acts: Lukan Narrative and Greco-Roman Discourse.* Edited by Todd Penner and Caroline Vander Stichele. SBLSymS 20. Atlanta: Society of Biblical Literature, 2003.

Pattemore, Stephen. *The People of God in the Apocalypse.* SNTSMS 128. New York: Cambridge University Press, 2004.

Patton, John H. "Causation and Creativity in Rhetorical Situations: Distinctions and Implications." *QJS* 65 (1979): 36–55.

Patton, Laurie L. *Bringing the Gods to Mind: Mantra and Ritual in Early Indian Sacrifice.* Berkeley and London: University of California Press, 2005.

Pelikan, Jaroslav. *Divine Rhetoric: The Sermon on the Mount as Message and as Model in Augustine, Chrysostom, and Luther.* Crestwood, N.Y.: St. Vladimir's Press, 2001.

Penner, Todd. "Civilizing Discourse: Acts, Declamation, and the Rhetoric of the Polis." Pages 65–104 in *Contextualizing Acts: Lukan Narrative and Greco-Roman Discourse.* Edited by Todd Penner and Caroline Vander Stichele. SBLSymS 20. Atlanta: Society of Biblical Literature, 2003.

———. *In Praise of Christian Origins: Stephen and the Hellenists in Lukan Apologetic Historiography.* ESEC 10. New York and London: T&T Clark, 2004.

Perelman, Chaim, and Lucie Olbrechts-Tyteca. *The New Rhetoric: A Treatise on Argumentation.* Translated by John Wilkinson and Purcell Weaver. Notre Dame: University of Notre Dame Press, 1969.

Translation from *La Nouvelle Rhétorique: Traité de l'Argumentation*. Paris: Presses Universitaires de France, 1958.

Peter, Hermann. *Der Brief in der römischen Literatur: Literargeschichtliche Untersuchungen und Zusammenfassungen*. Abhandlungen der Königlichen Sächsischen Gesellschaft der Wissenschaften, philologisch-historische Classe, 20.3. Leipzig: Teubner, 1901; repr., Hildesheim: Georg Olms, 1965.

Pilch, John J., and Bruce J. Malina, eds. *Handbook of Biblical Social Values*. Peabody, Mass.: Hendrickson, 1998.

Porter, Stanley E. "Paul as Epistolographer and Rhetorician? Implications for the Study of the Paul of Acts." Pages 98–125 in *The Paul of Acts: Essays in Literary Criticism, Rhetoric, and Theology*. WUNT 115. Tübingen: Mohr Siebeck, 1999. Repr. as *Paul in Acts*. Peabody, Mass.: Hendrickson, 1999.

———. "Paul of Tarsus and His Letters." Pages 533–85 in *Handbook of Classical Rhetoric in the Hellenistic Period 330 B.C.–A.D. 400*. Edited by Stanley E. Porter. Leiden and Boston: Brill, 2001.

———. "The Theoretical Justification for Application of Rhetorical Categories to Pauline Epistolary Literature." Pages 100–122 in *Rhetoric and the New Testament: Essays from the 1992 Heidelberg Conference*. Edited by Stanley E. Porter and Thomas H. Olbricht. Sheffield: Sheffield Academic, 1993.

Porter, Stanley, and Thomas H. Olbricht, eds. *Rhetorical Analysis of Scripture: Essays from the 1995 London Conference*. Journal for the Study of the New Testament: Supplement Series 146. Sheffield: Sheffield Academic, 1997.

———, eds. *Rhetoric and the New Testament 1992 Heidelberg Conference*. Journal for the Study of the New Testament: Supplement Series 90. Sheffield: Sheffield Academic, 1993.

———, eds. *Rhetoric, Scriptures and Theology: Essays from the 1994 Pretoria Conference*. Journal for the Study of the New Testament: Supplement Series 131. Sheffield: Sheffield Academic, 1996.

Porter, Stanley, and Dennis L. Stamps, eds. *Rhetorical Criticism and the Bible: Essays from the 1998 Florence Conference*. Journal for the Study of the New Testament: Supplement Series 195. Sheffield: Sheffield Academic, 2002.

———, eds. *The Rhetorical Interpretation of Scripture: Essays from the 1996 Malibu Conference*. Journal for the Study of the New Testament: Supplement Series 180. Sheffield: Sheffield Academic, 1999.

Reed, Jeffrey T. "Using Ancient Rhetorical Categories to Pauline Epistolary Literature." Pages 292–324 in *Rhetoric and the New Testament: Essays from the 1992 Heidelberg Conference*. Edited by Stanley E. Porter and Thomas H. Olbricht. JSNTSup 90. Sheffield: Sheffield Academic, 1993.

Reid, Marty L. "Paul's Rhetoric of Mutuality: A Rhetorical Reading of Romans." Pages 117–39 in *SBLSP* 34. Atlanta: Scholars Press, 1995.

———. "A Rhetorical Analysis of Romans 1:1-5:21 with Attention Given to the Rhetorical Function of 5:1-21." *PRS* 19 (1992): 255–72.

Reinhold, Meyer. *Classica Americana: The Greek and Roman Heritage in the United States*. Detroit: Wayne State University Press, 1984.

Richard, Carl J. *The Founders and the Classics: Greece, Rome, and the American Enlightenment*. Cambridge: Harvard University Press, 1994.

Richards, Earl Randolph. *Paul and First-Century Letter Writing: Secretaries, Composition and Collection*. Downers Grove, Ill.: InterVarsity, 2004.

———. *The Secretary in the Letters of Paul*. WUNT 42. Tübingen: Mohr-Siebeck, 1991.

Ricoeur, Paul. *The Rule of Metaphor: Multidisciplinary Studies of the Creation of Meaning in Language*. Translated by Robert Czerny, Kathleen McLaughlin, and John Costello. Toronto: University of Toronto Press, 1977.

Robbins, Richard. "Statement." No pages. Online: http://home.comcast.net/~rick1216/.

Robbins, Vernon K., ed. *Ancient Quotes and Anecdotes: From Crib to Crypt*. Sonoma, Calif.: Polebridge, 1989.

———. "Argumentative Textures in Socio-Rhetorical Interpretation." Pages 27–65 in *Rhetorical Argumentation in Biblical Texts: Essays from the Lund 2000 Conference*. Edited by Anders Eriksson, Thomas H. Olbricht, and Walter Übelacker. ESEC 8. Harrisburg, Pa.: Trinity Press International, 2002. Online: http://www.religion.emory.edu/faculty/robbins/Pdfs/LundArgument.pdf.

———. "The Chreia." Pages 1–23 in *Greco-Roman Literature and the New Testament*. Edited by David E. Aune. SBLSBS 21. Atlanta: Scholars Press, 1988.

———. "The Dialectical Nature of Early Christian Discourse." *Scriptura* 59 (1996): 353–62. Online: http://www.religion.emory.edu/faculty/robbins/dialect/dialect353.html.

———. "Enthymeme and Picture in the Gospel of Thomas." Pages 175–207 in *Thomasine Traditions in Antiquity: The Social and Cultural World of the Gospel of Thomas.* Edited by J. Ma Asgeirsson, A. D. DeConick, and R. Uro. NHMS 59. Leiden: Brill, 2006.

———. *Exploring the Texture of Texts: A Guide to Socio-Rhetorical Interpretation.* Valley Forge, Pa.: Trinity Press International, 1996.

———. "From Enthymeme to Theology in Luke 11:1-13." Pages 191–214 in *Literary Studies in Luke-Acts: A Collection of Essays in Honor of Joseph B. Tyson.* Edited by R. P. Thompson and T. E. Phillips. Macon, Ga.: Mercer University Press, 1998. Online: http://www.religion.emory.edu/faculty/robbins/Theology/theology191.html.

———. "From Heidelberg to Heidelberg: Rhetorical Interpretation of the Bible at Seven 'Pepperdine' Conferences from 1991–2002." Pages 335–77 in *Rhetoric, Ethic, and Moral Persuasion in Biblical Discourse.* Edited by Thomas H. Olbricht and Anders Eriksson. ESEC 11. New York: T&T Clark International, 2005.

———. *The Invention of Christian Discourse.* Vol. 1: *Wisdom, Prophetic, and Apocalyptic.* 2 vols. Blandford Forum: Deo Publishing, 2008.

———. *Jesus the Teacher: A Socio-Rhetorical Interpretation of Mark.* Philadelphia: Fortress, 1984.

———. "Narrative in Ancient Rhetoric and Rhetoric in Ancient Narrative." Pages 368–84 in *SBLSP* 35. Atlanta: Scholars Press, 1996.

———. "The Rhetorical Full-Turn in Biblical Interpretation: Reconfiguring Rhetorical-Political Analysis." Pages 48–60 in *Rhetorical Criticism and the Bible.* Edited by Stanley E. Porter, Dennis L. Stamps, and Thomas H. Olbricht. Journal for the Study of the New Testament: Supplement Series 195. Sheffield: Sheffield Academic, 2002.

———, ed. *The Rhetoric of Pronouncement. Semeia* 64 (1993).

———. *The Tapestry of Early Christian Discourse: Rhetoric, Society, and Ideology.* London: Routledge, 1996.

Roberts, R. H., and J. M. M. Good, eds. *The Recovery of Rhetoric: Persuasive Discourse and Disciplinarity in the Human Sciences.* Charlottesville: University of Virginia Press, 1993.

Roetzel, Calvin J. *The Letters of Paul: Conversations in Context.* 4th ed. Louisville, Ky.: Westminster John Knox, 1998.

Roncace, Mark. *Jeremiah, Zedekiah, and the Fall of Jerusalem.* Library of Hebrew Bible/Old Testament Studies. Journal for the Study of the Old Testament: Supplement Series 423. New York and London: T&T Clark, 2005.

Royalty, Robert M., Jr. "The Rhetoric of Revelation." Pages 596–617 in *SBLSP* 36. Atlanta: Scholars Press, 1997.

———. *The Streets of Heaven: The Ideology of Wealth in the Apocalypse of John*. Macon, Ga.: Mercer University Press, 1998.

Sampley, J. Paul. "The First Letter to the Corinthians: Introduction, Commentary, and Reflections." Pages 771–1003 in volume 10 of *The New Interpreter's Bible*. Edited by Leander E. Keck, et. al. 12 vols. Nashville: Abingdon, 2002.

———. "The Second Letter to the Corinthians: Introduction, Commentary, and Reflections." Pages 1–180 in volume 11 of *The New Interpreter's Bible*. Edited by Leander E. Keck, et. al. 12 vols. Nashville: Abingdon, 2000.

Sanders, E. P., and Margaret Davies. *Studying the Synoptic Gospels*. London and Philadelphia: SCM/Trinity Press International, 1989.

Sandness, Karl Olav. "Paul and Socrates: The Aim of Paul's Areopagus Speech." *JSNT* 50 (1993): 13–26.

Satterthwaite, Philip. "Acts Against the Background of Classical Rhetoric." Pages 337–79 in *The Book of Acts in Its Ancient Literary Setting*. Edited by Bruce W. Winter and Andrew D. Clarke. Volume 1 of *The Book of Acts and Its First-Century Setting*. Edited by Bruce W. Winter. Grand Rapids, Mich.: Eerdmans, 1993.

Schmidt, Daryl D. "Rhetorical Influences and Genre: Luke's Preface and the Rhetoric of Hellenistic Historiography." Pages 27–60 in *Jesus and the Heritage of Israel*. Edited by David P. Moessner and David L. Tiede. Volume 1 of *Luke the Interpreter of Israel*. Edited by David P. Moessner. Harrisburg, Pa.: Trinity Press International, 1999.

School-Janßen, Johannes. *Umstrittene "Apologien" in den Paulusbriefen. Studien zur rhetorischen Situation des 1. Thessalonicherbriefes, des Galaterbriefes, und des Philipperbriefes*. GTA 45. Göttingen: Vandenhoeck & Ruprecht, 1991.

Schubert, Paul. *The Form and Function of the Pauline Thanksgivings*. BZNW 20. Berlin: Töpelmann, 1939.

Schüssler Fiorenza, Elisabeth. "The Followers of the Lamb: Visionary Rhetoric and Socio-Political Situation." *Semeia* 36 (1986): 147–74.

———. *Revelation: Vision of a Just World*. Proclamation Commentaries. Minneapolis: Fortress, 1991.

———. *Rhetoric and Ethic: The Politics of Biblical Studies*. Minneapolis: Fortress, 1999.

Schweitzer, Albert. *The Quest of the Historical Jesus*. Translated by J. R. Coates, Susan Cuprit, and John Bowden. Edited by John Bowden. Minneapolis: Fortress, 2001.

Scott, Ian W. "Common Ground? The Role of Galatians 2.16 in Paul's Argument." *NTS* 53 (2007): 425–35.

Shiner, Whitney T. "Applause and Applause Lines." Pages 129–44 in *Rhetorics and Hermeneutics*. Edited by James D. Hester and J. David Hester. New York: T&T Clark, 2004.

———. *Proclaiming the Gospel: First-Century Performance of Mark*. Harrisburg, Pa.: Trinity Press International, 2003.

Shipp, Blake. "A Literary-Rhetorical Analysis of the Damascus Road Accounts in Acts." Ph.D. dissertation, New Orleans Baptist Theological Seminary, 2003.

———. *Paul the Reluctant Witness: Power and Weakness in Luke's Portrayal*. Eugene, Oreg.: Cascade, 2005.

Siew, Antonius King Wai. *The War Between the Two Beasts and the Two Witnesses: A Chiastic Reading of Revelation 11.1-14.5*. Journal for the Study of the New Testament: Supplement Series 283. New York: T&T Clark, 2005.

Smith, Donald K. "Origin and Development of Departments of Speech." Pages 447–70 in *History of Speech Education in America: Background Studies*. Edited by Karl R. Wallace. New York: Appleton–Century–Crofts, 1954.

Soards, Marion L. *The Speeches in Acts: Their Content, Context, and Concerns*. Louisville, Ky.: Westminster John Knox, 1994.

Solmsen, Friedrich. *Die Entwicklung der aristotelischen Logik und Rhetorik*. Berlin: Weidmann, 1929.

Spengel, Leonhard von. *Rhetores Graeci*. 3 vols. Leipzig: Teubner, 1854–1885.

Stewart, Douglas J. "On Ekphrasis: A Communication." *Arion* 5 (1966): 554–56.

Stowe, Harriet Beecher. *The Pearl of Orr's Island*. Sampson: Low, Son, 1862.

Stowers, Stanley K. *Letter Writing in Greco-Roman Antiquity*. LEC 5. Philadelphia: Westminster, 1986.

Strachey, Lytton. *Eminent Victorians*. Edited by John Sutherland. Oxford: Oxford University Press, 2003.

Strecker, Georg. *History of New Testament Literature*. Translated by Calvin Katter with the assistance of Hans-Joachim Mollenhauer. Harrisburg, Pa.: Trinity Press International, 1997.

———. *Literaturgeschichte des Neuen Testaments*. Gottingen: Vandenhoeck & Ruprecht, 1992.

Talbert, Charles H. *Literary Patterns, Theological Themes and the Genre of Luke-Acts*. SBLMS 20. Missoula: Scholars Press, 1974.

———. *What Is a Gospel? The Genre of the Canonical Gospels*. Philadelphia: Fortress, 1977.

Tannenhaus, Gussie H. "Bede's 'De schematibus et tropis'—A Translation," *QJS* 48 (1962): 237–53. Reprinted pages 96–122 in *Readings in Medieval Rhetoric*. Edited by Joseph M. Miller, Michael H. Prosser, and Thomas W. Benson. Bloomington: Indiana University Press, 1973.

Thaden, Robert von. "The Wisdom of Fleeing *Porneia*: Conceptual Blending in 1 Corinthians 6:12–7:7." Ph.D. dissertation, Emory University, 2006.

Thibeaux, Evelyn R. "'Known to Be a Sinner': The Narrative Rhetoric of Luke 7:36-50." *BTB* 23 (1993): 151–60.

Thiselton, Anthony C. *New Horizons in Hermeneutics: The Theory and Practice of Transforming Biblical Reading*. Grand Rapids, Mich.: Zondervan, 1992.

———. *The Two Horizons: New Testament Hermeneutics and Philosophical Description with Special Reference to Heidegger, Bultmann, Gadamer, and Wittgenstein*. Grand Rapids, Mich.: Eerdmans, 1980.

Thonssen, Lester. *Selected Readings in Rhetoric and Public Speaking*. New York: H. W. Wilson, 1942.

Thonssen, Lester, and A. Craig Baird. *Speech Criticism: The Development of Standards for Rhetorical Appraisal*. New York: The Ronald Press Company, 1948.

Thúren, Lauri. "Is There Biblical Argumentation?" Pages 77–92 in *Rhetorical Argumentation in Biblical Tests: Essays from the Lund 2000 Conference*. Edited by Anders Eriksson, Thomas H. Olbricht, and Walter Übelacker. ESEC 8. Harrisburg, Pa.: Trinity Press International, 2002.

———. *The Rhetorical Strategy of 1 Peter with Special Regard to Ambiguous Expression*. Abo: Academy, 1990.

Tompkins, P. K., John H. Patton, and Lloyd F. Bitzer. "Tompkins on Patton and Bitzer, Patton on Tompkins, and Bitzer on Tompkins (and Patton)." *QJS* 66 (1980): 85–93.

Trible, Phyllis. *God and the Rhetoric of Sexuality*. Philadelphia: Fortress, 1978.

———. "Muilenburg, James (1896–1974)." Pages 168–69 in volume 2 of *Dictionary of Biblical Interpretation*. Edited by John H. Hayes. 2 vols. Nashville: Abingdon, 1999.

———. *Rhetorical Criticism: Context, Method, and the Book of Jonah*. GBSOTS. Minneapolis: Fortress, 1994.

———. *Texts of Terror: Literary-Feminist Readings of Biblical Narratives*. Philadelphia: Fortress, 1984.

Vatz, Richard E. "The Myth of the Rhetorical Situation." *PR* 6 (1973): 154–61.

Veltman, Fred. "The Defense Speeches of Paul in Acts." Pages 243–56 in *Perspectives on Luke-Acts*. Edited by Charles H. Talbert. *PRS* 5. Edinburgh: T&T Clark, 1978.

Vickers, Brian. *In Defence of Rhetoric*. Oxford: Clarendon, 1988.

Volkmann, Richard. *Die Rhetorik der Griechen und Römer*. Leipzig: Teubner, 1885.

Votaw, C. W. "The Gospels and Contemporary Biographies." *AJT* 19 (1915): 45–73, 217–49.

Walz, Christianus. *Rhetores Graeci*. Stuttgart: J. G. Cottae, 1832–1836.

Wander, Philip. "An Ideological Turn in Modern Criticism." *CSSJ* 34 (1983): 1–18.

Watson, Duane F. "Chreia/Aphorism." Pages 104–6 in *Dictionary of Jesus and the Gospels*. Edited by Joel B. Green, Scot McKnight, and I. Howard Marshall. Downers Grove, Ill.: InterVarsity, 1992.

———. "The Contribution and Limitations of Greco-Roman Rhetorical Theory for Constructing the Rhetorical and Historical Situations of a Pauline Epistle." Pages 125–51 in *The Rhetorical Interpretation of Scripture: Essays from the 1996 Malibu Conference*. Edited by Stanley E. Porter and Dennis L. Stamps. Journal for the Study of the New Testament: Supplement Series 180. Sheffield: Sheffield Academic, 1999.

———, ed. *The Intertexture of Apocalyptic Discourse in the New Testament*. SBLSymS 14. Atlanta: Society of Biblical Literature, 2002.

———. *Invention, Arrangement, and Style: Rhetorical Criticism of Jude and 2 Peter*. SBLDS 104. Atlanta: Scholars Press, 1988.

―――. "James 2 in Light of Greco-Roman Schemes of Argumentation." *NTS* 39 (1993): 94–121.

―――. "Paul and Boasting." Pages 81–95 in *Paul in the Greco-Roman World: A Handbook*. Edited by J. Paul Sampley. Harrisburg, Pa.: Trinity Press International, 2003.

―――. "Paul's Appropriation of Apocalyptic Discourse: The Rhetorical Strategy of 1 Thessalonians." Pages 61–81 in *Vision and Persuasion: Rhetorical Dimensions of Apocalyptic Discourse*. Edited by Greg Carey and L. Gregory Bloomquist. St. Louis: Chalice, 1999.

―――. "Paul's Boasting in 2 Corinthians 10-13 as Defense of His Honor: A Socio-Rhetorical Analysis." Pages 260–75 in *Rhetorical Argumentation in Biblical Texts: Essays from the Lund 2000 Conference*. Edited by Anders Eriksson, Thomas Olbricht, and Walter Übelacker. ESEC 8. Harrisburg, Pa.: Trinity Press International, 2002.

―――. "Paul's Speech to the Ephesian Elders (Acts 20.17–38): Epideictic Rhetoric of Farewell." Pages 184–208 in *Persuasive Artistry: Studies in New Testament Rhetoric in Honor of George A. Kennedy*. Edited by D. F. Watson. Journal for the Study of the New Testament: Supplement Series 50. Sheffield: JSOT Press, 1991.

―――, ed. *Persuasive Artistry: Studies in New Testament Rhetoric in Honor of George A. Kennedy*. Journal for the Study of the New Testament: Supplement Series 50. Sheffield: JSOT Press, 1991.

―――. *The Rhetoric of the New Testament: A Bibliographic Survey*. Tools for Biblical Study 8. Blandford Forum: Deo Publishing, 2006.

―――, ed. *The Role of Miracle Discourse in the Argumentation of the New Testament*. SBL Symposium Series. Atlanta: SBL and Leiden: Brill, forthcoming.

Watson, Duane F., and Alan J. Hauser, eds. *Rhetorical Criticism of the Bible: A Comprehensive Bibliography with Notes on History and Method*. BIS 4. Leiden: Brill, 1994.

Weaver, Andrew Thomas. "Seventeen Who Made History—The Founders of the Association." *QJS* 45 (1959): 195–99.

Webber, Randall C. "'Why Were the Heathen So Arrogant?' The Socio-Rhetorical Strategy of Acts 3–4." *BTB* 22 (1992): 19–25.

Weiss, Johannes. "Beiträge zur Paulinischen Rhetorik." Pages 165–247 in *Theologische Studien: Herrn Wirkl. Oberkonsistorialrath Professor D. Bernhard Weiss zu seinem 70. Geburtstag*. Edited by C. R. Gregory. Göttingen: Vandenhoeck & Ruprecht, 1897.

White, John. *Light from Ancient Letters*. Foundations and Facets, New Testament. Philadelphia: Fortress, 1986.

Whitehouse, Harvey. *Arguments and Icons: Divergent Modes of Religiosity*. Oxford: Oxford University Press, 2000.

Who's Who in America: Geographic/Professional Index. Chicago: A. N. Marquis, Annual.

Wichelm, Herbert A. "The Literary Criticism of Oratory." Pages 181–216 in *Studies in Rhetoric and Public Speaking in Honor of James Albert Winans*. New York: The Century Company, 1925. Reprinted pages 3–27 in *Readings in Rhetorical Criticism*. 3rd ed. Edited by Carl R. Burgchardt. State College, Pa.: Strata, 2005.

Wilder, Amos N. *The Language of the Gospel: Early Christian Rhetoric*. London and New York: SCM/Harper & Row, 1964. Reprint. Cambridge: Harvard University Press, 1971.

———. "Scholars, Theologians, and Ancient Rhetoric." *JBL* 75 (1956): 1–11.

Wilke, Christian Gottlob. *Die neutestamentliche Rhetorik: Ein Seitenstück zur Grammatik des neutestamentlichen Sprachidioms*. Dresden and Leipzig: Arnold, 1843.

Wills, Lawrence. "The Form of the Sermon in Hellenistic Judaism and Early Christianity." *HTR* 77 (1984): 277–99.

Wilson, Edward O. *The Creation: An Appeal to Save Life on Earth*. New York: Norton, 2006.

Windt Jr., Theodore Otto. "Everett Lee Hunt on Rhetoric." *SpT* 21 (1972): 177–92.

———. "Hoyt H. Hudson: Spokesman for the Cornell School of Rhetoric." *QJS* 68 (1982): 186–200.

Winter, Bruce. "The Importance of the *Captatio Benevolentiae* in the Speeches of Tertullus and Paul in Acts 24:1–21." *JTS* 42 (1991): 505–31.

———. "Official Proceedings and the Forensic Speeches in Acts 24–26." Pages 303–36 in *The Book of Acts in Its Ancient Literary Setting*. Edited by Bruce W. Winter and Andrew D. Clarke. Vol. 1 of *The Book of Acts and Its First-Century Setting*. Edited by Bruce W. Winter. Grand Rapids, Mich.: Eerdmans, 1993.

Wisse, Jakob. *Ethos and Pathos from Aristotle to Cicero*. Amsterdam: Hakkert, 1989.

Witherington, Ben III. *The Acts of the Apostles: A Socio-Rhetorical Commentary*. Grand Rapids, Mich.: Eerdmans, 1998.

———. *Revelation*. New Cambridge Bible Commentary. New York: Cambridge University Press, 2003.
Wooten, Cecil W., ed. *The Orator in Action and Theory in Greece & Rome: Essays in Honor of George A. Kennedy*. Leiden: Brill, 2001.
Work, William, and Robert C. Jeffrey, eds. *The Past is Prologue: A 75th Anniversary Publication of the Speech Communication Association*. Annandale, Va.: The Speech Communication Association, 1989.
Wuellner, Wilhelm. "The Argumentative Structure of 1 Thessalonians as Paradoxical Encomium." Pages 117–35 in *The Thessalonian Correspondence*. Edited by Raymond F. Collins. BETL 87. Leuven: Leuven University Press and Peeters, 1990.
———. "Greek Rhetoric and Pauline Argumentation." Pages 177–88 in *Early Christian Literature and the Classical Intellectual Tradition*. Edited by William R. Schoedel and Robert L. Wilken. Théologie historique 54. Paris: Beauchesne, 1979.
———. "Paul's Rhetoric of Argumentation in Romans: An Alternative to the Donfried-Karris Debate over Romans," *CBQ* 38 (1976): 330–51. Reprinted pages 128–46 in *The Romans Debate*. Edited by Karl P. Donfried. Rev. and exp. ed. Peabody, Mass.: Hendrickson, 1991.
———. "Reading Romans in Context." Pages 106–39 in *Celebrating Romans: Template for Pauline Theology: Essays in Honor of Robert Jewett*. Edited by Sheila E. McGinn; Grand Rapids, Mich., and Cambridge: Eerdmans, 2004.
———. "Where Is Rhetorical Criticism Taking Us?" *CBQ* 49 (1987): 448–63.
Yeo, K. K. *Rhetorical Interaction in I Corinthians 8 and 10: A Formal Analysis with Preliminary Suggestions for a Chinese, Cross-Cultural Hermeneutic*. BIS 9. Leiden: Brill, 1995.
Young, Richard, and Maureen Daly Goggin. "Some Issues in Dating the Birth of the New Rhetoric in Departments of English: A Contribution to a Developing Historiography." Pages 22–43 in *Defining the New Rhetorics*. Edited by Theresa Enos and Stuart C. Brown. Newbury Park: Sage Publications, 1993.
Zulick, Margaret D. "The Active Force of Hearing: The Ancient Hebrew Language of Persuasion." *Rhetorica* 10 (1992): 367–80.
———. "The Agon of Jeremiah: On the Dialogic Invention of Prophetic Ethos." *QJS* 78 (1992): 125–48.

———. "The Ethos of Invention: The Dialogue of Ethics and Aesthetics in Kenneth Burke and Mikhail Bakhtin." Pages 34–55 in *The Ethos of Rhetoric*. Edited by Michael J. Hyde. Columbia: University of South Carolina Press, 2004.

Zweck, Dean. "The *Exordium* of the Areopagus Speech, Acts 17.22, 23." *NTS* 35 (1989): 94–103.

LIST OF CONTRIBUTORS

C. CLIFTON BLACK, Otto A. Piper Professor of Biblical Theology, Princeton Theological Seminary, Princeton, New Jersey

GREG CAREY, Associate Professor of New Testament, Lancaster Theological Seminary, Lancaster, Pennsylvania

JAMES D. HESTER, Professor of Religion Emeritus and Research Professor, University of Redlands, Redlands, California

FRANK W. HUGHES, Interim Priest, Church of the Holy Cross, Shreveport, Louisiana

GEORGE A. KENNEDY, Paddison Professor of Classics Emeritus, University of North Carolina, Chapel Hill, North Carolina; Visiting Professor of Speech Communication, Colorado State University, Fort Collins, Colorado

THOMAS H. OLBRICHT, Distinguished Professor of Religion Emeritus, Pepperdine University, Pepperdine, California

VERNON K. ROBBINS, Professor of Religion and Comparative Sacred Texts, Emory University, Atlanta, Georgia; Professor Extraordinary of New Testament, University of Stellenbosch School of Theology, Stellenbosch, South Africa

BLAKE SHIPP, Equipping Pastor, Browncroft Community Church, Rochester, New York

DUANE F. WATSON, Professor of New Testament Studies, Malone College, Canton, Ohio

MARGARET D. ZULICK, Associate Professor of Communication, Wake Forest University, Winston-Salem, North Carolina

INDEX OF PRIMARY SOURCES

I. Greek and Latin Authors

Aristotle, *Ars Rhetorica*
1.1.1354a	9, 31
1.1.1354b-1355a	9
1.2.8-22	79n43
1.9.32	93
2.1.5–2.11.7	167
2.22-25	79n43
3.14.6	128

Augustine, *De doctrina christiana*
4	42
4.3	10
4.29	10

Cicero
De inventione
1.20	128

De oratore
1.12.53	177n18
2.42.178	167
2.44.185	167
2.50.206	167

[Attributed to Cicero]
Rhetorica ad Herennium
4.38.51	79n43

Demetrius, *On Style*
223–35	59n46

Eusebius, *Historia Ecclesiastica*
3.39.15-16	65

Julius Victor, *Ars Rhetorica*
27	59n46

Justin Martyr, *Apology*
1.66.3	65
1.67.3	65

Philo
De Opificio Mundi
20	76

De Somniis
1.229-30	76

Plato, *Phaedrus*
259e-264e	9

Quintilian, *Institutio Oratoria*
5.14.29	167, 177n20
7.10.5-17	157n41
9.4.19	52
9.4.19-22	51

Tacitus, *Annals*
15.44	192

II. Biblical References
A. Old Testament

Genesis
- 1:1–2:3 — 75
- 28:10-17 — 74
- 31:11-16 — 74
- 37:5-11 — 74
- 40:1-19 — 74
- 41:14-36 — 74

Proverbs
- 8:22-31 — 76

Joel
- 2:28 — 74

B. Old Testament Apocrypha

Sirach
- 1:4 — 76
- 24:1-12 — 76

C. New Testament

Matthew
- 1:18-25 — 74
- 1:23 — 72
- 2:13-15 — 74
- 2:19-23 — 74
- 5:3 — 105n32
- 5:10 — 105n32
- 5:12 — 105n32
- 5:17 — 105n32
- 5:19 — 105n32
- 5:20 — 105n32
- 6:10 — 105n32
- 6:13 — 105n32
- 6:33 — 105n32
- 7:12 — 105n32
- 7:15 — 105n32
- 7:21 — 105n32
- 21–23 — 119n3
- 28:18-20 — 3

Mark
- 1–10 — 93
- 1:27 — 93
- 1:27a — 68
- 1:30-31 — 93
- 1:33 — 93
- 3:11 — 94
- 4:10-12 — 72
- 13 — 46, 58n21, 79n47
- 15 — 189
- 16:1-8 — 189
- 16:9-20 — 189

Luke
- 1:1-4 — 72
- 1:8-23 — 74
- 1:26-38 — 74
- 7:36-50 — 78n34
- 10:25-37 — 119n3
- 11:1-13 — 103n11
- 11:33-36 — 95
- 16:19-31 — 122n25

John
- 1:1-4 — 76
- 1:14 — 76
- 1:27 — 93
- 3:17-21 — 72
- 5 — 78n34
- 9:38-41 — 72
- 13–17 — 67, 92
- 14–17 — 46, 79n47
- 20:30-31 — 3, 72

Acts
- 2:17 — 74
- 3–4 — 61n72, 120n12
- 8:27-39 — 90
- 9:1-9 — 118
- 9:1-10 — 61n72, 120n12
- 9:1-12 — 111

9:1-26a	118	1 Corinthians	
9:1-22	111	1–4	133
9:10-16	118	2:1-5	133, 137n26
9:17-19a	118	6:9-10	105n36
9:19b-26a	118	6:12–7:7	106n55
10:1-16	74	8	128, 136n16
11:27–12:25	119n5	10	128, 136n16
13:16-41	121n15	15:50	105n36
15	121n14		
17:22-23	119n5	2 Corinthians	
20	49	1:1-2	149
20:18-35	49	1:3-8	90
20:17-38	58n37, 104n13, 110, 120n10	1:8–2:13	90
		1:14	91
21:33–22:24a	118	2:10	91
21:33-40	118	2:14-17	90
22:1	118	2:17	91
22:2	118	3:4–5:10	91
22:3-21	111	5:10	91
22:3-16	118	5:11	91
22:17-21	118	7:12	92
22:22-24a	118	10–13	53, 60n63
23:11	118	10:10	145
24–26	119n5	12:1-10	74
24	49	12:19	92
24:1-21	59n41		
25:23–26:32	118	Galatians	
26:2-33	111	1–2	38n56, 159n61, 160n64
28:16	90	1:1-5	149
		1:2	149
Romans		1:6	149
1:1–5:21	119n3	1:6-10	159n59
1:1-12	158n46	1:10	159n60
4:13	105n36	1:11–5:1	159n59
4:14	105n36	1:11–2:21	159n62
5:8-9	97	1:11–2:14	38n56
8:17	105n36	1:11–2:10	159n62
9–11	119n3	1:11	150
9	128, 136n16	1:12-17	150
10:14-17	3	1:13–2:14	159n59
15:24	90	1:18-24	160n62
15:28	90	1:18	150

2:1-10	150, 160n62	5:2-18	160n68
2:1	150	5:2	151, 160n67
2:7	160n63	5:7-8	152
2:9	160n63	5:7	159n60
2:11-21	159n62, 160n63	5:8-11	156n32
2:11-14	38n56, 150, 159n62, 160n62	5:11	159n60
		5:12	151
2:11	150, 160n63	5:13–6:10	159n60, 160n68
2:12	150	5:13	151
2:14	150	5:14	152
2:15-21	150, 159 nn. 59, 62	5:16-21	152
2:16	159n62	5:16	152
2:21	150	5:19-23	160n68
3:1–5:12	150	5:21	105n36
3:1–4:11	159n59	5:24–6:10	159n60
3:1-5	151	5:25	152
3:1	150, 159n60	6:10	152
3:6-14	151	6:11-18	159n59
3:15-18	151	6:11-17	149, 159n60
3:18	105n36	6:11	152
3:19-22	151	6:15	152
3:23–4:7	151	6:17	152
3:29	105n36		
4:1	105n36	Ephesians	
4:7	105n36	4–6	106n61
4:8-11	151		
4:8	159n60	1 Thessalonians	
4:9	152, 159n60	1:5	134
4:11	151	1:8	132
4:12-20	159n59	2:1-12	130
4:12	151	5:1	132
4:13-16	156n32	5:27	142
4:19-20	152		
4:20	151	Philemon	
4:21–5:1	151, 159n58	1-2	142
4:21–31	159n59		
4:21	159n60	Hebrews	
4:30	105n36	9:11-12	98
4:31	160n67		
5:1-12	160n67	James	
5:1	159n59	2	119n3
5:2–6:10	159n59		

2 Peter		4:1	172
3:15b-16	158n53	4:2	172
1 John		5:2	168
3:16	76	5:5	172
4:16b	76	5:6	172
4:7-12	76	5:7	172
		5:11	168
Revelation		5:13	172
1–3	176n4	6:2	172
1:1-9	168	6:5	172
1:1	164, 173	6:8	172
1:2	168, 173	6:9-11	173
1:3	164	6:9	173
1:4-5	172	6:10	174
1:5	173	7:3	173
1:7	172	7:4-9	173
1:9	173	7:9	172
1:11	168	7:10	172
2–3	168, 169	8:13	174
2:1-7	170	8:3-5	173
2:7	171	8:11a	177n22
2:8	170	9:4	174
2:10	170, 172	9:12	172
2:11	171	9:14	168
2:13	173	10:7	173
2:14-15	170	11:1–14:5	176n4
2:16	174	11:10	174
2:17	171	11:14	172
2:20	173	11:15–12:17	176n2
2:22	171	11:18	173, 174
2:22-23	174	12:3	172
2:23-25	170	12:11	169, 173
2:29	171	12:17	169, 173
3:4	173, 174	13:7	173
3:6	171	13:8	174
3:8-9	172	13:9-10	177n22
3:10	174	13:9	169
3:13	171	13:10	169, 174
3:14	173	13:12	174
3:20	172	13:14	174
3:21	172	13:15	173
3:22	171	13:18	169

14:1	172	20:15	174
14:11-12	169	21:3	172
14:14	172	21:5	172
15:2-8	173	21:8	174
16:5	168	21:9	178n25
16:6	169	22:1	172
16:15	171, 172	22:3-5	173
17:1	168	22:3	172, 173
17:2	174	22:6-21	178n25
17:6	169, 173	22:6-9	61n70
17:7	168	22:6-7	178n25
17:8	174	22:6	173, 178n25
17:9	169	22:7	164, 172, 178n25
18:1-2	168	22:7a	171, 178n25
18:4-8	171	22:7b	178n25
18:4-5	171	22:8-9	168
18:7	171	22:8	173
18:20	169, 173	22:9	173
18:24	169, 173	22:10	164
19	171	22:12-13	171
19:2	173	22:12	172
19:5	171, 173	22:16	171
19:10	164, 169, 173	22:17-19	168
20:4-5	169, 174	22:18-19	164, 177n22
20:4	173	22:20	171
20:6	169, 173	22:21	168
20:9	173		

SUBJECT INDEX

abolition movement, 15
aboriginals, Australian, 73, 74
Abraham, 151, 152
action, 13, 75; *see also* pragmatism
Acts of the Apostles, the, 48–50, 94, 107–18; speeches in, 48, 55, 82, 111–12, 113–14, 115–16, 122, 126, 132
Adams, John Quincy, 11–12
aesthetics, 16
Agricola, Rudolph, 10
allegory, 159
American Academy in Rome, 22
American Council of Learned Societies, 24
American Philological Association, 22, 24
American School of Classical Studies (Athens), 22, 24
amplification, 45, 47, 67
Ananias the Apostle, 118
ancient Near East, 180, 182, 187
angel(s), 71, 74, 170, 173, 178, 188
Anglican Church; *see* Church of England
anthropology, 2, 31, 74, 184
aphorism(s), 70
apocalypse, apocalyptic, 14, 54, 55–56, 70, 82, 85, 87–88, 90–92, 97–98, 100, 163–75; *see also* eschatology; revelation

Apollonius of Tyana, 189
apomnēmoneumata (memoirs), 64
Apostles' Creed, 180; *see also* doctrine, Christian
argument; *see* invention (of arguments)
Aristophanes, 64
Aristotle, 8, 9, 12, 13, 14, 16, 23, 30, 68, 107, 126, 128, 133, 135, 140, 144, 164, 165, 166, 167, 170, 173
Arlington Street Church (Boston), 181
Arnold, Carroll C., 30, 31, 38
Arnold, Matthew, 183
Arnold, Thomas, 183
arrangement, 9, 10, 12, 27, 34, 42, 43, 45, 46, 47, 49, 50–53, 57, 69, 74, 85–86, 116, 119, 126–27, 132–33, 140–43, 147, 156
Asia Minor, 164, 174
Asklepios, 94
Asmis, Elizabeth, 127
assumption of the Virgin Mary, 185
Athanasian Creed; *see* doctrine, Christian
audience, 14, 27, 45, 54, 67, 81, 83, 140, 141, 142, 143, 144, 146, 152, 166, 167–75, 177, 186
Augustine of Hippo, 3, 10, 42, 85, 133
authority, 54, 67, 72, 86, 132, 169

Baird, A. Craig, 27
baptism, 152
Basil the Great, 37
Bates College, 28
Bauer, Bruno, 184
Bauer, Karl Ludwig, 42
Baur, Ferdinand Christian, 131
Beatitudes, 71, 89
Bede the Venerable, 42
belief; *see* faith
benevolence, 10, 167, 177; *see also captatio benevolentiae*
Betz, Hans Dieter, 33–34, 42, 126, 130
Beutler, Johannes, 128
Bingham, Caleb, 13
biogenetics, 74
biography, 46, 47, 64, 70, 190–91
Bios; *see* biography
Bitzer, Lloyd, 14, 15, 28
Blair, Hugh, 3
blame (rhetorical strategy), 54, 132, 150
blessing, 168, 169, 170, 171, 173, 175
Bloomquist, L. Gregory, 131
Body, 56, 87, 91–95, 100, 116, 150, 152, 159
Boethius, 10
Booth, Wayne A., 29
Brandt, W. J., 33
Bryant, Donald, 23, 28, 29
Buddhism, 102
Bullinger, E. W., 32
Bultmann, Rudolf, 32
bureaucracy, 189
Burke, Kenneth, 13, 14–15

Cadbury, Henry J., 182
Cambridge University, 22
Caplan, Harry, 23, 27

captatio benevolentiae, 128; *see also* benevolence
Carleton College, 25
Cato, 12
Center for Byzantine Studies (Dumbarton Oaks), 22
Center for Hellenic Studies (Washington), 22–23, 24
Cephas; *see* Simon Peter
charisma; *see* Spirit, Holy
Chatman, Seymour, 70
Chicago Formalists; *see* University of Chicago
Child, Francis James, 25
chreia, 46–47, 48, 140, 150, 160, 187
Christ; *see* Jesus of Nazareth
Christian Science, 180
Chrysostom, John, 3, 133
church, 53, 149, 151, 160, 164, 168, 170, 171, 172, 174, 179, 186, 190
Church of the Advent (Boston), 181
Church of England, 181, 183
Cicero, 11, 12, 13, 22, 42, 68, 107, 128, 132, 133, 140, 145, 164, 167, 170, 173
circumcision, 149–52
city-state, 82, 83, 84, 87–89, 91–93, 126
Civil War (American), 25
classical world, classics, 4, 9, 11, 13, 14, 21, 22–24, 27, 28, 30, 31, 32, 33, 34, 41, 43, 45, 46, 47, 50, 54, 63, 64, 70, 73, 75, 79, 82, 83, 84, 112, 118, 125–35, 139–40, 143, 163, 165, 175, 180, 182, 187, 189, 191
Clement of Alexandria, 133
code, coding, 145–48, 156, 158, 160, 169
Coleman-Norton, Paul R., 180
Collins, Raymond F., 128

Colloquium Biblicum Lovaniense, 127
colonialism, 75
Colorado State University, 28, 183
Columbia University, 28
Columbian Orator, The (1797), 12
commandment(s), 159; *see also* law
communication, 29, 111, 153; *see also* oratory; speech, speeches
composition, 4, 21, 26, 28, 29–31, 32, 33, 35, 51, 53, 65, 85, 81, 140, 157, 182, 186, 187; *see also* English, composition
Conference on College Composition and *confirmatio* (*narratio*, narration), 51, 90, 140, 150, 159, 160
Congregational Church, 179–80
controversy, 3, 14, 46–47, 183, 187
conversion, 118, 120, 181, 183
Cooper, Lane, 27
Corbett, Edward P. J., 29, 33
Corinthians, the First Epistle to the, 52, 126
Corinthians, the Second Epistle to the, 50, 52, 53, 90
Cornell University, 22, 26–27, 28, 30; Cornell School, 13, 26–28
counter-identification, 167; *see also* identification
court, courtroom; *see* law, law-court
Cowley Father's (monastery in Boston), 181
Crane, Ronald S., 29
Cranmer, Thomas, 131
creation, 45, 75–76, 84, 94–96, 152, 184; *see also* precreation
creed; *see* doctrine, Christian
criticism, biblical, 2, 11, 21, 31–34, 45, 74, 79, 102, 131, 139, 184–86; *see also* discernment; hermeneutics
Crosby, Harry, 29

cross-cultural investigation, 73–74, 175
cross-disciplinary studies; *see* interdisciplinary studies
crucifixion; *see* Jesus of Nazareth
curse, 168, 170

Damascus Road narratives (in Acts), 111, 118
Day of the Lord, 91
death, 47, 85, 93, 104, 173, 174, 184, 187, 189
De doctrina christiana, 133
declamation; *see* oratory
Deissmann, Adolf, 42
deliberative (species of rhetoric), 50, 54, 67, 81–84, 86–90, 95, 100, 126, 164–65; *see also* rhetoric, species of
delivery, 11, 12, 13, 25, 27, 133, 147
Demetrius, 76
Democracy, 12, 190; *see also* federalism (American), government
demonstrative; *see* epideictic (species of rhetoric)
Demosthenes, 13, 23, 51, 126, 132
DePauw University, 26
Derrida, Jacques, 70
devil; *see* Satan
dialectic, 9, 10–11, 117
diatribe, 160
Dio Chrysostom, 157
discernment, 168, 169; *see also* criticism, biblical; hermeneutics
disciples; *see* Jesus of Nazareth
discourse, 3, 15–16, 26, 54, 55, 56, 65, 69, 71, 73, 75, 81–102, 115, 118, 141–43, 144, 148, 160, 165–71, 178, 182, 187
dispute; *see* controversy

distress, 169, 170, 171
doctrine, Christian, 87, 100–02, 132, 180, 183, 184, 189, 190
Donfried, Karl Paul, 130
Douglass, Frederick, 12
Dow, Sterling, 23
Doyle, Arthur Conan, 63
drama, dramatism, 25, 54, 70, 117, 158, 165–66, 172, 174
dream(s), dreamtime, 74–75
Drummond, Alexander, 26, 27
Duhammel, P. Albert, 29
Duke University, 32, 41, 127, 128

ekphrasis (vividness), 81
eclecticism, 108, 111
education, 43, 47, 52–54, 94–96, 140, 148, 186, 187, 189
Elder, J. Peterson, 23
elegance; *see* style
Elijah the prophet, 94
Eliot, George, 184
Elisha the prophet, 94
elocution; *see* delivery
eloquence; *see* style
Else, Gerald F., 28
Emerson, Ralph Waldo, 181
Emory University, 126
emotion(s), 9, 30, 46, 79, 102, 144, 151, 166–67
encomium, 47, 140
encouragement, 167–68, 172, 173, 174, 175
Energeia, 8, 17
English; composition, 28, 29–31; departments of, 25, 26, 29, 33; literature, 13, 21, 25, 20; *see also* composition
enthymeme, 9, 45, 52, 70, 71, 79, 84, 85, 86, 89, 99, 100, 102–4
environmentalism, 190
epic; *see* poetics, poetry

epicheireme, 159
epideictic (species of rhetoric), 50, 54, 67, 75, 81–86, 88, 92–97, 98, 100, 104–5, 126, 132, 164–65; *see also* rhetoric, species of
epilogue, 159
Episcopal Church, 180, 182
epistemology, 10, 153–54
epistles; *see* letters
Ernesti, J. C. G., 31
error; *see* falsehood
eschatology, 75, 152, 186; *see also* apocalypse, apocalyptic; revelation
ethics, 16, 190
Ethopoeia, 187, 188
ethos, 14, 54, 67, 71, 75, 82, 83, 147, 152, 157, 165, 166, 186
Eusebius of Caesarea, 65, 66, 182
evil, 54, 91, 100, 132, 174
exegesis; *see* criticism, biblical
exhortation, 120, 151–52, 160, 171–72, 178
exigence, 14, 44, 45, 115, 140, 141–42, 143, 146–47, 149–52, 154, 155
existentialism, 84
exorcism, 94
exordium, 51, 127
eyewitness(es); *see* witness

faith, 72, 151, 169, 171, 173, 180, 184, 185
faithfulness, 171, 173, 185
falsehood, 10
family, 55–56, 87, 94–96, 100, 180
Farewell Discourse (John), 45, 46, 67
Farrell, Thomas B., 34, 127, 128
fear, 54, 91, 150, 167, 170, 171, 173, 174, 175, 178
federalism (American), 11; *see also* democracy; government

SUBJECTS

Fédération Internationale des Associations des Etudes Classiques, 24
feminism, 16
Feuerbach, Ludwig, 184, 189
fiction, 166, 183
figures (rhetorical), 27, 42, 46, 55, 147
First Parish Church (Boston), 181
Fisher, Walter R., 28
forensic rhetoric; *see* judicial (species of rhetoric)
forgiveness, 190
form criticism, 7, 32, 69, 128, 131, 139, 140, 163
formalism, 69–70, 108, 110, 115
freedom, 23, 64, 190
fundamentalism, 84
Fuscus, 157

Galatians, the Epistle to the, 3, 33, 42, 50, 88, 126, 139, 149–53
Garrett-Evangelical Theological Seminary, 126
genre, 48–52, 55, 56, 64, 115, 143
Gentile(s), 118; *see also* pagan culture
Gildersleeve, Basil L., 22
glory; *see* God, glory of
Gnosticism, 187
God; begotten of, 76; as creator, 76; disobedience to, 118; as father, 101, 180, 185, 190; glory of, 76–77; honor of, 54; as human projection, 184; image of, 75–76; judgment of, 54, 91, 152, 167, 174, 175, 190; kingdom of, 75, 88–90, 100, 187, 172, 187 [*see also* heaven(s); mystery; parable(s); riddle; secrecy]; obedience to, 54, 118; power of, 76; praise of, 54, 171; seal of, 174; Son of, 94, 101, 185; speech of, 10; voice of, 172; word of, 89; worship of [*see* worship]; wrath of, 97; *see also* Spirit, Holy
Goodwin, William Watson, 22
gospel(s), 45–48, 55, 63–77, 82, 94, 126, 134, 145, 149, 150, 152, 160, 184, 186, 191, 192; *see also* Jesus of Nazareth; mission; witness
government, 12; *see also* democracy, federalism (American)
grace, graciousness, 72, 76, 118, 168
grammar, 11, 25, 187
Greco-Roman culture; *see* classical world, classics
Griesbach, Johann Jakob, 64
Griffin, Leland, 127, 128
Grube, G. M. A., 23, 24

Haberman, Fred, 23
Hale, William, 22
Hall, Robert, 41
Harshbarger, H. Clay, 27–28
Harvard University, 22, 23, 25, 26, 63, 181
Haverford College, 181–82
healing, 92–94, 100, 185, 189
heaven(s), 87, 90, 91, 98, 101, 168, 171–75, 185, 189; *see also* God, kingdom of
Hebrew Bible, 7–8, 11, 17, 32, 42, 72, 76, 184
Hebrews, the Epistle to the, 71, 98
Hellenism, 8, 9, 23, 42, 43, 49, 76, 85, 87, 101, 128, 139, 140; *see also* Judaism, Hellenistic
heresy, 174
hermeneutics, 10, 45, 69, 82; *see also* criticism, biblical; discernment
Hermes, 188
Herod the Great, 188–89
Herodotus, 22

Hinduism, 102
historical criticism; *see* criticism, biblical
historiography, 49, 64, 182, 187, 191
holiness, holy, 98, 173; *see also* Spirit, Holy
homiletics, 2, 182; *see also* preaching
honor (rhetorical strategy), 55, 132, 167, 175; *see also* God, honor of
hope, 165, 166, 167, 170, 171, 175, 180, 184
Horace, 22
household; *see* family
Hudson, Hoyt H., 27
Hughes, Frank Witt, 34, 128
humanism, 11, 77, 184, 189, 190
Hunt, Everett, 26, 27
Huron College, 27
hypomnēmata (note-taking), 64–65, 145, 182
hypsos; *see* sublimity

icon, iconography, 81–82
identification, 167; *see also* counter-identification
ideology, 15, 16, 45, 55, 116–17, 164
ignorance, 10, 69
illusion, 189
Ilongots (Philippine), 73
image, 81–82
imitation (*imitatio*), 50
immaculate conception (of Mary), 185
Immanuel; *see* Jesus of Nazareth
immortality of the soul, 180, 189
imperial court, 56, 87, 98, 100
Indians, North American, 73, 75
infancy narratives; *see* Jesus of Nazareth
inheritance, 90, 151
Institute for Advanced Studies (Princeton), 22

interdisciplinary studies, 1, 7, 8, 16, 21, 31, 41, 64, 70, 72–73, 128
interpretation; *see* criticism, biblical; discernment; hermeneutics
invention (of arguments), 8, 9, 10, 11, 12, 16, 17, 30, 42, 43–44, 45, 47, 49, 50, 51, 52, 53, 60, 69, 71, 74, 82, 83, 112, 126, 133, 140, 143, 148, 150–52, 156, 157
irony, 147, 151
Islam, 102, 156, 182
Isocrates, 27, 133

Jaeger, Werner, 23, 34, 63
James, Proto-Gospel of, 185, 189
Jebb, Richard C., 24
Jerusalem, 118, 150, 160, 173
Jesus of Nazareth, 45; authority of, 71, 89, 93, 172, 187; crucifixion of, 189, 190; death of, 187; deeds of, 72; disciples of, 72, 145, 150, 189; discourse of, 171; divinity of, 188; historical reconstruction of, 47–48, 184–85, 186, 191; as God's incarnation, 75–76; as Immanuel, 72; infancy narrative about, 4, 73, 187, 188–89; as Lamb of God, 172, 173; as messiah, 74, 89, 172; as miracle-worker, 189; name of, 180; presence of, 91, 94, 189; resurrection of, 187, 188, 189; return of, 168; rhetoric of, 47–48; as risen Christ, 168, 170, 188; sayings of, 48, 72, 84; as social reformer, 187; teachings of, 46–47, 75, 184, 186, 191; tradition about, 48; voice of, 168, 170, 171, 175, 178; will of, 186; *see also* gospel(s)
Jesus Seminar, 187, 189, 191
Jewett, Robert, 126, 130

SUBJECTS

John, the Gospel according to,
 64, 70, 75, 96–97, 188, 191;
 relationship to the Synoptics, 66
John, the Revelation to, 3, 54–55,
 83, 163–75, 186
John, Seer of Patmos, 167, 169, 170,
 171, 172, 175
John the Baptist, 187, 189
Johns Hopkins University, 22
Johnstone, Henry W., Jr., 29, 30, 31
Joseph, husband of Mary, 74
Joseph, son of Jacob, 74
Josephus, 147, 188
Jowett, Benjamin, 183
Judaism, Hellenistic, 76, 85, 125,
 185; *see also* Hellenism
judgment; *see* God, judgment of
judicial (species of rhetoric), 50,
 51, 70, 75, 82, 83–92, 100,
 126, 164, 165; *see also* rhetoric,
 species of
justification, 131, 151
Justin Martyr, 64
Justinian, 22

Kant, Immanuel, 190
Kennedy, George A., 1–4, 7–11,
 16–17, 21–24, 28, 29, 31–34,
 37, 41–56, 63–77, 81, 84–104,
 107–18, 125–35, 139–53, 163–75,
 179–90, 193–203
Kierkegaard, Søren, 180
king, kingship, 56, 168, 169
kingdom of God; *see* God, kingdom of
kingdom of heaven; *see* God,
 kingdom of
King's Chapel (Boston), 181
knowledge, 1, 13, 16, 22, 44, 45, 52,
 56, 64, 88, 95–96, 101, 129, 154,
 156, 169, 186, 187
König, Eduard, 32

Krentz, Edgar, 128
kyori; *see* wrapped words

Lamb of God; *see* Jesus of Nazareth
lament, 10
Lampe, Peter, 130
language, 8; performative aspect of,
 164
Lausberg, Heinrich, 128
law, law-court, 30, 47, 49, 53, 70,
 82, 83, 87, 90–92, 100, 150–51
Leff, Michael C., 34, 127, 128
Leon, Judah Messer, 11
letters, 42, 43, 49, 50–54, 55, 70, 71,
 82, 108, 113, 115–16, 125–35,
 164, 170, 171, 172, 186; process
 of composing, 145–46
Levison, John R., 41
linguistics, 31, 33, 103, 111, 164
literary criticism, 69, 131, 139, 154,
 163
literary-rhetorical criticism, 111–12
Livy, 107
loci; *see* topics (topoi)
logic, 30–31, 45, 54, 67, 71–72, 74,
 84–86, 117, 143, 168
logos, 14, 54, 71, 75–76, 82, 83, 85,
 147, 166, 186, 189, 186
Lombard College, 26
Longenecker, Richard N., 126–27
"Longinus," 3
love, 76, 152
Lowth, Robert, 11
loyalty; *see* faith
Lucretius, 22
Luke, the Gospel according to,
 45–46, 73, 188, 191
Luther, Martin, 131
Lutheran Church, 180
Lycurgus, 188
Lyons, Joseph A., 12

McCarthyism, 15
McKeon, Richard, 29, 30
magi, 188–89
Manifest Destiny, 15
Mark, the Gospel according to, 45, 72, 94, 96, 187, 188, 189, 191
Martin, Clarice, 41
martyr, martyrdom, 169, 173, 174, 175, 185
Mary, mother of James, 189
Mary, mother of Jesus, 74, 185, 188
Mary Magdalene, 189
Matthew, the Gospel according to, 45, 73, 96, 188, 191
Matthews, Jack, 23
Melanchthon, Philip, 31, 42
memory, 133, 147
Menander Rhetor, 68, 92, 126
Merry, Glenn N., 26
message; *see* gospel; witness
messiah; *see* Jesus of Nazareth
metaphor(s), 74, 99
metaphysics, 185
Methodist Episcopal Church, 179
metonym, 99
Michigan State University, 28
millennialism, 75, 165, 173, 191
ministry, 65, 133–34
miracle, 10, 55–56, 81, 84–85, 87, 88, 89, 92–94, 100–5, 144, 185, 188, 189
mirror-reading, 44
mission, 3, 118; *see also* gospel; witness
Mithraism, 188
Modern Language Association, 25
modernism, 184
monarchy; *see* king, kingship
monotheism, 185
motion pictures, 70
mourning; *see* lament

Muilenburg, James, 7, 32, 39
Murphy, James J., 38
Mursi (Ethiopian), 73
mystery, 101; *see also* God, kingdom of; parable(s), riddle; secrecy
mysticism, 186
myth, 76, 85, 86, 184, 187, 188, 189

narration (*narratio*); *see confirmatio*
narrative, 46, 48–49, 69, 71, 82, 83, 86, 90, 93, 84, 113–14, 164, 172, 175
Natanson, Maurice, 30
National Association of Academic Teachers of Public Speaking, 25; *see also* National Communication Association
National Association of Elocutionists, 25
National Communication Association, 25
National Council of the Teachers of English, 25
National Humanities Center (North Carolina), 23
neo-Aristotelians, 16, 29
New Criticism, 69–70
New Old South Church (Boston), 181
New Rhetoric; *see* rhetoric
New Testament, 8, 15, 32, 41–56, 69, 74, 83, 84–85, 86, 108, 126, 128, 131–35, 164, 179, 180, 184, 186
Newman, Francis, 183
Newman, John Henry, 183
Nicea-Chalcedon; *see* doctrine, Christian
Norden, Eduard, 24, 32, 42
Northwestern University, 7–8, 26, 28, 126
novels, 70, 187

obedience, 54, 118
Olbrechts-Tyteca, Lucie, 33
Olbricht, Thomas H., 131
Old North Church (Boston), 181
Old Testament; *see* Hebrew Bible
Oliver, Robert T., 30
Olivet Discourse (Mark), 46
O'Neill, James M., 26
ontology, 10
orality, 44, 76, 112
oratory, 10, 12, 14, 25, 47, 75, 92, 156, 167, 186; *see also* communication; speech, speeches
orthodoxy; *see* doctrine, Christian
Oxford University, 22, 184; Oxford movement, 183

P (hypothetical Pentateuchal source), 76
Pacific School of Religion, 126
pagan culture, 10, 133, 187; *see also* Gentile(s)
paideia, 143, 147, 152, 154, 159
pain, 163, 176, 189
Papias of Hierapolis, 65, 66
parable(s), 72, 75, 187; *see also* God, kingdom of; Jesus of Nazareth; mystery; riddle; secrecy
paraenesis, 151
parousia; *see* Jesus of Nazareth, return of
partition, 90, 91
pathos, 3, 14, 29, 30–31, 54, 82, 83, 163–75, 186
patristics, 10–11, 37, 64
Paul the Apostle, 4, 42, 49, 74, 125–35, 139–54, 186; *see also* Saul of Tarsus
Paulson, Stanley, 31
peace, 12, 100, 184, 189
Pennsylvania State University, 30, 31, 38

Pepperdine University, 43, 131
Perelman, Chaim, 30, 33
peroratio, 51
persecution, 23, 118
personification, 49, 140
persuasion, 3, 8, 11, 12, 13, 30, 47, 53, 54, 67, 72, 75, 110, 113, 115, 117, 130, 132, 133, 134, 141, 148, 151, 152, 154, 163, 165, 166, 174
Peter the Apostle; *see* Simon Peter
Pharisee(s), 72
Philemon, the Epistle to, 126, 142, 146
Philo of Alexandria, 76, 147, 188–89
philology, 25
philosophy, 2, 9, 11, 30, 31, 44, 47, 53, 54, 76, 85, 101 125, 145, 154, 188
Philostratus, 192
physiology, 13
Plato, 9, 23, 26, 27, 64–65, 134
pleasure, 167, 179
Pliny the Younger, 157
plot; *see* narrative
Plutarch, 22, 64, 107
poetics, poetry, 11, 74, 187
pointing, 165, 166, 170, 171–72; *see also* showing
polemic; *see* controversy
polytheism, 185
Pontius Pilate, 190, 192
postmodernism, 110, 164
poverty, 189
power(s), 11, 51, 53, 64, 67, 71, 74, 76, 90, 97, 101, 118, 133–34, 148, 154, 167, 174, 187, 174, 187; *see also* God, power of
praise, 19, 54, 92–93, 104–05, 121, 132, 173–74, 132; *see also* God, praise of
pragmatism, 12, 153
praeteritio, 132

prayer, 127, 128, 173, 174, 180, 181, 185
preaching, 4, 15, 72, 145, 148, 179, 180, 181, 182, 186; *see also* homiletics
precreation, 55–56, 88, 96–97; *see also* creation
preexistence, 76–77
Presbyterian Church, 179
priest, priesthood, 55–56, 87, 88, 97–98, 100, 105, 168, 169; *see also* sacrifice; worship
Princeton University, 22, 23, 179, 190
proem, 90, 159
progymnasmata, 46–47, 48, 49, 50, 54, 55, 69, 81, 111, 112, 118, 140, 187
pronouncement stories, 47
proof, 9, 27, 45, 90, 147, 159
prophet, prophecy, 14, 17, 54, 55–56, 87–90, 100–1, 104–5, 164, 169, 173, 176, 186, 187, 189, 164, 169, 187, 189
propositio, 159
prosopopoeia, 45–46
Puritans, 15, 22
psychology, 13, 31, 54, 166, 188, 189
psychosomatic healing, 189

Q (hypothetical gospel source), 48, 64
Quakers, 15, 181–82
Quintilian, 11, 12, 23, 26, 70, 107, 126, 164, 167
Qumran, 154
Qur'an, 156

rabbis, 89, 154
radio, 28
Ramsey, Paul, 180
Ramus, Peter, 10

rationalism, 184, 185
Raubitschek, A. E., 23
recapitulation, 92
Reformation (Protestant), 42, 131, 185
Reimarus, Herman Samuel, 184
relics (religious), 185
religion, 3, 7, 21, 75, 76, 82, 189
religious studies, 132, 182
resurrection, 85, 104, 169, 173, 184, 187, 189; *see also* Jesus of Nazareth
revelation, 10, 54–55, 72, 132, 171; *see also* apocalypse, apocalyptic; eschatology
Revelation, the Book of; *see* John, the Revelation to
Revolutionary War (American), 181
rhetography, 4, 55, 81–102
rhetology, 82, 83, 98, 99
rhetoric; comparative, 17, 63, 108, 109–10, 165; critical methodology, 43–44, 46, 48, 128; as a form of energy, 75–77, 144–46, 148, 150–53, 157, 186; handbooks of, 9, 43–44, 47, 49, 51, 55, 70, 74, 109, 110, 112, 120, 126, 140, 148, 153, 154, 159, 167; history of, 2, 4, 7–17, 29, 30, 132–33, 134–35; imperial, 55, 56, 81, 87, 90–92, 96–97, 100, 105, 175; Jewish rhetoric, 11, 44, 45, 100–01; "New Rhetoric," 44; philosophical, 72; poetic, 165; political motives of, 15, 75, 83, 87; radical, 45, 56, 67, 81, 84, 86–99, 143, 147, 154; social situation of, 14, 15, 43, 44, 45, 49, 51, 69, 140, 175 [*see also* socio-rhetorical analysis]; sophistic [*see* sophist, sophistry]; species of, 45, 52, 54, 140 [*see also* deliberative, epideictic, judicial];

SUBJECTS

suspicion of, 10, 23, 133–34;
  teaching of, 4, 13, 14, 26, 22–31,
  51–53, 187; technical, 72;
  universality of, 2, 8, 73, 147, 153,
  165; worldly, 83–99
Rhetorica ad Herennium, 126, 140
rhetorical situation, 14, 17, 43–45,
  49, 89, 118, 126, 140–43, 146–54,
  152, 156, 157, 158, 160
Rhetorical Society of America, 29
rhetorical unit, 14, 32, 43, 46–47,
  49, 109, 110, 114–15, 126, 140,
  141, 143, 144, 149–52, 159, 160,
  171, 186, 187
rhetórolect, 85–88, 91, 99–102
riddle, 169–70; *see also* God,
  kingdom of; mystery; parable(s);
  secrecy
righteousness; *see* justification
ritual, 82, 151, 183
Robbins, Vernon K., 127, 130–31
Roman Catholic Church, 183, 185
Romans, the Epistle to the, 33, 42,
  50, 130, 146
Rome, 54, 90, 118, 140, 169, 186
Romulus, 188
Rostovzeff, Michael, 23

sacred language, 67, 84–88, 143
sacrifice, 87, 97–98, 101; *see also*
  priest, priesthood; worship
saint, 169, 173, 174, 175, 185, 186
Sallust, 107
Salome, 189
salvation, 100, 151
Sampley, J. Paul, 130
Santa Claus, 188
Satan, 54
Saul of Tarsus, 118; *see also* Paul the
  Apostle
Schweitzer, Albert, 184, 185,
  186–87

science(s); natural, 189, 190; social,
  13, 125
scribal transcriptions, 66, 157, 189
Scripture(s), 2, 11, 31–34, 108, 117,
  131, 132, 181, 183, 187
secrecy, 187; *see also* God, kingdom
  of; mystery; parable(s); riddle
semiotics, 11; *see also* sign,
  signification
Seneca, 12, 146
sermon; *see* preaching
Sermon on the Mount (Matthew),
  45, 47, 67, 71, 82, 88–90
Sermon on the Plain (Luke), 45, 47,
  67, 71, 88
service; *see* ministry
Seymour, Thomas Day, 22
shame (rhetorical strategy), 167, 177
Sheridan, Thomas, 12
Shorey, Paul, 22
showing, 165, 167, 170, 171–72; *see
  also* pointing
sight; *see* vision
sign, signification, 10, 81–82, 93, 97,
  99, 144–45, 150, 175, 187; *see also*
  miracle; semiotics
Simeon, 188
Simon Peter, 74, 91, 150, 160
sin(s), 174, 190
Smith, D. Moody, 32
Smyth, Herbert, 22
Society for the History of Rhetoric,
  29
Society of Biblical Literature, 2, 25,
  32, 63, 68, 69, 130, 131
sociology, 15, 31, 49
socio-rhetorical analysis, 49–50,
  55–56, 82, 84, 86, 88, 92, 98–100,
  108, 110–11, 116–17, 120–21; *see
  also* rhetoric, social situation of
Socrates, 64–65
Solmsen, Friedrich, 23, 24

Son of God; *see* God, Son of
Son of Man, 87
sophist, sophistry, 9, 27, 72, 133
source criticism, 64–66, 112, 145, 187
speaker, 14, 27, 72, 75, 81–83, 88–90, 97, 99, 141–49, 157, 165–67
speech, speeches, 13, 14, 30, 43, 46, 47, 50, 51, 53, 67, 70, 71, 75, 76, 82, 85, 126, 132, 133, 143, 145, 146, 147, 171, 186, 188; *see also* Acts of the Apostles, speeches in; communication; oratory
Speech Association of America, 28
speech communication, 2, 4, 8, 14, 17, 21, 25–28, 33, 34, 73
Speech Communication Association, 25, 28, 37, 38; *see also* National Communication Association
Spirit, Holy, 101, 134, 147, 150–52, 155, 171; *see also* God; holiness, holy
Stanford University, 22
stasis, 43, 112, 115, 140, 186
Stowe, Harriet Beecher, 188
Strauss, David Friedrich, 184
Studiorum Novi Testamenti Societas, 127, 130
style, 7, 9, 10, 11, 12, 17, 27, 42, 43, 45, 46, 47, 49, 50, 51, 52, 53, 67, 69, 74, 115, 126, 132, 133, 140, 143, 147, 151, 156, 160, 163, 181
sublimity, 46
Suetonius, 64
suffering, 104, 189
supernaturalism, 184, 187, 188, 189
syllogism, 9, 45, 71
symbol, symbolism, 14–15, 169, 173
symbouleutic; *see* deliberative (species of rhetoric)
synoptic problem, 64–66

Tacitus, 22, 192
teach, teaching; *see* doctrine, Christian
Teachers College of Columbia, 26
temple, 56, 87
television, 70
Tertullian, 133
thanksgiving, 127–28
theology, 2, 76–77, 102, 125, 128, 131–33, 190
Theon of Alexandria, 107, 118
Theseus, 188
thesis, 46, 85, 160, 187
Thessalonians, the First Epistle to the, 50, 88, 126, 127, 130, 131
Thessalonians, the Second Epistle to the, 126, 131
Thirty-Nine Articles, 183
Thomas, (Coptic) *Gospel of*, 86, 187
Thonssen, Lester, 27
Thucydides, 22, 107
topics (topoi), 46, 47, 50, 51, 54, 67, 85, 92, 97–98, 132, 147, 187, 191
tradition criticism, 112, 132
transcendentalism, 184
Trinity Church (Boston), 181
Trinity University (San Antonio), 64, 182
trope(s), 27, 42, 74
trust; *see* faith
truth, 10, 72, 76, 134
Twain, Mark, 1
two-gospel hypothesis, 64; *see also* synoptic problem
two-source theory, 64; *see also* synoptic problem

Union Theological Seminary (New York), 28, 32
Unitarian Church, 181
University of Chicago, 22, 30, 126, 127, 128; Chicago Formalists, 29

SUBJECTS 255

University of Cincinnati, 26
University of Florence, 131
University of Göttingen, 127
University of Heidelberg, 131
University of Illinois, 26, 28
University of Iowa, 23, 26, 27, 28, 29
University of London, 131
University of Malibu, 131
University of Miami (Ohio), 25
University of Michigan, 26, 37
University of Minnesota, 25, 28
University of Nebraska, 39
University of North Carolina (Chapel Hill), 28, 32, 68, 127, 179, 182, 183
University of Pittsburgh, 23
University of Pretoria, 131
University of Southern California, 26, 28
University of Toronto, 128
University of Uppsala, 127
University of Wisconsin, 23, 26, 28
utopianism, 165, 186

Vietnam, 15
Vinson, Richard B., 41
Virgil, 22
Virgin Mary, the; *see* assumption of the Virgin Mary; immaculate conception; (of Mary) Mary, mother of Jesus
virtue(s), 132, 167
vision(s), 74, 168, 171, 172, 173, 188
vita; *see* biography
vocalization, 145, 156
vocation, 54, 91
voice(s), 11, 12, 163, 168, 171, 172, 173, 175, 177, 178; *see also* God, voice of; Jesus of Nazareth, voice of

Volkmann, Richard, 24
Von Spengel, Leonhard, 24

Wabash College, 28
Walz, Christianus, 24
Wana, Indonesian, 75
Wanamaker, Charles A., 128
war, 184
Ward, Mrs. Humphrey, 183
Washington, George, 12, 181
Watson, Duane F., 32, 34, 131, 179
Weinrich, Carl, 180
Weiss, Johannes, 32
Wicheln, Herbert A., 14, 27
wickedness; *see* evil
Wilke, Christian Gottlob, 31
Winans, James A., 26, 27
Winona State University, 25
wisdom, 11, 55–56, 76, 85, 88, 94–96, 147, 169
witness, 169, 173, 174; *see also* gospel; mission
wonder; *see* miracle
Woolbert, Charles H., 26
word, word of the Lord; *see* God, word of
World War II, 23
worship, 97–98, 171; *see also* priest, priesthood; sacrifice
wrapped words (*kyori*), 75
Wuellner, Wilhelm, 33, 137
Wycliffe College, 126, 128

Xenophon, 64

Yale University, 22, 30, 39
Young, Cuyler, 180

zealotry, religious, 184
Zechariah, 74, 188
zoology, 74